Handbook to
Life in America

Volume VI

The Roaring Twenties
1920 to 1929

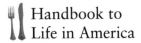

Handbook to Life in America

Volume VI

The Roaring Twenties 1920 to 1929

Rodney P. Carlisle
GENERAL EDITOR

Facts On File
An imprint of Infobase Publishing

Handbook to Life in America: The Roaring Twenties, 1920 to 1929

Facts On File, Inc.
An Imprint of Infobase Publishing
132 West 31st Street
New York, NY 10001

Library of Congress Cataloging-in-Publication Data
Handbooks to life in America / Rodney P. Carlisle, general editor.
v. cm.
Includes bibliographical references and index.
Contents: v. 1. The colonial and revolutionary era, beginnings to 1783—v. 2. The early national period and expansion, 1783 to 1859—v. 3. The Civil War and Reconstruction, 1860 to 1876—v. 4. The Gilded Age, 1870 to 1900—v. 5. Age of reform, 1890 to 1920—v. 6. The roaring twenties, 1920 to 1929—v. 7. The Great Depression and World War II, 1929 to 1949—v. 8. Postwar America, 1950 to 1969—v. 9. Contemporary America, 1970 to present.
ISBN 978-0-8160-7785-4 (set : hc : alk. paper)—ISBN 978-0-8160-7174-6 (v. 1 : hc : alk. paper)—ISBN 978-0-8160-7175-3 (v. 2 : hc : alk. paper)—ISBN 978-0-8160-7176-0 (v. 3 : hc : alk. paper)—ISBN 978-0-8160-7177-7 (v. 4 : hc : alk. paper)—ISBN 978-0-8160-7178-4 (v. 5 : hc : alk. paper)—ISBN 978-0-8160-7179-1 (v. 6 : hc : alk. paper)—ISBN 978-0-8160-7180-7 (v. 7 : hc : alk. paper)—ISBN 978-0-8160-7181-4 (v. 8 : hc : alk. paper)—ISBN 978-0-8160-7182-1 (v. 9 : hc : alk. paper) 1. United States—Civilization—Juvenile literature. 2. United States—History—Juvenile literature. 3. National characteristics, American—Juvenile literature. I. Carlisle, Rodney P.
E169.1.H2644 2008
973—dc22

2008012630

Facts On File books are available at special discounts when purchased in bulk quantities for businesses, associations, institutions, or sales promotions.

Please call our Special Sales Department in New York at (212) 967-8800 or (800) 322-8755.

You can find Facts On File on the World Wide Web at http://www.factsonfile.com

Printed in the United States of America

MP GB 10 9 8 7 6 5 4 3 2

This book is printed on acid-free paper.

Contents

Volume VI
The Roaring Twenties
1920 to 1929

Preface

"It is the soothing thing about history that it does repeat itself."
—Gertrude Stein

THE FLAVOR OF daily life in previous eras is usually only vaguely conveyed by examining the documents of state and the politics of the era. What people ate, how they spent their time, what entertainment they enjoyed, and how they related to one another in family, church, and employment, constituted the actual life of people, rather than the distant affairs of state. While governance, diplomacy, war, and to an extent, the intellectual life of every era tends to be well-documented, the way people lived is sometimes difficult to tease out from the surviving paper records and literary productions of the past.

For this reason in recent decades, cultural and social historians have turned to other types of physical documentation, such as illustrations, surviving artifacts, tools, furnishings, utensils, and structures. Statistical information can shed light on other aspects of life. Through examination of these and other kinds of evidence, a wholly different set of questions can be asked and tentatively answered.

This series of handbooks looks at the questions of daily life from the perspective of social and cultural history, going well beyond the affairs of government to examine the fabric and texture of what people in the American past experienced in their homes and their families, in their workplaces and schools. Their places of worship, the ways they moved from place to place, the nature of law and order and military service all varied from period to period. As science and technology advanced, the American contributions to those fields became greater and contributed to a different feel of life. Some of this story may be familiar, as historians have for generations commented on the disparity between rural and city life, on the impact of technologies such as the cotton gin, the railroad and the steamboat, and on life on the advancing frontier. However in recent decades, historians have turned to different sources. In an approach called Nearby History, academic historians have increasingly worked with the hosts of professionals who operate local historical societies, keepers of historic homes, and custodians of local records to pull together a deeper understanding of local life. Housed in thousands of small and large museums and preserved homes across America, rich collections of furniture, utensils, farm implements, tools, and other artifacts tell a very different story than that found in the letters and journals of legislators, governors, presidents, and statesmen.

FRESH DISCOVERIES

Another approach to the fabric of daily life first flourished in Europe, through which historians plowed through local customs and tax records, birth and death records, marriage records, and other numerical data, learning a great deal about the actual fabric of daily life through a statistical approach. Aided by computer methods of storing and studying such data, historians have developed fresh discoveries about such basic questions as health, diet, life-expectancy, family patterns, and gender values in past eras. Combined with a fresh look at the relationship between men and women, and at the values of masculinity and femininity in past eras, recent social history has provided a whole new window on the past.

By dividing American history into nine periods, we have sought to provide views of this newly enriched understanding of the actual daily life of ordinary people. Some of the patterns developed in early eras persisted into later eras. And of course, many physical traces of the past remain, in the form of buildings, seaports, roads and canals, artifacts, divisions of real estate, and later structures such as railroads, airports, dams, and superhighways. For these reasons, our own physical environment is made up of overlapping layers inherited from the past, sometimes deeply buried, and at other times lightly papered over with the trappings of the present. Knowing more about the many layers from different periods of American history makes every trip through an American city or suburb or rural place a much richer experience, as the visitor sees not only the present, but the accumulated heritage of the past, silently providing echoes of history.

Thus in our modern era, as we move among the shadowy remnants of a distant past, we may be unconsciously receiving silent messages that tell us: this building is what a home should look like; this stone wall constitutes the definition of a piece of farmland; this street is where a town begins and ends. The sources of our present lie not only in the actions of politicians, generals, princes, and potentates, but also in the patterns of life, child-rearing, education, religion, work, and play lived out by ordinary people.

VOLUME VI: THE ROARING TWENTIES, 1920–1929

The years from 1920 to 1929 were fondly remembered in later decades, as Americans looked back from the somber years of the Great Depression, World War II, and the Cold War to an earlier time. The trends of the 1920s that seemed to define the era—Prohibition, bootleggers and bathtub gin, the Harlem Renaissance, the Lost Generation, the Jazz Age, flaming youth, flappers, and the Florida land boom—represented different aspects of profound shifts in values away from the staid and stern morality of the 19th century. With nostalgia, evident even as early as 1930, after the Great Crash, Americans looked back at the 1920s as an age of breaking with the past, and of a clash between an older "Victorian" or "Puritan" generation and a young, 20th-century generation. Disillusioned with grand causes and reforms, young men and women turned away from political parties to cocktail parties, away from reformers to performers, and away from social causes to socializing. Whether the youth were more liberated and vibrant, or more hedonistic and self-indulgent, was a matter of point of view. But that popular image of the Roaring Twenties caught in the literature of the day, some by expatriate American writers who chose to live in Europe, reflected only a part of the transformation of life in the decade.

Technological changes, some of them springing from earlier innovations and inventions, continued to revolutionize daily and family life. With increasing distribution of electric power and gas lines to residences, the ordinary household took on a look more familiar in later decades, with electric washing machines for clothes, electric vacuum cleaners, electric and gas stoves replacing wood-burning ranges, with hot-water heaters and hot and cold running water in kitchens and bathrooms. While many middle-class homes still proudly displayed pianos, player pianos, and even organs, increasingly, compact phonographs and then radios provided the music. Although sewing machines, clothing patterns, and bolts of cloth sold in dry-goods stores still provided the means to make clothing at home, ready-made outfits at department stores and dress shops became cheaper and more available.

Henry Ford took the lead in producing a cheap automobile for the masses, but newly-organized General Motors and Plymouth-Dodge also sought to mass-produce inexpensive cars for the less affluent. Buying "on time" with monthly payments made the purchase of automobiles, household appliances, clothing, and other products much easier for average and low income families. Canned and packaged foods, introduced in earlier decades, continued to proliferate, making food preparation far easier and more convenient.

With these changes in material culture came numerous social consequences, some profound, some obvious, some trivial or almost unnoticed. It was possible for low-income families to emulate the comforts and lifestyle of the upper middle classes, with labor-saving appliances making it easier to maintain a family in some comfort without the assistance of domestic servants such as cooks and maids. Cooking, laundry, cleaning, ironing, and other household work could now be accomplished by one or two family members, still leaving time for leisure and play. The 1920s were also an age of apparent prosperity, with booming employment, and hundreds of thousands of families found the combination of slightly improved wages, new products, and time-purchases as an introduction to the consumer lifestyle. The phenomenal rise in prices of corporate stocks tended only to affect the wealthy and upper middle class, but the psychology of economic boom was infectious. Caught up in the swirl of apparent easy money, thousands invested savings in stocks and bonds or in Florida real estate, often buying lots sight unseen.

The proliferation of cheap automobiles stimulated the spread of roadhouses, tourist camps, motels, juke joints, and remote speakeasies. A young couple with access to an automobile could escape not only the supervision of parents, but could also evade the prying eyes of gossiping neighbors, finding seclusion and entertainment miles from home. Although college campuses still sought to regulate the morality of students, escape from restriction was facilitated by the auto and its growing infrastructure of roads, fuel stations, and remotely located hot-spots.

RURAL VERSUS URBAN CONFLICTS

The clash between rural and urban life, already apparent in the politics, protests, and social clashes of earlier eras, continued with new intensity in the 1920s. Adhering to more fundamentalist religious views, rural Americans tended to resent and resist many of the social and intellectual trends that swept the urban areas.

Some of these conflicts surfaced in famous events, such as the Scopes Trial in Dayton, Tennessee, in July 1925, that tested a state regulation prohibiting the teaching of Darwinian theories of evolution in school. The carnival atmosphere surrounding the test case was stimulated by the news media, including the daily press, the newsreel movie industry, and radio broadcasters. Regarded as great fun by many cynical reporters like H.L. Mencken, the trial did in fact represent many sharp divisions in American culture.

The effort to preserve what many perceived as traditional American values against the spread of a more relaxed moral standard surfaced in other ways. Advocates of immigration reform succeeded in establishing a system of quotas that limited immigrants from southern Europe and elsewhere in an effort to preserve a core Anglo-Saxon and northern European ethnic dominance. For a few years in the early and mid 1920s, the revived Ku Klux Klan terrorized not only African Americans, but also Catholics and Jews.

Prohibition, of course, was an effort to force, by legislation, the abstinence from alcohol. While it had some success in reducing the availability of liquor, beer, and wine, by outlawing their consumption, it had the unintended consequence of converting hundreds of thousands of otherwise law-abiding citizens into participants in criminal behavior. Respect for and support for government regulation suffered. In the south, institutionalized racial segregation continued to exclude African Americans from exclusively white use of public spaces, including separate railroad cars, buses, waiting rooms, restaurants, movie theater seating, public parks, and swimming pools. Perhaps most importantly, public schools and colleges remained rigidly segregated throughout much of the nation, with the facilities for African-American children and college students decidedly underfunded, poorly maintained, and understaffed.

Along with these fundamental divisions in society, some stimulated and enhanced by the new means of transportation and communication, other transformations and long-term trends gave life in 1920s America a decidedly 20th-century look and feel. Radio and film helped transform sports and entertainment, enhancing the trend already apparent in earlier decades, to nationalize, homogenize, and professionalize those fields. Movie stars, pop musicians, and sports heroes were recognized nationwide, and as icons of popularity, Rudolph Valentino, Bessie Smith, and Babe Ruth replaced the earlier celebrities of stage, print, and the lecture circuit. Competitions and prizes offered for long-distance airplane flights made national and international celebrities out of pilots like Charles Lindbergh and Amelia Earhart.

Less noticed by the popular media, other great advances went on in the fields of science, medicine, and public health. Experiments with rocketry by Robert Goddard, with nuclear physics by Robert Oppenheimer and Werner Heisenberg, with birth control by Margaret Sanger, with cellophane and rayon at DuPont, with vitamins by researchers at Yale and the University of Wisconsin, and with television by Vladimir Zworykin all presaged developments that would transform life in America and the world over the next decades.

A DISTINCT ERA IN AMERICAN LIFE

Echoing the sense of prosperity and break with tradition, and stimulated by a flurry of investment, commercial buildings reflected a wide proliferation of "modern" styles, including Art Deco motifs, Egyptian revival, Beaux-Arts, and other departures. Office buildings, auto sales rooms, even warehouses and factory buildings sprouted decorative design elements reflecting architects' conceptions of a break from the constraints of tradition.

Although only a decade, the years from 1920 to 1929 represented a distinct era in American life, with the flourishing of changes that represented the end of many earlier styles and cultural norms, and the transition to new ones. Thus the hectic events that crowded the news media: the sports, the fads, the show-trials, the celebrities and the notorious, the scandals and the outrages, were not simply the product of yellow journalists' desire to shock and outrage. Rather, they represented fundamental transformations in American life. Many of those changes could be attributed to the new developments in technology that erased regional differences, brought sectors and peoples into closer contact with each other, and that created a ferment as the new consumer culture emerged. New institutions of national corporations, advertising agencies, national regulatory agencies, and national communications media attempted to adapt to and build on the transformations, foreshadowing the distinctly American lifestyle that would more fully emerge in later decades.

RODNEY CARLISLE
GENERAL EDITOR

Chapter 1

Introduction

"The world, as a rule, does not live on beaches and in country clubs."
—F. Scott Fitzgerald, in a letter to his daughter

NO AMERICAN IS as associated with a specific decade as F. Scott Fitzgerald is with the 1920s. Perhaps no other American writer wrote as eloquently of an era and for such a wide audience, which helps us understand his celebrity status. In the Progressive Era, the nature of celebrity in America had changed: national media carried words to all corners of the country, Mark Twain's lecture tours had helped turn writers into public figures rather than persons behind closed doors, and the increasing quality and affordability of photography meant that the public could better see its idols. The prosperity brought by the end of the Great War and the fruits of the Industrial Revolution meant that the wealthy could be very wealthy indeed, without needing to rely on the accumulated splendor of "family money," and the lavish lifestyles of the wealthiest celebrities held the public fascination.

The story of Scott and Zelda Fitzgerald personifies an elite version of American life in the Roaring Twenties, or the Jazz Age, as Scott referred to the decade. Scott and Zelda were the First Couple of the Jazz Age, stylish and wealthy, drinkers and world travelers, frank and sometimes scandalous, managing simultaneously to enjoy great self-made success while seeming to lead lives of idle decadence.

Of course, much of that was an illusion. Each had significant bouts with alcohol, each was unfaithful to the other, and the pettiness of their squabbles was

F. Scott Fitzgerald, the writer who defined his generation and the Roaring Twenties, in 1937, just three years before his death.

interrupted by Zelda's frequent stays in mental health facilities. They often lived beyond their means, forcing Scott to ask editors for advances on stories not yet written or to demand more money for stories he had already sold. But he was well-liked as well as respected for his talent and skill. He was simply terrible with money, and perhaps some of that image of the Jazz Age couple owes itself to his and Zelda's difficulty moving on from their own early 20s to a more mature and grounded life.

Though Fitzgerald's work was never quite as autobiographical as is sometimes claimed—not as much as his audience sometimes thought—the lives of both the Fitzgeralds and his most famous protagonist, Jay Gatsby, offer fascinating parallels to the American condition throughout the Jazz Age. Fitzgerald and Gatsby were both Catholic midwesterners, though unlike Gatsby, Fitzgerald spent considerable portions of his youth in New York and attended prestigious eastern prep schools before enrolling in Princeton. Both American Catholicism and the midwest had recently gained more power, becoming more mainstream. America was no longer northeastern and Protestant, even when it held those qualities as part of its idealized self-image. Though immigration continued in force, Catholicism was no longer the province of ethnic ghettos where everyone spoke in an accent and cooked strange food—an image that was very much present in the early part of the century.

Both Fitzgerald and Gatsby served in the U.S. Army in World War I, a war that separated them from their significant others. But while Gatsby lost Daisy for the next few years, Scott had only to prove to Zelda that he could be a successful writer and support her financially. Thus came *This Side of Paradise*, his novel about love, greed, materialism, pretensions, and status among the college-age youth of his time. The book is frankly a mess, never sure whether it wants to laud or needle its protagonist, reading like a thinly connected maze of everything Fitzgerald had ever wanted to put into words. But it worked. It captured the spirit of the time and the generation in a way nothing else yet had. He wrote two more novels in the next few years—*The Beautiful and*

Politics of the Times

Republican Warren Harding won the election in November 1920 by 16 million votes to Democrat James Cox's nine million. Eugene Debs, still in prison for exercising his right to free speech by opposing the draft, polled over 900,000 votes for president on the Socialist ticket. President Harding pardoned Debs as part of a general amnesty for imprisoned radicals on Christmas Day, 1921.

Even with Harding's pleasant style and his assurances of normalcy, the years that followed were marked more by departure from the past than by any return to a bygone era. In fact, Republicans began to describe their economic plan and the apparent prosperity that evolved from it as the New Era. New Era prosperity was reflected in rising stock prices, greater volume of stock market trade, and a boom in real estate values in Florida and elsewhere. The prosperity gave rise to new fortunes and new ways of spending money.

The New Era was new in more profound ways. Prohibition, enacted during Woodrow Wilson's tenure of office, engendered a strange legal climate in which otherwise law-abiding citizens found ways to break the law in order to get a cocktail, a bottle of beer, or a party lubricated with scotch, bourbon, or gin. Overnight, it seemed, ordinary behavior had become criminalized, wrenching social and cultural values in a new direction. The nation turned inward to consumerism and a cultural clash over manners and morals, and away from a focus on issues of world peace, democracy, and justice.

Although the disillusionment in foreign affairs ushered in a period of isolationism, many Americans still kept a nervous eye on developments abroad. Small wars racked Europe, between Greece and Turkey, and between Russia and Poland, and military dictators emerged to stifle budding democracies. Vladimir Ilyich Lenin's Bolshevik brand of Communism came to dominate the newly formed Soviet Union.

Affability and amiability had served as assets during the presidential campaign, but proved to be severe liabilities for Harding in the office of the presidency, as scandals dominated his administration. By contrast, his successor Calvin Coolidge maintained a taciturn, quiet, and often solemn manner. Coolidge became notorious for his low-key style.

Coolidge handily won the 1924 election, as the Democrats were in disarray, divided between those who supported William Gibbs McAdoo and those backing Al Smith. Progressives rallied around the third-party candidacy of Robert LaFollette in 1924. The election seemed a confirmation of confidence in the New Era, with Coolidge taking about 15 million votes and Davis about eight million. LaFollette polled over four million. Al Smith won the Democratic nomination in 1928 and that campaign reflected the difficult issues that served as an undercurrent to the era. Herbert Hoover won the presidency with over 21 million popular votes to Smith's 15 million votes.

Damned and *The Great Gatsby*—after which his production screeched to a halt. His friend and colleague Ernest Hemingway later said that Fitzgerald's talent was a wild thing and the smarter he got at taming it and putting it to his own devices, the less he managed to produce with it.

The Progressive Era had redefined the United States in ways both formal (a rash of constitutional amendments, the integration of the Confederacy and of the Mormon community) and informal (the organizational and psychological shift from the regional to the national level). If that was the childhood of the redefined United States, the 1920s were its adolescence. The many suggested reforms of the frantic Progressive Era had largely slowed down, and what hadn't been enacted (or remained a continuing issue) tended to coalesce around core concerns like human rights, consumer protections, and the general betterment of the common man. The structural changes of the progressives had already gone into effect, as illustrated by the direct election of senators and the modernization of voting rights and citizenship.

What remained was for the country to step into the shoes it had made for itself. The path had been set. The Industrial Revolution provided cars, and the 1920s put them to use on federally-funded highways. The previous decades had invented movies, and the Hollywood of the 1920s adopted the feature film as their primary expression. The 19th century forwarded the core ideas of modern sciences, and the 1920s argued evolution in court and derived quantum mechanics from modern physics. Socialism as an American concern came and went like a teenager going through a phase, just as 19th-century style imperialism and new political parties. It is no coincidence that after shifting constantly during the first half of the country's history, the effective political parties of the United States have remained the same since World War I. With that war and its aftermath, the nation came of age.

"How You Gonna Keep 'Em Down on The Farm After They've Seen Paree?" asked a 1919 song by Joe Young and Sam Lewis, written as American boys came back from the war. As reluctant as Americans had been to enter it—or to repeat it—the war had been a chance to flex American muscle and find out just what the nation was capable of achieving, and even those who were not surprised by the results had to be affected by having their beliefs confirmed. Even fighting a war on another continent, the United States had shown its strength, and had come home the richest nation in the world. Just as adolescents are prone to extreme mood swings as they adjust to themselves and their world, it is almost poetically inevitable that the decade ended with the Great Depression.

FLAPPERS AND PHILOSOPHERS

After the publication of *This Side of Paradise*, Scott and Zelda became celebrities as famous for being themselves as for his work. His short stories—especially for the *Saturday Evening Post* and *The Smart Set*—actually accounted for a good deal more of his financial success than his novels in this pre-television Golden Age of magazines. Zelda in particular, along with silent film star Clara Bow, was the public face of the "flapper generation." Flappers were young women, especially those from late teenage years to 30, who engaged in a score of scandalous activities and flouted the conventions of the previous generations. While every generation has its rebellious teenagers, there was a common thread among flappers that went beyond their bobbed hair and cigarette holders: they openly and proudly disdained authority, presumably in response to the obvious ubiquity of drinking despite Prohibition, and the signal therefore that authority was limited in its real power. They were the first generation of women to vote, but they did so in a climate tainted by the widespread contempt for Prohibition, which other than suffrage itself had been the first significant political change brought about by female activists. They knew they had more power than women before them, in other words, but had even more reason to distrust that power.

Flappers did away with the old-fashioned clothing of previous generations, favoring clothes and styles that made them look boyish, even to the extent of popularizing bras and corsets that reduced their curves as much as possible. At the same time, they were the first generation for which the use of make-up was widespread, especially lipstick (often "kiss-proof") and eyeliner. Skirts became shorter, arms were bared, and fashionable new dances took advantage of the increased mobility and flexibility that clothes gave women. Of all the unlikely developments, the knee—emblematic of those shorter skirts and sights previously unseen in public—became a sexualized body part, to the

The growing prosperity of the Jazz Age gave more people the buying power to afford what might have once been out of reach, such as this 1928 Oldsmobile.

A group of flappers with bobbed hair, short skirts, and stockings rolled down below their knees gathered around a man at a piano in Washington, D.C., in October 1923.

point that magazine articles reported young women rouging their knees to draw attention to them. In many ways, flappers' fashion choices took things that were acceptable for children (who were allowed to be less covered up, and rarely put their hair up) and made them adult—part of the decade's glorification of youth.

Though all teenagers of the time were known for it, flappers seem to be the originators of much of the specialized slang of the day. To the untrained ear, flapper conversation could be as dense and inscrutable as Cockney rhyming slang—while "petting" may have an intuitive meaning, there is no inherent clue to whether something that's "jake" is good, bad, or something else altogether. Calling boys "sheikhs," money "berries" or "clams" or "voot," and attractive girls "tomatoes" was a sort of code, a conscious artifice. Though the word would not be popularized in this context for another generation, the Jazz Age kids had invented "cool": you had it or you didn't, you knew it or you didn't, and if you had to ask, you would never know.

Flappers and their male counterparts patronized jazz clubs, which had often previously been considered "race clubs" meant only for blacks, and were the

The Lost Generation

Reacting to a rejection of "provincial" American values, Gertrude Stein coined the term *Lost Generation* to refer to those Americans who came of age during and just after World War I, though the term is most useful when applied specifically to those who, like her, expatriated themselves to Europe. The subculture of American expatriates in western Europe (and especially France) is generally associated with the modernists and the major young novelists and poets of the day: Stein herself and her lover Alice B. Toklas (who popularized marijuana brownies for more than one generation); Scott and Zelda Fitzgerald (his novel *Tender is the Night* and hers *Save Me the Waltz* are both largely inspired by their expatriate experiences); poet-critic T. S. Eliot; Ezra Pound, the central poet of modernism and precursor to the Beats and the bulk of the experimental poets of the 20th century; Ford Madox Ford, an English novelist who spent considerable time in Paris with the Americans and James Joyce; John Dos Passos, a politically active novelist who continually experimented with different methods of constructing a novel; and Ernest Hemingway. Hemingway wrote a memoir about the 1920s expatriates, *A Moveable Feast*, but it was not published until 1964, after his death.

The Lost Generation was not an artistic movement, though its members were generally modernist in persuasion (though there was a vast difference in style and content between, say, Fitzgerald and Dos Passos, or Hemingway and Pound).

They were a clique, really, in which some members might come and go but everything revolved around the core. As a result, much of what we know about their personal lives amounts to gossip: men slept with each others' wives, perhaps by consent; arguments over sex and politics turned into fistfights; and everyone drank far too much. Of those things we can be confident.

Less clearly, accusations of homosexuality were rampant. It should be noted that this is one of the rare times in American history when homosexuality enjoyed a certain amount of mainstream acceptance: so-called "pansy bars" operated in every major city, and certain Hollywood actors were open with the public about their homosexual relationships.

So "accusation" may be an inappropriate term here—maybe "report" would be better. Hemingway is the exception—Zelda accused him of having an affair with Scott, and many members of the Lost Generation scoffed that his over-the-top masculinity was just a guise to cover up his fear of being discovered as a homosexual or bisexual. Though most of the writers were avid letter-writers and diary-keepers, there is really no way to know what happened, what was merely suspected, and what was gossip.

Clara Bow in a daring backless gown. Bow became known as the first "It Girl" after starring in the silent film It*—the title was the period's coy way of referring to sex appeal.*

first generation to openly declare that dating had an object other than the pursuit of marriage. A couple might enjoy one another's company for a few months, or a few weeks, without any designs on marriage. Dating was an end unto itself, not simply a means to find a husband or wife. Though it was rarely spoken of, the increased availability of condoms may have played a role, particularly given the number of veterans of World War I and the fact that at this point in history, soldiers had a greater awareness of the existence of condoms than the general population. The disconnect between courtship and marriage may have also contributed to the popularity of petting parties: social gatherings for teenagers and college-age young adults revolving around fully or partially clothed petting or "fooling around." While magazines exaggerated the prevalence of these parties in order to sensationalize them, they were a real phenomenon, and not at all limited to "wayward youth" or the decadent city.

BEYOND FITZGERALD

Of course, Fitzgerald captured only a portion of the age—a vital portion, and perhaps its newest and most vibrant in his eyes, but the Jazz Age was still an incomplete model of the decade. Xenophobia was rampant in the wake of the Great War, and influenced everything from foreign policy to rural violence. The decade would not have been nearly as prosperous if the United States had used more of its newfound wealth to help rebuild Europe, but Americans had no interest in that—not because of a lack of charity *per se*, but because European wars were still seen as European concerns, and it was best to just stay out of the whole mess. Many Americans had not wanted to go to war to begin with, and had done so only because it became clear it was inevitable.

The Crash

The stock market suffered unheard of losses on "Black Thursday" (October 24, 1929), rallied briefly on Friday and Monday, and then suffered a total collapse on Tuesday, October 29. Excerpted below is an article from the afternoon edition of the *Minneapolis Star* published on October 24.

BILLIONS AGAIN CLIPPED FROM VALUES
AS STOCKS GO INTO NEW TAILSPIN

LEADERS CRASH IN ONE OF
WORST BREAKS IN HISTORY

TRADES AT RATE OF
14 MILLION SHARES

TRADERS SURGE ABOUT
BROKERAGE HOUSES—SEE
HOLDINGS WIPED OUT

"Wave after wave of selling again moved down prices on the Stock Exchange today and billions of dollars were clipped from values. Traders surged about the brokerage offices watching their holdings wiped out, and scenes on the floor of the Exchange were of the kind never before witnessed. It was one of the worse breaks in history, with all leaders crashing down through resistance barriers.

"The reaction came with the same abruptness as the one yesterday in which billions of dollars in value were lost. For a time, in the morning, the market was showing signs of rallying power. Banking support was given the leaders, and U.S. Steel staged a substantial recovery that was carried over to the other pivotal shares. Then new waves of selling out of poorly margined accounts started another reaction. Tickers at 12:20 were 68 minutes behind. All records for volume were being broken. Sales to noon amounted to 5,711,200 shares. This was at the rate of 14,000,000 shares for a full day. At 12:20, U.S. Steel was down to 195, off 9; Consolidated Gas, 111, off 11 ½; Montgomery Ward, 60, off 23 ¼; Johns Manville, 145, off 35; General Electric, 289, off 25; Westinghouse, 165, off 25; Sears Roebuck, 117, off 17 ¼; American Can, 138, off 16 ½; American Telephone, 250, off 21 ½; American & Foreign Power, 93, off 21; Radio Corp., 49 ¼, off 18 ¼; Columbia Gas, 83, off 14 ¼; National Cash Register, 83, off 17; General Motors, 50, off 7 1/8; Standard Oil of New Jersey, 67, off 6 ½.

"Nervousness was still apparent in many quarters. An evidence of this was the trading in American Water Works, which declined 17 ¼ points to 103."

Though immigration had already changed the face of America, the push to limit it reached its height in the 1920s, when the law was explicitly phrased to preserve the current ethnic makeup of the country. Quotas were imposed on the number of immigrants allowed from each country, based on how many people of that nationality already lived in the United States. The effect was to drastically slow the immigration of southern Europeans in favor of northern Europeans (especially the British, French, and Germans, who had all arrived in great numbers before the later waves of immigration), and to nearly halt the immigration of Asians. The rights of resident aliens were restricted, especially where property was concerned.

Lynching continued to be a problem, and the overwhelming majority of lynching victims were blacks. Anti-black racism was far from an exclusively southern problem, as the Great Migration of blacks to the northern industrial cities had caused resentment there, and both cities and small towns across the midwest made it clear that blacks were unwelcome.

The membership of the Ku Klux Klan rose to unfathomable numbers—millions of American men—and admitted members of the Klan included Indiana Governor Edward Jackson. The Klan included or influenced a number of the delegates to the 1924 Democratic Convention, opposing the Catholic New York Governor Alfred Smith, and ensuring that the party did not condemn the Klan. President Warren G. Harding is sometimes claimed to have been inducted into the Klan sometime after his inauguration.

Hundreds of Ku Klux Klan members marched down Pennsylvania Avenue in Washington, D.C., in this parade on September 13, 1926.

This second Klan was not simply an anti-black organization. Once it attained such extraordinary numbers, it acted as a sort of moral police for a very specific set of issues. In fact, many progressive reforms had Klan support—Prohibition, the funding of public schools, and aid to poor whites (sometimes viewed as balancing out the "unfair assistance" received by poor blacks) were all causes the Klan endorsed and provided money for. But the Klan would go further, sending vigilante groups to deal with moonshiners and houses of prostitution, harassing teenagers engaged in "immoral behavior," and so on. Its concerns went far beyond racism, without reducing the role racism played in Klan philosophy: this was a broader, larger, more dangerous Klan than the Klan of Reconstruction.

In his fascination with the "flaming youth" of the period, Fitzgerald's vision failed to encompass many other social and cultural developments of the era. Across the nation, as the older generation of immigrants found jobs in cities and in rural areas, they and their rapidly Americanizing children sought to attain the prosperity, comfort, and "respectability" of the middle class. The process of homogenizing and developing a national, rather than a regional culture was further advanced by the combination of new media and thriving businesses that sought to expand a consumer base, coupled with the effect of public education and the revolution in transportation.

With radio and newspapers flooding the public with advertising, and with movies depicting and replicating ideas of style, manners, and vocabulary, the distinct variations of ethnicity, class, and region became further blurred. As rural isolation broke down, so also did some of the distinctions between regions.

CULTURE AND VALUES

Schools provided, along with their formal function of education, institutional frameworks for acculturation to the American way of life. The fact that the same textbooks were used across the nation in public grammar schools and high schools meant that the schools inculcated roughly similar content. Perhaps more important than the material taught was the underlying message of education, which valued respect for and obedience to authority, rewarded hard work, diligence, and proficiency in skills, and enforced adherence to a rigid time schedule marked by bells and wall clocks. Such values did not always "take" on recalcitrant youth, but everyone attending public school learned, whether they liked it or not, that such values would be expected in the workplace.

It was not only prosperous youth depicted by Fitzgerald who experienced the revolution in lifestyle brought on by the automobile and by the other transformations of transportation. In rural districts the automobile, long-distance bus, and railroad rapidly broke down traditional isolation. Young women from the countryside were able to commute by train or bus to work or pursue higher education, and young men, searching for employment, moved to distant cities. City and suburban life also changed with the automobile. Suburbs that had relied on streetcars, trains, and busses for their communication with hub cities now expanded further as automobiles added further reach. It became common for city workers to drive a few miles from their home to a rail station, leave their car there, or be dropped off by a spouse, and then commute into the city workplace by rail.

Part of the popularity of professional sports in the era can be attributed to the desire to identify with a major city in a region, and to take vicarious pride, as Cincinnati took on Chicago or Boston in a baseball game. Rather than simply representing a fad, professional sports fitted exactly into the changing cultural milieu as a means of preserving a sense of regional identity even as that identity was being threatened by the forces of commerce, the leveling of education, the images of the media, and the power of transportation.

BILL KTE'PI

Further Readings

Alexander, Michael. *Jazz Age Jews.* New York: Princeton University Press, 2003.

Carlisle, Rodney. General Editor, *Day By Day: The Twenties*. New York: Facts On File, 2007.

Carse, Robert. *Rum Row: The Liquor Fleet That Fueled the Roaring Twenties.* Mystic, CT: Flat Hammock Press, 2007.

Dolan, Mark. *Modern Lives: A Cultural Re-reading of the Lost Generation.* West Lafayette, IN: Purdue University Press, 1996.

Fitzgerald, F. Scott. *This Side of Paradise, Tales of the Jazz Age, Flappers and Philosophers.* New York: Scribner, 1920.

Hemingway, Ernest. *A Moveable Feast.* New York: Scribner's, 1964.

Kyvig, David. *Daily Life in the United States, 1920–1940: How Americans Lived Through The Roaring Twenties and The Great Depression*. New York: Ivan R. Dee, 2004.

Latham, Angela. *Posing a Threat: Flappers, Chorus Girls, and Other Brazen Performers of the American 1920s*. Middletown, CT: Wesleyan University Press, 2000.

Merwin, Ted. *In Their Own Image: New York Jews in Jazz Age Popular Culture.* New Brunswick, NJ: Rutgers University Press, 2006.

Rhodes, Chip. *Structures of the Jazz Age: Mass Culture, Progressive Education, and Racial Discourse in American Modernism*. New York: Verso, 1998.

Zeitz, Joshua. *Flapper: A Madcap Story of Sex, Style, Celebrity, and the Women Who Made America Modern*. New York: Three Rivers Press, 2007.

Chapter 2

Family and Daily Life

"A family is . . . composed not only of children but of men, women, an occasional animal, and the common cold."
—Ogden Nash

THE ROARING TWENTIES were a tumultuous time for American families. The horrors of World War I had shattered the comfortable Victorian certainties regarding morality and proper behavior upon which families of the Gilded Age and the Progressive Era had modeled themselves. As a result, many people pursued pleasure in a way that would have been considered shameful even a decade earlier. The well-intentioned experiment of Prohibition and the resultant hypocrisy of large numbers of Americans who continued to drink alcohol illegally contributed further to a general atmosphere of hedonism.

However, not all the changes in family life in the Jazz Age were necessarily negative. The general increase in disposable income enjoyed as a result of prosperity translated into an improved standard of living for all classes. The fruits of the technological innovation of the previous decade became available not merely to the wealthy few, but to the laboring classes as well, resulting in major improvements in the quality of life.

AT WORK IN THE JAZZ AGE

The tone of the blue-collar workplace of the 1920s was by and large set by the 1919 Steel Strike, in which U.S. Steel responded ruthlessly to crush the last vestiges of unionization in that industry. With anti-Communist feelings running high as a result of the 1917 Bolshevik Revolution in Russia, Attorney General

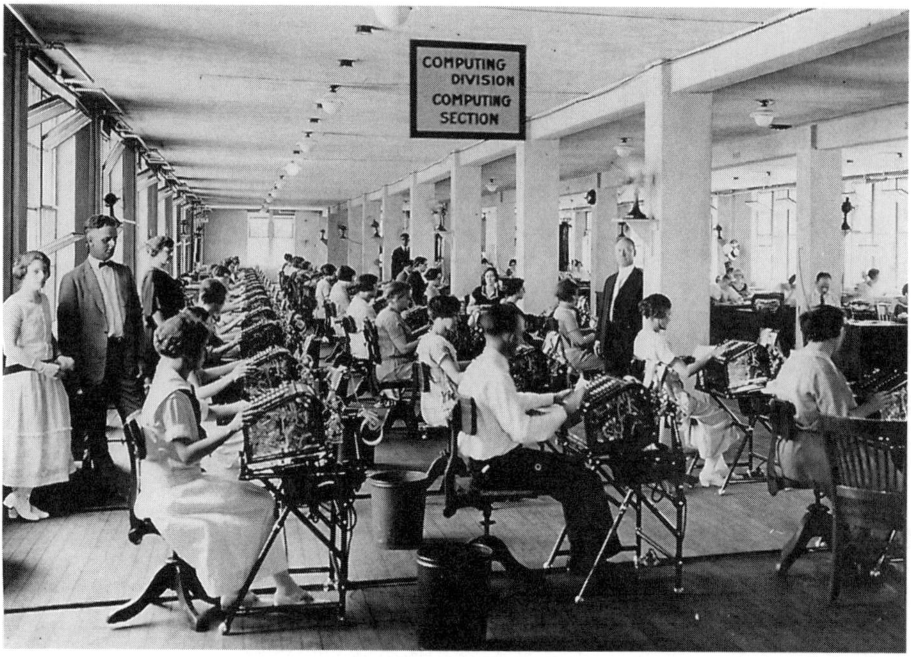

These mostly female government employees worked in long, uniform rows in an open room, where they used machines to calculate veterans' bonuses.

Mitchell Palmer set off the "Palmer Raids" against suspected anarchists and Communist sympathizers who were regarded as responsible for urging strikes.

Although these policies ensured that America's economic future would be capitalist, it did not mean a return to the wholesale exploitation of workers that had characterized the Gilded Age. The gains of the Progressive Era could not be wiped away, and the middle class had taken note of how bad conditions were for the millions of workers who toiled in America's factories and would not simply look the other way as the screws were put back on. Instead of coercion, the captains of industry increasingly turned to incentives, reasoning that if the workers could be brought to see the industrialist as the source of their new prosperity, the blandishments of Communist agitators with their talk of class warfare would be less attractive.

The 1920s saw the end of the seven-day workweek for the blue-collar laborer, although the steel industry was one of the last holdouts. Judge Elbridge Gerry, the head of U.S. Steel, claimed that the workers themselves wanted the seven-day week in order to earn more money. His argument was somewhat disingenuous, since the main reason steelworkers opposed the reduction of their workweek was the resultant reduction in their already meager wages. With pressure from the press, U.S. Steel agreed to give workers a raise to ensure they continued to take home the same amount of pay in spite of working fewer hours.

In fact, workers of all industries enjoyed a real increase in income during the 1920s. This gain was at least partly the result of Prohibition, which demolished the industrialists' old argument that higher wages would simply vanish down the "rum hole," and that only holding wages at bare subsistence levels would keep workers reasonably sober and reliable. With wages going up for all income groups, such durable goods as automobiles and household appliances became affordable for lower middle-class and working-class families.

For the white-collar worker, the shifts in the workplace experience were more complex. White-collar workers did enjoy increased prosperity in the 1920s, but not to the same extent as working-class people, for the simple reason that white-collar workers had already enjoyed relatively high compensation in previous decades. The relatively safe nature of office work compared to factory labor meant that it had not been as heavily transformed by the reformers, although efficiency experts such as Frederick W. Taylor applied their efforts to improving workflow in the office as well as the factory floor. For instance, the roll-top desk with its myriad of pigeonholes for storing papers had been a fixture of 19th-century offices and became regarded as a barricade to efficient movement of paperwork. A vital paper could easily become mislaid in one of those pigeonholes, and the ability of clerks to pull the top closed and lock it also enabled them to hoard essential paperwork and use it to manipulate their employers. As a result, the roll-top desk was replaced by a flat-top desk with only a few large drawers, and papers were moved to central filing areas, accessible to the entire office. Employees of all ranks were firmly discouraged from keeping papers in their own desks, and could be required to produce them at any moment. A tidy workspace was one of the essential factors in a positive work evaluation.

Performance evaluation became a source of steadily increasing anxiety for white-collar workers. Unlike manufacturing, office work did not lend itself to objective metrics of productivity. As a result, success in the office environment was increasingly based upon matters of appearance, personal grooming, deference, and general ability to get along with colleagues and supervisors. Worse, there was little transparency in the reviewing process, and employees were seldom told the reasons for their being turned down for a promotion or a raise, leaving them to worry over all their possible shortcomings. Purveyors of personal-grooming products were able to capitalize upon this new anxiety, even highlighting problems such as halitosis and body odor to be solved by their wares.

THE NEW WOMAN AND THE WORKPLACE

The 1920s marked an increasing movement of women into the workplace, and particularly of educated women into the professions. Although they still faced opposition from conservatives who believed women should focus on the domestic sphere, they faced fewer formal barriers than women of the Progressive Era.

A liquor business hidden underneath a lunchroom being raided by Prohibition officers in Washington, D.C., on April 25, 1923.

Prohibition and the Invisible Workplace

One of the most remarkable aspects of the Roaring Twenties was the enormous expansion of the "invisible economy" as a result of nationwide Prohibition. Whereas previously most criminal business enterprises had been related to prostitution, and as such were regarded by the general public as disreputable, no such stigma adhered to the myriad shady drinking establishments that sprang up after the Volstead Act went into force. Even respectable people saw no problem with obtaining a bottle on the sly.

As a result, large numbers of people were employed in illegal bars known as speakeasies. The air of risk that adhered to these establishments gave their patrons a certain thrill of the forbidden, but for the people behind the bar, it was just a job, and a dangerous one at that. Since illegal watering holes were in constant danger of being raided by enforcement agents, the workers had to develop methods of recognizing desirable customers and identifying undercover police officers. Most of them depended upon various code phrases, which were passed by word of mouth. However, the most frequent method of keeping an illegal drinking establishment from being shut down was to turn to the mob for protection. Organized crime had started with brothels and gambling establishments, and had developed connections with corrupt police and government officials. In almost all the major cities, there were multiple rival gangs, and no matter which gang a given speakeasy turned to for protection, there was still a constant danger that it might become a target of a rival's attention. Unlike the revenuers, rival mobsters had no rules of engagement or worries about due process of law. Attacks on rival properties could involve "motorcade" shootings in which cars filled with thugs would drive by and fire thousands of rounds from Thompson machine guns. Such attacks were rare, but they were widely publicized and contributed to the sense of general lawlessness associated with the Roaring Twenties.

However, there were still plenty of informal barriers that made it difficult to break into any of the major career fields. In particular, male gatekeepers who controlled hiring and admission to professional schools often dismissed women's career aspirations and passed them over in favor of men.

Still, it could not be ignored that during World War I women had proven themselves adequate to many lines of work that had been exclusively male. They had driven trucks, made deliveries of ice and milk and other prosaic necessities in order to free up men needed on the fighting front. Certainly opponents of women's work could no longer fall back on claims of frailty to "protect" women from remunerative employment.

Furthermore, women with ambitions to careers beyond wife and mother no longer regarded it as a given that working outside the home would necessarily mean resigning oneself to a life of celibacy. Although it had been completely unremarkable in the Gilded Age for married women of the working class to hold a full-time job at the factory, it was generally expected that a woman of the middle class who went to college and took paid employment thus had forsaken the possibility of marriage. However, women of the 1920s were no longer satisfied with having to make a choice between career and true love. In keeping with the new social climate that abandoned the old notion of sex as male privilege and female chore, middle-class women insisted that having a career did not mean surrendering their rights to intimacy and affection.

Middle-class women who did try to combine marriage and career generally found little social support. Not only were they criticized for having abandoned their wifely and maternal duties by working for pay, but they also found little help at home. Most men of the 1920s were not yet ready to set their hands to work that was still considered not only the sole province of women, but demeaning for a man.

AT HOME IN THE JAZZ AGE

The prosperity that characterized the 1920s completed the shift that had begun in the Progressive Era from a traditional patriarchal family to a companionate family in which husband and wife participated equally in the marriage. Rising wages meant that life was no longer a continual struggle for survival, leaving time and energy for couples to enjoy one another's presence. The shift of the role of child from economic asset to emotional treasure was complete for all but the poorest of families.

The wife of the 1920s no longer thought of herself primarily in terms of mother and homemaker, operating principally in the domestic sphere and leaving the outside world to men. The growing availability of birth control meant she would not face an endless series of pregnancies, nor have to raise a large brood of children. Instead, a woman could devote her time and energy to making herself an interesting and enjoyable partner for her husband. Better educated than her foremothers, she was an interesting conversationalist who

Women finally won the right to vote on August 26, 1920, with the ratification of the Nineteenth Amendment. These three suffragists demonstrated casting their votes in New York City in 1917.

could talk comfortably with her husband and his associates about a variety of topics. She moved freely in a wider world that women of earlier eras had regarded as the prerogatives of men.

The most significant legal victory for women was the ratification of the Nineteenth Amendment on August 26, 1920, which gave women the right to vote. However, the sweeping social changes that some reformers of the Progressive Era had imagined as a result of women having a voice in the political process did not come about. By the 1920s, people were no longer interested in grand schemes of social reform on abstract principles; a far more practical transformation was coming about as a result of economic shifts and technological changes.

Some of the technological advances, such as the automobile or domestic appliances, had been developed in earlier decades and simply became more widespread in the 1920s as a result of increasing financial availability. However, one of the greatest technological transformers of daily life in the

Appliances and Housework

The 1920s saw almost universal urban electrification, largely as a result of the increase in prosperity. Although electricity had originally been viewed primarily in terms of illumination, by 1920 a wide variety of household appliances were powered by electricity. The growing acceptability of purchasing consumer goods on credit combined with the general prosperity of the era to allow even families of modest means to acquire them.

However, the proliferation of household appliances did not necessarily free women from their prosaic duties as some more starry-eyed commentators had hoped. Although it was true that the new domestic technologies had eliminated many onerous chores, they also enabled women to undertake new ones. While gas and electric ranges did not require the carrying of fuel or the removal of ashes, their more precise temperature control enabled women to substitute a more complex cuisine for the stews and roasts that had formerly dominated American cooking. Washing machines with electric agitators and wringers spared women the back-breaking labor of the washboard, but also made it possible for people to change their clothes on a daily basis.

Furthermore, appliances actually tended to concentrate housework upon the woman, by relieving men and children of chores they had formerly done. Chopping firewood for a hearth or wood-burning stove had typically fallen upon the adult male, as a result of his greater upper-body strength. When the stove and furnace no longer required wood to be chopped, the husband generally did not replace that task with another one, but instead regarded the time thus freed as his for leisure activities.

Not only did appliances create a household in which the homemaker toiled while her husband and children took their ease, but it also put an end to a large number of businesses dedicated to providing the heavier and more onerous tasks. Once every woman had her own washing machine, the steam laundry could no longer find enough customers. Vacuum cleaning services, which could be called in once a week to clean one's carpets, were displaced by the individual vacuum cleaner.

This pre-electric iron had a bulky attachment for steam.

Jazz Age actually appeared on the commercial scene in that decade. In the first two decades of its existence, radio had been considered primarily as a wireless telegraph, a means of sending commercial and military messages to individual recipients. Even when Reginald Fessenden demonstrated that a properly modulated carrier wave could reproduce complex sounds, including music and the human voice, the management of American Marconi regarded it as a curiosity.

In 1915 David Sarnoff, a forward-looking young executive at American Marconi, saw the commercial potential of what he termed the "magical music box." However, World War I interrupted his efforts, and it was not until July 2, 1921, that he was able to arrange the first radio broadcast of a sports event. Although there were only a few sets capable of receiving the historic transmission, the effect upon American society could only be described as electrifying. Suddenly radio became the rage, and manufacturers of receiving sets sprang up all over the country to supply the demand, as broadcasting stations appeared in all the nation's major cities.

Although the telephone had already pierced the boundary between the private and public spheres, it was a person-to-person medium and generally enabled people to talk with others they already knew, such as friends and busi-

Radio transformed daily life in the 1920s and brought the world to those who stayed home. This photo of a woman wearing a radio headset in 1923 was entitled "The Shut-in's Sunday Service."

ness associates. Radio broadcasting brought the world into the home, enabling people to listen to a symphony, a drama, a comedy, or even that new jazz music right in their own living rooms. For the first time, people heard news of distant events as it happened, rather than through a friend or a newspaper.

FLAPPERS AND COEDS

Although women of all ages enjoyed greater freedoms in the 1920s, the young were the most adamant in claiming it as their own. Even in the final years of the previous decade, a new style had emerged among young women, emphasizing freedom of movement. Instead of the voluminous skirts that had previously characterized women's dresses, the new style featured straight lines and much higher hemlines. Similarly, sleeves and necklines were reduced, until some of the most daring young women bared almost their entire backs. The corset, a restrictive undergarment that tightly bound the waist in order to enhance the idealized hourglass figure, was definitively abandoned in favor of minimal undergarments that created a slim, boyish figure.

The Invention of the Adolescent

One of the most striking developments of the 1920s was the rise of a distinctive youth culture. Teens and young adults no longer looked primarily to their families for their sense of identity, but instead to their peers. Young people developed distinctive slang that was not merely regional, but shared across the country. Young people adopted distinctive styles not shared by older adults, and began to have social activities directed primarily to people their own age, such as school dances and social clubs aimed entirely at young people.

The rise of youth culture was largely the result of the rise of radio, which enabled young people across the country to share common references instead of being restricted to the knowledge available in their own communities. Dance crazes such as the Charleston and the bunny hug could spread across the nation in a matter of weeks or even days, rather than having to percolate over months.

However, adolescence was made possible only because young people no longer had to assume adult responsibilities at an early age. The combination of prosperity and reforms against child labor meant that there was a large pool of young people with money and spare time, caught in a twilight period between childhood and adulthood. They had money to spend and were hungry for diversions to take their minds off the frustration of enforced dependence upon their parents, while not yet facing the ties of real responsibility.

As women modeled their lives after popular icons in the 1920s, fashion and cosmetics became more important in their lives. This illustration captures one version of the flapper ideal.

This new style was called the flapper, and such bold fashions scandalized many members of the older generation. Churches and city governments sought to compel a return to the old standards of dress by rigorous mandates specifying acceptable lengths of skirts, sleeves, and necklines. However, the flappers were not discouraged by the opprobrium of their elders, and if anything, became more adamant to have their own distinctive way of living.

And their behavior was even more shocking to the staid sensibilities of their elders. In earlier generations, a young woman protected her reputation, and thus her marriage prospects, by the careful regulation of all contact with non-family males. Ideally she did not even permit herself to be kissed until she was married. Some Victorian thinkers held that a woman who once had fallen in love with a man must never give her heart to another lest she become spiritually shopworn. By contrast, the flapper regularly displayed her affection for her beau, to the point that terminology developed to distinguish between various forms of kissing: necking and petting. A necking couple confined their kisses to the face and neck, whereas petting involved allowing one's lips to stray lower, perhaps upon the breasts and shoulders, or even further if one were truly daring.

The 1920s saw young women attending college in unprecedented numbers. Furthermore, they were not only attending the women's colleges or state teachers' colleges, but studying alongside young men in the various state universities and even prestigious private institutions. As such, they were able to meet with young men out from under the watchful eyes of their parents, leading to a major shift in the manner in which young people chose their future spouses.

Nineteenth-century courting customs, which had continued to prevail through the first two decades of the 20th century, centered on the young woman's home and family. A young man could call upon her if she had expressed her willingness to receive him. Generally they would visit in the parlor or sitting room of the young woman's family home. By contrast, dating centered entirely upon men inviting women to public functions, particularly the cinema, generally followed by a restaurant meal. The automobile was a large factor in this shift, since it gave young people the necessary mobility to go places, while increased prosperity made it easier for young men to pay for entertainment activities. However, the most critical shift was the simple fact that a woman no longer risked ruining her reputation by the simple act of being alone with a young man.

DOWN ON THE FARM

Farmers entered the Jazz Age on a definite downswing, particularly when compared to the prosperity enjoyed by workers in the city. During World War I there had been high demand for food combined with a severe shortage of labor, so many farmers had made major capital investments, particularly the new all-purpose tractors like the Fordson or International Harvester's Farmall. But the armistice brought a sudden collapse in grain prices, and many farmers who had bought machinery on credit suddenly found it difficult to keep up with their loans.

However, all was not entirely grim for the farmer. Enough farmers were able to buy tractors in the 1920s that virtually every agricultural machinery company put serious effort into developing small tractors to compete with Henry Ford's sturdy and nimble Fordson. Mechanization made the farmer's life easier, with less backbreaking work.

Some farmers were even prosperous enough to be able to afford an automobile as well as a tractor. But even a tractor allowed farmers to go into town with a frequency that simply was not possible with horses. Emotional attachments that one developed with the creatures aside, one simply did not abuse so valuable a productive resource as a team of horses. After working the beasts all day in the field, it would not be good practice to then hitch them to a buggy, for they needed rest. By contrast, the internal combustion engine was tireless, needing only fueling and periodic maintenance. Thus farm families were able to participate in the life of the nearby town to a far greater extent, and even to take trips to the city in an automobile.

But the greatest factor in changing the experience of daily life on the farm was the radio. In many ways it was an even more potent agent of change for farm families than for urban ones. Although the telephone had already broken down some of the isolation that had made farm life so difficult in the 19th century, it was a point-to-point communication device, connecting individuals. The telephone might have facilitated gossip among farm families, but the radio connected them with cultural events in the big city. Farm families could now laugh along with the antics of Amos and Andy, or listen to a symphony orchestra. Young people in Idaho and Utah were dancing the Charleston like their urban contemporaries.

However, the cultural transfer was not entirely one-way. Radio took the musical styles that had been popular among rural people and presented them to a broader audience. People across the nation tuned into *National Barn Dance* on Chicago's WLS, which along with Nashville's *Grand Ole Opry* helped to solidify Country-Western as a distinct musical genre.

Of course radio was not entirely an unmixed blessing. Although it connected rural communities with the larger national culture and helped to popular-

In 1923 this dairy farmer had an antenna and headphones rigged up in the barn so he could tune in to the radio while milking cows.

ize rural musical forms, it also eroded local cultures. People who could turn on the radio and listen to a big-name performer were perhaps less likely to learn to make music on their own.

Operating a radio on the farm was not so simple as it was in the city. Because most farms still lacked electricity, radios had to be run with batteries. Those batteries were expensive, so farm families would generally try to extract every bit of power before replacing them. Thus the radio could become the agent of a most unusual form of family togetherness as family members moved their chairs closer to the radio, to the point their heads were fairly touching, just inches from the speaker.

THE CRASH AND THE END OF PROSPERITY

Although the stock market crash of October 1929 was catastrophic for investors, the ripple effects upon the nation as a whole took time to develop. The first and most obvious effect was upon banks, who had lent large amounts of money for speculators to buy stock on margin. When all that paper wealth evaporated in a few disastrous days of trading, banks were left with worthless notes. As a result, depositors became concerned whether the banks would remain solvent, leading to frenzied attempts to recover one's savings. These runs on banks often triggered the very failures people had been fearing, and as a result people who had nothing to do with stock speculations lost their life's savings.

By the end of 1929, people were cutting back on their spending, which actually exacerbated the effects of the stock market crash by reducing the amount of money with which the economy had to work. The failure of the economy to rebound only confirmed people's loss of confidence, which created a devolutionary spiral of economic shrinkage that culminated in the Great Depression. The energy and excitement that had characterized daily life in the 1920s was gone, replaced by a new grimness and conservatism that hearkened back to the values of an earlier, less consumerist era.

LEIGH KIMMEL

Further Readings

Allen, Frederick Lewis. *Only Yesterday: An Informal History of the 1920s.* New York: John Wiley & Sons, 1997.

Carter, Paul. A. *Another Part of the Twenties*. New York: Columbia University Press, 1977.

Douglas, Emily Taft. *Margaret Sanger: Pioneer of the Future*. New York: Holt, Rinehart and Winston, 1970.

Ertel, P. W. *The American Tractor: A Century of Legendary Machines*. Osceola, WI: MBI Publishing, 2001.
Gordon, Bob. *Early Electrical Appliances*. Princes Risbourough, Buckinghamshire: Shire Publications, 1998.
Gray, Madeline. *Margaret Sanger: A Biography of the Champion of Birth Control*. New York: Richard Marek Publishers, 1979.
Haber, Barbara. *From Hardtack to Home Fries: An Uncommon History of American Cooks and Meals*. New York: The Free Press, 2002.
Hanson, Erica. *The 1920s*. San Diego, CA: Lucent Books, 1999.
Harriss, John. *The Family: A Social History of the Twentieth Century*. Oxford: Oxford University Press, 1991.
Hoover, Robert and John. *An American Quality Legend: How Maytag Saved our Moms, Vexed the Competition, and Presaged America's Quality Revolution*. New York: McGraw-Hill, 1993.
Kyvig, David E. *Daily Life in the United States, 1920–1939: Decades of Promise and Pain.* Westport, CT: Greenwood Press, 2002.
Litshey, Earl. *The Housewares Story: A History of the American Housewares Industry.* Chicago, IL: National Housewares Manufacturers Association, 1973.
Lynd, Robert S. and Helen Merrell Lynd. *Middletown: A Study in American Culture.* New York: Harcourt, Brace & World. 1929.
———. *Middletown: in Transition: A Study in Cultural Conflicts*. New York: Harcourt, Brace and Company, 1937.
Matthews, Glenna. *Just a Housewife: The Rise and Fall of Domesticity in America*. New York: Oxford University Press, 1987.
Mintz, Steven. *Huck's Raft: A History of American Childhood*. Cambridge, MA: Harvard University Press, 2004.
Root, Waverly and Richard de Rochemont. *Eating in America: A History*. New York: Ecco Press, 1997.
Rubin, Susan Goldman. *Toilets, Toasters & Telephones: The How and Why of Everyday Objects*. San Diego, CA: Browndeer, 1998.
Shearer, Stephen R. *Hoosier Connections: The History of the Indiana Telephone Industry and the Indiana Telephone Association*. Indianapolis, IN: Indiana Telephone Association, 1992.
Shepard, Sue. *Pickled, Potted and Canned: How the Art and Science of Food Preservation Changed the World*. New York: Simon and Schuster, 2000.
Strasser, Susan. *Never Done: A History of American Housework*. New York: Pantheon, 1982.
Swisher, Clarice. *Women of the Roaring Twenties*. Detroit, IL: Lucent Books, 2006.
Tone, Andrea, ed. *Controlling Reproduction: An American History*. Wilmington, DE: S.R. Books, 1997.

Chapter 3

Material Culture

"So popular has installment buying become ... that it is possible today to buy almost everything from candy to private yachts."
—Hawthorne Daniel

THE THIRD DECADE of the 20th century was a time of contrast and dramatic change in the United States, resulting in the rise of a material culture that was unprecedented in American history. The 1920s began with a post–World War I depression, which gave way to widespread prosperity, and ended with the Great Depression, the most devastating economic downturn ever experienced in America. The years in between were filled with prosperity and improved standards of living for many Americans. Work weeks were shorter, prices were stable, and wealthy Americans had money to burn. New technologies and innovative products offered diverse ways of spending both money and time. Prohibition had taken effect at the turn of the century, precipitating widespread rebellion. For the first time since the founding of the republic, women had been granted the right to vote with the passage of the Nineteenth Amendment in 1920. The evolving culture of the Roaring Twenties, with its strong emphasis on youth, created a generational divide that was virtually impossible to reconcile. The 1920s also introduced a "new morality" that brought about a sexual revolution.

The most popular image of the Roaring Twenties is of flappers with bobbed hair and knee-length fringed skirts listening to jazz and dancing the Charleston. Other images are of Americans drinking bathtub gin or hanging out at one of the many speakeasies that sprang up in the United States during Prohibition.

Virtually all images of the period symbolize the materialist culture and consumer revolution of the 1920s. Despite the image of widespread prosperity, the consumer revolution bypassed the poorest Americans. Many of the images of the Roaring Twenties have an element of truth, but they tend to be exaggerated. Movies and television are in large part responsible for the exaggeration because they depict the affluent, glamorous American as the norm. Although much attention has been paid to the speakeasies of the period, most Americans did not drink alcohol during Prohibition. The home brew known as bathtub gin was sometimes viewed as a way to bypass restrictions on alcohol, but hundreds of individuals paid a high price for their lighthearted consumption, discovering that bathtub gin could cause blindness, brain damage, and death. In speakeasies, the quality of drinks was often poor since bartenders liberally diluted drinks with orange juice and ginger ale.

Images concerning jazz and dancing are generally accurate because both were part of the fabric of life in the Roaring Twenties, and both were linked to speakeasies. However, dancing was also a favorite activity in homes and at music halls, private parties, and night clubs. So many new dances were introduced in the 1920s that schools began offering classes in social dances such as the square dance, ballet, fox trot, camel walk, toddle, and tango. The Charleston was introduced in 1924 in the black musical *Runnin' Wild*. Many people remained convinced that jazz was responsible for the "decadent" materialism and immorality of the day and tried to ban it. Nevertheless, radio proved an excellent resource for bringing jazz to the general public. White composer George Gershwin (1898–1937) helped to complete the transformation to mainstream with songs that became American standards, including "Sewanee" and "Someone to Watch over Me."

AMERICAN URBANIZATION

For the first time in American history, more people lived in cities than in rural areas. This urbanization was partially responsible for the discarding of Victorian mores in favor of the "new morality," precipitating a major transformation in women's roles and appearance. Many people were scandalized by the new short skirts and what they viewed as loose behavior. Some cities passed ordinances mandating that women's skirts be a certain length below the knee. Even sophisticated New York City banned "risqué" dances. By 1923 the economy had recovered, and incomes rose at the same time that employees were given more leisure time to enjoy their new affluence.

The rapid industrialization of the United States had resulted in a surplus of ready-made products, and manufacturers who realized that their employees were potential customers turned to advertisers to convince Americans that these products were necessary to happiness and success. In 1924 Congress reduced the tax burden of the most affluent Americans by passing the Revenue Act, slashing income taxes, estate taxes, and the surtax on large incomes.

CONSUMPTION IN DAILY LIFE

Americans continued to spend a large part of their budgets on food and food-related products in the 1920s. In 1921 $44 million was spent on chewing gum, $408 million on candy, and $448 million on soft drinks. The number of smokers was increasing, and $1.7 billion was spent on tobacco products in 1921. By 1929 Americans were consuming 998 cigarettes per capita. The consumer revolution resulted in major changes in American home life. In 1920 35 percent of all homes were wired for electricity. Forty-eight percent of homes had ice boxes, but only one percent had a refrigerator. Less affluent Americans continued to store perishable food in underground storage containers or insulated chests. Eight percent of homes had washing machines, and nine percent had vacuum cleaners.

As the decade progressed, consumption increased as more items became affordable. Sewing machines, electric toasters and irons, pastel-colored kitchen and plumbing fixtures, improved phonographs and records, egg beaters, food grinders, mixers, and blenders were common household purchases. Home expenditures increased accordingly. Installment plans were available for virtually all purchases, including furniture, appliances, sewing machines, pianos, clothing, books, kitchen utensils, and luxury items. A fifth of all retail sales were a result of installment-plan purchases.

By 1927 two-thirds of all automobiles were bought on credit. Even Henry Ford caved in and established the Universal Credit Corporation in 1928. At the end of the decade, personal debts were rising 2.5 times faster than incomes.

In addition to large department stores that had become staples of American shopping culture, consumers in the 1920s had the option of buying household needs at "five and dimes" where a variety of budget items were sold. Chain stores

Eighty percent of all household purchases in the 1920s, including large items like furniture, were made by women.

Two dress styles from the 1920s with the typical straight lines, low waists, and bare arms.

such as A&P and Woolworth's significantly increased profits in response to consumer demands. Between 1920 and 1929, the percentage of chain stores in relation to total retail grew from four to 20 percent. Mail-order catalogs continued to gain in popularity, and Chicago became the catalog capital of the United States. Some companies introduced specialized catalogs to lure customers. In 1926 Montgomery Ward introduced the *Ward Way Home Catalog*. The following year, the *Sears Modern Homes Catalog* became available, with 144 full-color pages that offered a plethora of items and an installment plan. Sears sold 73 complete homes with detailed plans, ranging in price from $474 for the "Hanson," which had two bedrooms, a living room, a kitchen, a bathroom, and a porch, to $4,319 for the two-story Colonial Revival "Lexington." Garages could be purchased for as low as $82.50. Apartment buildings sold for $2,099 and commercial structures for $2,240.

The 1920s ushered in a period in which clothes were increasingly bought off the rack, and class distinctions blurred as shop girls began to dress fashionably. Based in part on European fashions of the period, women's clothing signified a major departure from those of the previous century. Hemlines were raised, and clothing was loose. Hair was bobbed; stockings were rolled down; galoshes were floppy; jewelry was prominent; hats were strange; lips were painted, and eyes were kohl-rimmed. Transparent silk stocking replaced the cotton lisle of the past, and clothing manufacturers began researching cheaper, more durable materials such as rayon.

Because women were modeling their lives after popular icons, rather than on their mothers and grandmothers, fashion became increasingly important in their lives. This insistence on fashion sometimes had devastating consequences. American dancer Isadora Duncan (1877–1927) became enamored of the long, flowing scarves that were popular in the 1920s and made them her trademark. While in France, on September 14, 1927, Duncan was riding in a car going at full speed. The wind caught her scarf and wrapped it around the automobile's wheels, propelling Duncan out of the car to her death.

In the spring of 1929, the Waldorf Hotel, a New York City landmark, went out of business, offering 2.4 million pieces of its history for sale. At the end of the first day, $25,000 had been spent on items ranging from tables and lamps to bedroom furniture and rugs. For $1 souvenir seekers could take home artifacts that included ash trays, candlesticks, and cups. Bargain hunters flocked to the roof garden to browse tables offering items from $2 to $20.

MARKETING MATERIAL CULTURE

In 1926 in an address to the American Association of Advertising Agencies, President Calvin Coolidge (1872–1933) grandiosely proclaimed that advertising was essential to the "regeneration and redemption of mankind" because it ministered to the "spiritual side of trade." The consumer revolution of the Roaring Twenties helped to turn advertising into a highly developed science. Advertising agencies began adapting the ideas of behaviorist John B. Watson (1878–1958) and iconic psychiatrist Sigmund Freud (1856–1939), devising new strategies for reaching consumers and generating high profits. One of the major elements of the strategy was convincing consumers of the importance of brand names in their lives.

By the mid-1920s, the J. Walter Thompson Company had become the most successful advertising agency in the world by virtue of placing $230,000 worth of advertising in the April issue of the *Ladies Home Journal*. The boy wonder of the advertising field, however, was Albert Lasker (1880–1952), who helped to shape modern advertising. Lasker is credited with creating the "reasons why" style of advertising that gave consumers explicit reasons why one product was better than another. He also created the first training program for advertising copywriters through Lord and Taylor, the advertising agency he had owned since the age of 23. Once assured of success, Lasker began paying himself a salary of over a million dollars a year. Lasker's efforts to professionalize advertising were so successful that Harvard Business School created the annual Advertising Awards in 1923. During the 1920s, advertising copy comprised more than half of all material produced on American printing presses.

A velvet and mesh hat from the 1920s. The modern flapper look was distinctly different from that of the corsets and wide hats of 1900.

Sinclair Lewis and 1920s Materialism

Sinclair Lewis, who critiqued the consumerism of the 1920s, in 1914.

Some scholars maintain that Sinclair Lewis (1888–1951) is the fiction writer who most realistically captured the aura of the 1920s. *Main Street*, published in 1920, painted a devastating portrait of middle-class Americans who had been corrupted by industrialization. *Babbitt*, a social satire published in 1922, dealt directly with the materialism that had become a way of life in the United States.

George Babbitt's determination to own the correct brand of all consumer items was considered so symbolic of the materialistic culture of the 1920s that the word "Babbitt" was added to the dictionary to describe a self-satisfied person enamored with middle-class values and materialism. With this exaggerated love of consumer items, Babbitt represented all American businessmen who had become so caught up in selling their products that they became victims of the consumerism they promoted. When Lewis was awarded the Pulitzer Prize in 1925 for *Arrowsmith*, he refused it.

An excerpt from *Babbitt* follows:

"Babbitt moaned, turned over, struggled back toward his dream. ... A dog barked in the next yard. As Babbitt sank blissfully into a dim warm tide, the paper-carrier went by whistling, and the rolled-up *Advocate* thumped the front door. Babbitt roused, his stomach constricted with alarm. As he relaxed, he was pierced by the familiar and irritating rattle of some one cranking a Ford: snap-ah-ah, snap-ah-ah, snap-ah-ah. ... He glanced once at his favorite tree, elm twigs against the gold patina of sky, and fumbled for sleep as for a drug. He who had been a boy very credulous of life was no longer greatly interested in the possible and improbable adventures of each new day. He escaped from reality till the alarm-clock rang, at seven-twenty.

"It was the best of nationally advertised and quantitatively produced alarm-clocks, with all the modern attachments, including cathedral chime, and a phosphorescent dial. Babbitt was proud to be awakened by such a rich device. Socially it was almost as creditable as buying expensive cord tires."

Since manufacturers needed to sell surplus products, they were only too glad to turn to professionals for help, and advertising agencies willingly accepted the lion's share of preparing advertising copy and graphics. This process allowed them to target consumers according to both personality traits and social values. Advertisers promoted consumerism by insisting that specific products could generate happiness, success, youth, beauty, and make consumers more feminine, masculine, sexually appealing, and stronger. Many ads were aimed at making consumers transform their appearances by losing weight, building muscle, growing hair, or enhancing their busts, raising grave concerns about self-image in the process. Lucky Strike cigarettes, for instance, were touted as weight-loss aids. A 1925 ad for a hair treatment product asked men if they would still be loved if they went bald.

In keeping with the widespread advertising and media emphasis on youth, the flapper image was heavily promoted in the movies and magazines of the Roaring Twenties to the extent that it came to be virtually synonymous with consumer culture. *Vanity Fair* assured American women that their products were worn by all flappers. A series of films about flappers were essentially used as wish lists for American women. To accompany *The Perfect Flapper* (1924) starring Colleen Moore, Associated First National Pictures issued a press book with ties to 12 separate fashion and beauty products. Celebrities were increasingly called on to convince consumers to use certain products. Fake doctors were employed to give medical advice on manufacturers' products. Despite objections from environmentalists, billboards also became a popular and effective source of advertising.

Advertising, including packaging and point-of-purchase displays, grew more sophisticated and ubiquitous in the 1920s.

A Coca-Cola ad on a serving tray from the 1920s—an example of the many attempts to convince consumers of the importance of brand names.

Ads were also used to convince Americans that they *needed* certain products. Advertisers became adept at scaring Americans into buying items such as toothpaste, mouthwash, deodorant, and bath salts to ensure clean breath and destroy body odors. A 1925 ad for Odorono deodorant, appearing in *Motion Picture Magazine*, cautioned consumers that perspiration posed a serious threat to romance. Another deodorant ad warned that body odor could suddenly come "creeping in" and threaten happiness. Ads for Woodbury Facial Soap and Jergens lotion emphasized the importance of soft, touchable skin that encouraged intimacy. The introduction of sanitary napkins in the 1920s presented advertisers with a major dilemma. Ultimately, ads were devised that gave the necessary information without using explicit words. To save women the embarrassment of asking for the products, Kotex wrapped them in plain brown paper and placed a coin box directly beside the boxes.

The first commercial radio broadcast took place in November 1920, and 10 stations were on the air within a year. In 1924 consumers spent $3.58 million purchasing radios. By 1928 radios were able to run on electricity. Radios that could be left on for longer periods opened up greater opportunities for hawking consumer products. The possibilities seemed endless when the first car radio was marketed that same year. Mass magazines continued to be a valuable resource for selling products, both to the general public and to specific audiences.

In this way, advertisers sold the materialistic culture, as well as particular products. By the early 1920s, advertisers had recognized that most purchasing decisions were made by females, and women's magazines provided a showcase for a myriad of products. Studies show that 80 percent of all household purchases in the 1920s were made by women. Females regularly purchased food, clothing, electrical appliances, linoleum, rugs, and home furnishings. They also purchased automobiles and accessories, which had been considered a male province in the past.

TRANSPORTATION

By 1920 the automobile had become an integral part of American life. In 1921 there were a reported nine million cars traversing the roads. In 1923 and 1924 Ford sold two million vehicles. Priced at $290, the Model T Touring car made up more than half of all cars in operation and was made to last a lifetime. Since they were more expensive, Buicks, Pierce Arrows, Cadillacs, and Oldsmobiles were considered status symbols. Consumers of the previous decade had generally settled for conservative black automobiles and uncomfortable interiors. In the 1920s, automobile designers discarded the low-hung models of the past and offered customers a range of colors. The most popular new colors were conservative browns, tans, and grays, but custom-made vehicles often mirrored the tastes of owners. A famous actress, for instance, ordered a robin's egg blue town car with a border of deeper blue and a pin line of deep coral. Dark red leather interiors and nickel hardware became common. The more expensive models had two rear-seat compartments, one for storing a small ice box, and the other for holding luggage. Some models had large tonneau seats that were as comfortable as arm chairs.

Automobiles had a major impact on all aspects of life in the United States. The middle-class migration to the suburbs that had begun in the previous decades accelerated in the 1920s, and roads were improved to handle increased traffic. Automobiles also helped to precipitate the sexual revolution of the Roaring Twenties. In the past, young people had generally socialized in groups, and young women were often under the watchful eyes of parents or chaperones.

A 1927 automobile with a two-toned body built by the Stutz Motor Company, whose models were known for speed and luxury.

A woman picnicking at a public auto camp in Yellowstone National Park beside an older car with an attached foldout tent in 1920.

The closed automobile allowed courting couples an unprecedented privacy. Automobiles also reduced distances between rural areas and large cities, propelling even isolated areas into the materialistic culture of the day.

Automobiles also made it easier for Americans to enjoy picnicking, which had become a national passion, encouraging picnickers to drive for miles in order to find the ideal spot. Some manufacturers offered models with special features designed for camping, including a foldout tent that attached directly to an automobile. Motor homes were built on the chassis of automobiles to make campers.

One of the most popular was the 1928 Nomad motor coach that was promoted as "A Highway Home Uniting Comfort with Economy." Manufacturers used the love of the outdoors to increase profits by offering picnicking accessories. The Gold Medal Folding Camp Chair, which was promoted as adjusting to any body size and holding any weight, was especially popular. The Upton Kamp Kook Kit, containing a grill, two cups, two frying pans, and a coffee boiler, also sold well. Coleman became the leading producer of camp stoves. By the mid-1920s, Everywoman's Garment Company was selling knickers designed to make camping easier and more comfortable for women.

Air travel became more readily available in the 1920s, even though it was beyond the means of most Americans. On April 13, 1925, Henry Ford announced that he was sponsoring the first commercial air flight between Chi-

Transporting British Homes

One of the most glaring examples of the materialism of the 1920s arose in response to events taking place in Europe. In the 1920s much of Europe was still recovering from World War I, and many British families were forced to sell homes dating back to the 15th and 16th centuries. Other homes were moved when industrialization resulted in railroads and street car lines cutting into private property.

While some Americans settled for transporting interiors and furnishings from Britain, others, eager to highlight their connection to European society, began buying British homes and transporting them in entirety to the United States. Most of those dwellings were moved to New York or California. Homes were meticulously dismantled in Britain, with each part numbered and packaged to facilitate reconstruction. The homes were generally sent to London where they were displayed, complete with lawns and flower beds, to attract potential buyers. If a buyer already existed, homes and interiors were shipped directly to America.

The cost of these transported homes was enormous. Buyers paid not only the original purchase price but also transportation costs, high tariffs, and costs of rebuilding homes once they arrived in the United States. The price of transporting interiors ranged from $2,000 to $75,000. One Connecticut buyer paid to have an entire Elizabethan manor with half a dozen rooms, a hallway, woodwork, and shingles shipped America. The oldest of these transported homes was Nordland Hall, a castle that had stood in Halifax, Yorkshire, for five centuries. The castle was moved to Liverpool by truck before being shipped to San Francisco via New York. The buyer paid $150 a ton in shipping costs alone.

One of the most famous transported homes, a Soho mansion designed by Sir James Thornhill in 1702, had been owned by William Hogworth. The home originally had 20 rooms, but only 15 were shipped to the United States, along with all of their accoutrements, leaving only brick walls behind. In New York, the entrance hall, grand staircase, paneled oak walls, windows, mantles, fireplaces, and frescoes were painstakingly reassembled. The project was completed by adding period furniture throughout the house.

cago and Detroit. By 1929 Ford had introduced the Ford Tri-Motor plane, christened the "City of Philadelphia." The plane was designed to ensure passage from the Atlantic to the Pacific Coast in 48 hours. On the first sojourn, Ford transported passengers by train from New York to an Ohio airport where they boarded the plane and flew to Kansas, seated in roomy wicker seats. After traveling by train to New Mexico, passengers flew to Los Angeles, meeting the 48-hour deadline.

MATERIALISM AND ARCHITECTURE

During the 1920s, 5.7 million new homes were built in the United States. Architect Frank Lloyd Wright (1856–1924) continued to be the foremost American architect, and his prairie-style homes remained popular throughout the 1920s, particularly in the suburbs. As more homes were wired for electricity, Wright and other architects began using electricity in their designs. Many architects adopted the open interior plan in which living areas, dining rooms, and kitchens flowed into one another. Only bedrooms and bathrooms were isolated from family areas. Bathrooms with indoor plumbing were still a novelty in the Roaring Twenties and were a major improvement over the outhouses of past generations. Because of the easy availability of hot water, Americans of the 1920s bathed more often than their ancestors. One- and two-story bungalows continued to sell well among American homeowners. In the south the architectural trend was toward one- and two-story bungalows with large front porches where families gathered in warm weather.

The style of architecture that came to be most closely identified with the Roaring Twenties was art deco, a style that combined elements of ancient architecture with modern futuristic forms. Art deco received international attention after it was introduced at the Exposition des Arts Decoratifs in Paris in 1925. Art deco was heavily influenced by the ancient architecture of the Far East, Greece, Rome, Africa, India, and the Mayan and Aztec styles of the South American continent. The Egyptian artifacts found in 1922 in the tomb of young King Tutankhamen, who had remained entombed in the Valley of the Kings for some 3,300 years, were arguably the greatest influence. In the United States the most renowned architect of the art deco style was Raymond Hood (1881–1934), who designed buildings for the *Chicago Tribune* (1924) and the *New York Daily News* (1929) in the art deco style.

AMUSEMENTS

In the 1920s, the amount that Americans spent on recreational pursuits rose by 300 percent. As a result of political and social reforms and changing lifestyles, Americans of the 1920s had more leisure time than at any time in American history. In towns around the United States, the public flocked to bandstands, clubhouses, pavilions, picnic tables, outdoor grills, and refreshment stands. The World's Columbian Exposition that took place in Chicago in 1893 served as a model for the building of amusement parks throughout the 1920s. Unlike more expensive entertainments, amusement parks continued to be popular during the Great Depression.

Most children's toys of the 1920s were manufactured. Cast-iron and pull-toys continued to be popular, but they were made of lighter materials, making them safer for small children. Banks, automobiles, buses, airplanes, and fire engines remained favorite items. Yo-yos had originated in ancient Greece and China, but they attained new popularity in the 1920s after Donald Duncan began

A detail from an Egyptian Revival doorway. The Egyptian craze of the 1920s sparked by the discovery of King Tut's tomb also influenced Art Deco buildings of the era.

manufacturing a cheap wooden model. Adults also loved yo-yos and enjoyed inventing new tricks to impress others. Electric trains had been gaining in popularity since the turn of the century, but they achieved new market status in the 1920s with the introduction of sturdy Lionel trains, complete with power stations, automatic switches, and warning signals. These trains were accessorized in great detail, and they had real headlights that lit up as trains traveled past toy farms and villages. After newspapers began publishing *Little Orphan Annie* in 1924, comic strips became popular among children and adults. Comic books came into their own in the 1920s, generally evolving from comic strips or from radio shows such as *The Lone Ranger*. The longer medium allowed cartoonists to develop more detailed plot lines than in short comic strips.

Music was an essential element of the material culture of the Roaring Twenties. In 1921 $232 million was spent on musical instruments. For those who preferred listening to music rather than playing it, the radio offered a variety. On November 28, 1925, the *Grand Ole Opry* began a regular broadcast of its Saturday night show from Nashville, Tennessee, and fans of country and bluegrass helped to increase the sale of radios and phonographs. In the 1920s some 200 phonograph companies were producing two million phonographs a year, and consumers could purchase records to suit individual tastes. Improved technologies introduced at mid-decade vastly improved the quality of these recordings.

JAZZ AND SPORTS

The defining music of the decade was jazz, and the 1920s are often referred to as "The Jazz Age," symbolizing not only a musical style, but the rebellion of young white Americans, northern blacks, and the anti-Prohibition population. Jazz evolved in New Orleans as a mixture of other musical styles, including slave spirituals, minstrel music, vaudeville, rag time, and brass band. Blues, with its tendency toward improvisation and personal expression, was a significant musical influence, and blues singers such as Bessie Smith (1894–1936) and Ma Rainey (1886–1939) drew large crowds as they traveled around the country. Jazz became the first American music to break down racial barriers. By 1920 New York and Chicago had emerged as the music centers of the United States, and large jazz bands propelled jazz into the mainstream. In New York, where the Harlem Renaissance was in full swing, pianist and composer Eubie Blake (1887–1983) and bandleaders Fletcher Henderson (1897–1952) and Duke Ellington (1899–1974) were the major attractions. In Chicago, trumpet player Louis Armstrong (1901–71) and bandleader Joe "King" Oliver (1885–1938) held center stage.

Spectator sports continued to draw large audiences in the 1920s, and large sums were spent on tickets and sports equipment and memorabilia. Baseball had become a national passion. On January 5, 1920, the Boston Red Sox traded Babe Ruth to the New York Yankees for $125,000. It was a move that changed baseball history, because Ruth led the Yankees to 39 American League Pennants and 26 World Series Titles. Yankee Stadium became known as "the house that Ruth built." Other sports heroes of the day included boxer Jack Dempsey (1895–1983) and football player Knute Rockne (1888–1931). College football, boxing, golf, and tennis also drew large crowds throughout the decade.

Although gambling was not a new pastime in the United States, it reached new heights in the 1920s, partly because the telephone made it much easier to place bets. When governments attempted to regulate the industry, gambling establishments sought greener pastures on river boats and trains, which were not restricted by local laws. The 1920s were considered the "golden age" of horse racing in the United States, and some states imitated the example of Kentucky, which guaranteed a share of profits from the Kentucky Derby by legalizing para-mutual betting. This practice allowed race tracks to earn a percentage of all winnings, generating taxable income. Even churches and community organizations gave their stamp of approval to gambling by organizing bingo games, for which participants purchased playing cards.

MOVIES AND OTHER ENTERTAINMENT

Movies, theaters, and concerts attracted large audiences in the 1920s. In 1921 alone, Americans spent $800 million on these activities. The movies were by far the most popular entertainment venue of the day. In 1922 20 million people per day went to the movies. With the advent of perfected sound techniques at mid-decade, attendance improved significantly. By 1929 95 million tickets per week were purchased. The most popular stars of the day were Theda Bara, Charlie Chaplin, Rudolph Valentino, Joan Crawford, Clara Bow, Mary Pickford, Douglas Fairbanks, Gloria Swanson, Greta Garbo, John Gilbert, and Colleen Moore. Because of the studio system, a few companies produced, exhibited, and distributed the majority of the 600 or so movies that were made each year.

Mary Pickford, one of the biggest film stars of the era, standing beside a movie camera on a California beach.

In 1920 producers such as Cecil B. DeMille developed a new formula for making movies by highlighting the rich and fashionable in cinematic fantasies that dealt with sex, romance, marriage, glamour, and money. The stars as well as the characters they played were offered up as ideals for mainstream America, establishing new moral standards and promoting consumer goals. In DeMille's 1921 release *Forbidden Fruit,* for instance, Agnes Ayres played Mary Mardock, the wife of an alcoholic. After finding work as a seamstress, Mary is forced into service as a paid escort to a millionaire who falls in love with her. After her husband is conveniently killed by the police who are trying to arrest him for blackmailing the millionaire, Mary marries her prince and lives happily ever after. Such films allowed producers to promote consumption by convincing women they could look like movie stars if they bought the right products and wore the right clothes. At the same time, producers transmitted the message that money paved the way to true happiness.

Films of the 1920s were generally categorized by genre to attract specific audiences. The most popular genres were westerns, comedies, mysteries, romances, and horror. Some movies of the 1920s, such as the comedies of Laurel and Hardy and Buster Keaton, are still considered classics. In 1928 Walt Disney introduced Steamboat Willie, the forerunner of Mickey Mouse, to American audiences, establishing one of the most extensive consumer empires in American history. Television was still in the experimental stage in the 1920s; but by 1928, a few Americans had sets in their homes.

The dining experience had been honed to an art in the 1920s. Much of that entertainment took place at restaurants and tea rooms such as the Tea Court of New York's Plaza Hotel, where the materialism of the age was reflected in the opulent décor of Tiffany glass, caen stone, Brech violet marble, and hand woven Savonnerie rugs. Tables in the Tea Court were graced with Baccarat crystal and gold-encrusted china. Americans of the 1920s entertained both lavishly and informally in their homes, at clubs, in rented halls, and at lawn parties and picnics. Regular social events included luncheons, suppers, balls, house parties, bridge games, and benefits.

CONCLUSION

After the trauma of World War I, many Americans were ready to abandon Progressive Era ideas of social reform in favor of self-indulgence. This, combined with greater income and leisure, the spread of radio, and the growing sophistication of marketing led to a surge in consumption. Widespread automobile ownership brought a new feeling of freedom and mobility, but also helped make consumer debt more common. When marketers picked up the imagery of the times, especially of the flapper, and used it to promote products, American culture gained an indelible set of images from a brief but memorable era. What Americans were also left with was the fallout from massive stock speculation and a growing habit of buying on credit.

ELIZABETH R. PURDY

Further Readings

Adams, Judith. *The American Amusement Park Industry: A History of Technology and Thrills.* Boston, MA: Twayne, 1991.

Allen, Frederick Lewis. *Only Yesterday: An Informal History of the 1920s.* New York: Wiley, 1997.

Braden, Donna R. *Leisure and Entertainment in America.* Dearborn, MI: Henry Ford Museum, 1988.

Desser, David and Garth S. Jowett, eds. *Hollywood Goes Shopping.* Minneapolis, MN: University of Minnesota Press, 2000.

Dumenil, Lynn. *The Modern Temper: American Culture and Society in the 1920s.* New York: Hill and Wang, 1995.

Ewen, Stuart and Elizabeth Ewen. *Channels of Desire: Mass Images and the Shaping of American Consciousness.* New York: McGraw-Hill, 1982.

Eyvig, David E. *Daily Life in the United States, 1920–1940.* Chicago, IL: Ivan R. Dee, 2004.

Goldberg, David J. *Discontented America: The United States in the 1920s.* Baltimore, MD: Johns Hopkins University Press, 1999.

Kronzberg, Melvin and Joseph Gies. *By the Sweat of Thy Brow: Work in the Western World.* New York: Putnam's, 1975.

Mailer, Nathan. *New World Coming: The 1920s and the Making of Modern America.* New York: Scribner, 2003.

Meade, Marion. *Bobbed Hair and Bathtub Gin: Writers Running Wild in the Twenties.* New York: Doubleday, 2004.

"Old English Homes Imported." *New York Times* (January 21, 1923).

Perrett, Geoffrey. *America in the Twenties: A History.* New York: Simon and Schuster, 1982.

Schlereth, Thomas J. *Cultural History and Material Culture: Everyday Life, Landscapes, Museums.* Ann Arbor, MI: University of Michigan Press, 1990.

Schuller, Gunther. *Early Jazz: Its Roots and Musical Development.* New York: Oxford University Press, 1968.

Strasser. *Satisfaction Guaranteed: The Marking of the American Mass Market.* New York: Pantheon, 1989.

Streissguth, Tom. *The Roaring Twenties: An Eyewitness to History.* New York: Facts on File, 2001.

Tedlow, Richard S. *New and Improved: The Story of Mass Marketing in America.* New York: Basic Books, 1990.

Chapter 4

Social Attitudes

"We're coming, we're coming, our brave little band;
On the right side of temp'rance we now take our stand."
—Irwin Silber

THE TEN YEARS between 1920 and 1930 saw significant changes in American social attitudes, beliefs, and practices. The writer F. Scott Fitzgerald described this time as "the gaudiest spree in history." Whether or not this is true, the decade was certainly colorful. Descriptions of this time—Roaring Twenties, the Jazz Age, the Prohibition Era, the Age of Intolerance—all suggest qualities that have captured the popular imagination and remain as lasting memories.

The election of President Warren G. Harding (1865–1923) in 1920 provided still another identity for both his administration and the era: the Return of Normalcy. This "normality" was in reaction to the extraordinary events and disappointments brought about by World War I. It was also a reaction against the previous Progressive Era, which had expanded the role of the federal government and its regulatory powers. During his presidency Harding embraced an older, politically conservative worldview that relied on laissez-faire approaches to business and life in general. His election also marked the beginning of Republican domination of the presidency throughout the 1920s under the later presidencies of Calvin Coolidge (1872–1933) and Herbert Hoover (1874–1964).

The 1920s were a time not only of conservative policies but of a general inward focus on parochial American political issues rather than international affairs. This internal focus remains a characteristic of America to this day.

Labeled "isolationism," America's absorption with domestic issues had a great impact on the social development of the decade and the various behaviors that were represented. Although the outside world did not disappear (nor did America's responsibilities to it), these years shaped an internal belief in the superiority of American democratic institutions, ideas, science, literature, and society over those of other countries. In such a situation, nationalist and patriotic attitudes would play a major part in the emerging social mix.

Although there was a substantial desire by many people and politicians for a return to "old time" values and traditions, the decade represented a time of considerable and dynamic change that created substantial tensions and challenges in American society as a whole. The national psyche craved certainty, predictability, and nostalgia, but new social developments undercut the old certainties, making life more complex.

POPULATION AND URBANIZATION

One of the most critical factors affecting social attitudes resulted from a shift in the location of the American population, and this change would reverberate through the social history of the period. For the first time in American history the 1920 census revealed that the population of cities now outnumbered that of rural areas. Of a population of 106 million, 54 million now lived in cities and the trend would continue throughout the decade. By 1930, out of 138 million people, 70 million were city residents. The impact of this mass movement of people created challenges as well as opportunities.

Urban life offered possibilities for improving one's economic position in a rapidly expanding economy. It also offered greater freedoms and attractions, both positive and negative. Urban life provided activities in the form of museums, galleries, theatres, universities, libraries, restaurants, cinemas, and sports. The technological developments of the period, such as food refrigeration, household appliances, ready-made clothing, and canned goods, allowed people to live more easily. The expansion of transport services in terms of railroads, subways and elevated railroads, not to mention the decisive arrival of the automobile, meant that movement was possible even in the midst of increased congestion and overcrowded housing. The pressure on housing would be constant throughout the decade.

To offset growing congestion, cities built upwards, making use of elevators and the steel frame to create high-rise offices and residences. With living space there also came a demand for recreation and employment, pushing more people into restricted spaces and producing tensions in the process. Factories moved to outlying areas, the value of city lands increased, and many of the less affluent had to live in overcrowded tenements, giving rise to poor hygiene and disease, and having a dramatic social impact on the quality of life for many of the new urban residents. Though the move to the city could be liberating for some, it could also mean poverty and sacrifice for others. Yet the

Ford Model T

The Ford Model T dramatically contributed to the changing social attitudes and new freedoms of the 1920s and became a symbol of the decade. Between 1909 and 1927, the Ford Motor Company built 15 million cars and made America accessible to the masses. Henry Ford was able to do this by transforming the nature of the assembly line, reducing cost, and contributing to the prosperity of investors and workers alike. Originally assembled at the Piquette Avenue Plant in Detroit, assembly time was reduced by 1913 to one hour and 33 minutes. By the end of production in 1927, Ford was producing a car every 24 seconds. All models had basically the same chassis and engine. Being an early example of a vanadium steel car, Ford made the Model T so strong it endured the rough dirt road conditions of the day.

Driving the Model T was not easy. Acceleration and braking were slow and cumbersome. The brakes worked by a system of restrictive bands on the 2-speed transmission, not by callipers on the wheels. With three floor pedals, two steering levers, and one floor lever, and given the different pedal and lever functions, driving required considerable hand and leg coordination. The Model T relied on a 4-cylinder engine that could reach a top speed of 45 mph and it ran on narrow pneumatic tires. Completely interchangeable parts made repair routine. Over a 19-year period, the Model T changed very little and was clearly outdated and outperformed by the end of its run. Even with its fading design, reliance on hand cranking to start, and its universal black color scheme (black paint dried faster), the Model T's cost made up for its many deficiencies. From its original $850 starting price, the Model T's cost fell to under $300 by 1927. With credit terms, it was easily affordable. Its popularity even brought it nicknames like Tin Lizzie and Flivver. Finally replaced by the more stylish and modern Model A in 1927, the durability of the Model T has meant that many of these cars can still be found.

Five people in a Ford Model T touring car in 1923. Ford produced 15 million Model Ts over 18 years before introducing the Model A.

era was supposed to be the best time in American history. As a popular song of the period proclaimed: "Ain't We Got Fun?" The reality suggested something different. According to some estimates, a majority of the population fell below the not-yet-clearly-defined poverty line.

IMMIGRATION, NATIVISM, AND RACISM

In addition to the shift in population from the more established countryside to new urban areas, America experienced massive immigration in the latter decades of the 19th century and in the opening decades of the 20th. Over one million immigrants a year came to America in the years from 1905 to 1914. Immigrants made up 15 percent of the total population in the early 1900s. In some cities, New York City being the most prominent example, immigrants made up 40 percent of the population. Besides contributing to the urban swell, immigrants came to symbolize for some a threat to the basic homogeneity of the American republic. Many wanted the preservation of a perceived past, characterized by greater harmony and conformity. As a result, pressures were exerted to amend the immigration policies that had previously amounted to an open door.

In 1921 the Emergency Quota Act was introduced to restrict immigration to three percent of those nationalities living in the United States in 1910. This act was further strengthened by the Immigration Quota Act of 1924, which reduced the quota to two percent and made 1890 the year for determining numbers. In effect this act attempted to halt the influx of those immigrants who were deemed most disparate, largely in terms of nationality and religion. Yet even after 1920s restrictions, over four million immigrants came to America. Many Americans saw it as a patriotic duty to insist on restrictions, as did some unions who saw lower-paid immigrants as competitors for employment in a market that, though expanding, still had significant pockets of unemployment.

Klan leaders marching without masks in Washington, D.C., on September 13, 1926.

The nativist attitude against immigration was matched by a rising tide of racism against the nation's African-American population. In the course of the urbanization of America, there had been a migration of hundreds of thousands of African Americans from the segregated south to the north, initially inspired by the greater opportunities that came with economic expansion during World War I. This population influx, like that of the immigrant migrations, produced a negative reaction in many quarters. Ethnic hostility was now combined with racism as a notable fact in the cultural life of the 1920s.

All of these groups were seen as a threatening foreign presence, whether they were Jews, Catholics, or African Americans, and their presence was resisted, discriminated against, and feared. The most vocal and radical organization to articulate such feelings was the Ku Klux Klan (KKK). The Klan claimed over five million members in 1923 and had political influence not only in the south but in the midwest and parts of the west.

The Klan laid claims to protecting core American values, although in practice it preached racial and religious superiority and hatred. The KKK hid behind white sheets and used terror and lynching to achieve their objectives. Although the number of lynchings in America declined in the 1920s, the problem remained a concern, and the Dyer Anti-Lynching Bill was introduced in 1918. This bill passed the House in 1922 before being blocked in the Senate. The Dyer Act nevertheless represented a step toward reversing a blot on the American landscape. The exposure of corruption inside the Klan in 1925 reduced its membership and influence during the latter years of the decade.

MIGRATION AND RIOTING

The increased African-American migration northward challenged social attitudes and produced new social tensions and insecurities. Existing white populations saw the movement in terms of racist stereotypes, and as a competition for jobs and housing. Such tensions could explode, as they did in East St. Louis in 1917 when 39 African Americans died as a result of rioting. In such an unwelcome climate, organizations such as the United Negro Improvement Association (UNIA), founded in 1914 by Jamaican-born Marcus Harvey (1887–1940), gained an appeal in many of the emerging black communities. In its promotion of racial pride, culture, and economic development, the UNIA underwent a major expansion during the 1920s. However with its nationalist themes and money-raising projects it produced suspicions and government investigations, which led in 1923 to Marcus Garvey's conviction for fraud. Following his release from jail, Garvey was deported in 1927 and the movement fell into disarray.

Other African-American organizations such as the National Association for the Advancement of Colored People (NAACP), founded in 1909, campaigned to protect African Americans by calling for greater integration and full civil rights protection. Ultimate success in reversing legal and other forms of racial discrimination did not overcome this social issue until the arrival of the civil rights movement in the 1950s.

The fear of the foreigner also took the form of resentment and hostility directed against external ideologies, particularly those proposing radical social change and revolution. The 1917 Russian Revolution gave reality to these fears, particularly the idea that such an upheaval could be transported to American shores. This trepidation was not restricted to a fear of Bolshevik Communism but was extended to concern over the spread of anarchism, which challenged the very existence of many American institutions. A series of strikes and bombings during 1919 saw the launch of the 1919 Red Scare led by the Attorney General, A. Mitchell Palmer (1872–1936). The Red Scare actions essentially ended in the summer of 1920. It was estimated that during this time there were as many as 150,000 such radicals at large in America, and the political climate called for their suppression and, if foreign-born, exile. At the height of this affair in 1920 as many as 6,000 accused radicals were rounded up. Few were ever convicted and most were later released; however, several hundred would be deported.

The most famous product of these times was the Sacco and Vanzetti case, which symbolized the unsettled climate of this decade. The case revealed the divisions within society and manifested the extremes in public reaction to the competition between Americanism and radicalism. Nicola Sacco (1891–1927) and Bartolomeo Vanzetti (1888–1927) were Italian immigrants and anarchists living in Massachusetts who were arrested in May 1920 for payroll robbery and murder. Their politics seemed to be a factor in the evidence of their crime, and challenged the idea of a fair trial, given the pre-existing prejudices against them. They became *causes célèbres* in liberal-left circles, but their convictions were upheld and they were executed on August 23, 1927, in the face of worldwide, although primarily European-led protests.

Although the immediate Red Scare soon passed from the front pages, there remained within American society a deep suspicion of the Communist menace that would remerge after World War II. Xenophobia became part of the social landscape of the 1920s and all foreigners could be subjected to periodic mistrust. This could have a regional focus as well and include groups as disparate as the Japanese and Mexicans who primarily settled on the west coast of America.

Other organizations such as the American Legion emerged at the end of World War I, and as prominent defenders of the American Constitution, contributed to the drive for 100 percent Americanism. The American Legion along with the Rotary clubs, founded in Chicago in 1905, became increasingly influential in the decade as vehicles that served the American way of life.

THE PROHIBITION EXPERIMENT

The most critical determinant of American social attitudes in the entire decade was undoubtedly the Prohibition experiment, which symbolized the coming of age of a long-established crusade against the evils of alcohol. The passage of the

Eighteenth Amendment to the Constitution in 1919, which prohibited the manufacture, transport, and consumption of intoxicating liquor, would confound and challenge the very nature of America's social fabric. Prohibition came into effect on January 16, 1920, and its enforcement mechanism was the Volstead Act, enacted October 28, 1919, which provided penalties for violations.

Prohibition was the end-product of a long drive by Wayne Wheeler's (1869–1927) Anti-Saloon League and by Christian forces such as the Women's Christian Temperance Union that saw alcohol as a social evil. Alcohol was blamed for poverty and violence, particularly domestic violence, and was believed to be the primary cause of national immorality. Prohibition was seen as a magical cure and important evangelists such as Billy Sunday (1862–1935) preached of a new world and a new beginning. By ending demon drink, salvation was at hand.

Prohibition gained the support of the majority of politicians in both parties, that is, those outside of heavily immigrant urban areas such as Chicago, New York, Boston, and Philadelphia. Behind this political upheaval was, for the first time, the appearance of women as a force for change. American women increased their influence and powers of persuasion by embracing Prohibition as part of the reform process. Their voices had gained a new resonance following the ratification of the Nineteenth Amendment on August 26, 1920. Women now had the vote and they would be heard, and for many women banning drink was key to their moral agenda.

Prohibition officers dismantling a still in San Francisco in the 1920s. Metal stills like the one at right were used in the production of moonshine.

Unfortunately in practice Prohibition did not prove to be a social panacea. While arguably lowering American alcohol consumption during this era, Prohibition corrupted many of the institutions Americans valued, such as the court system, police force, and local government. Enforcement directly led to bootlegging and the rise of organized crime, producing the gangster legend in the process. Murder and mayhem followed and crime became a way of doing business in many American cities. Famous gangsters such as Al Capone (1899–1947) became national celebrities who enforced their rule in cities like Chicago with bribery and violence. They undercut the very nature of municipal democracy, providing what the bootleggers called "hospitality" to those who could afford it. With bars and saloons illegal, there arose a new facility for the sale of alcohol, the speakeasy. Chicago alone had over 7,000 in the 1920s. Chicago also became synonymous for gang warfare with approximately 800 gangsters killed in the period from 1920 to 1933.

Rapid fortunes were made in the illegal booze trade and bootleggers such as Cincinnati's George Remus (1876–1952) accumulated a fortune of over $5 million. Some critics suggest that he was the inspiration for F. Scott Fitzgerald's (1896–1940) famous novel *The Great Gatsby*. One persistent opponent of Prohibition was the notable writer H.L. Mencken (1880–1956) of the *Baltimore Sun*, who saw the entire enterprise as a waste of time and energy, driven forward by ignorance and hypocrisy. Prohibition hurt the public welfare in

Prohibition before the Eighteenth Amendment

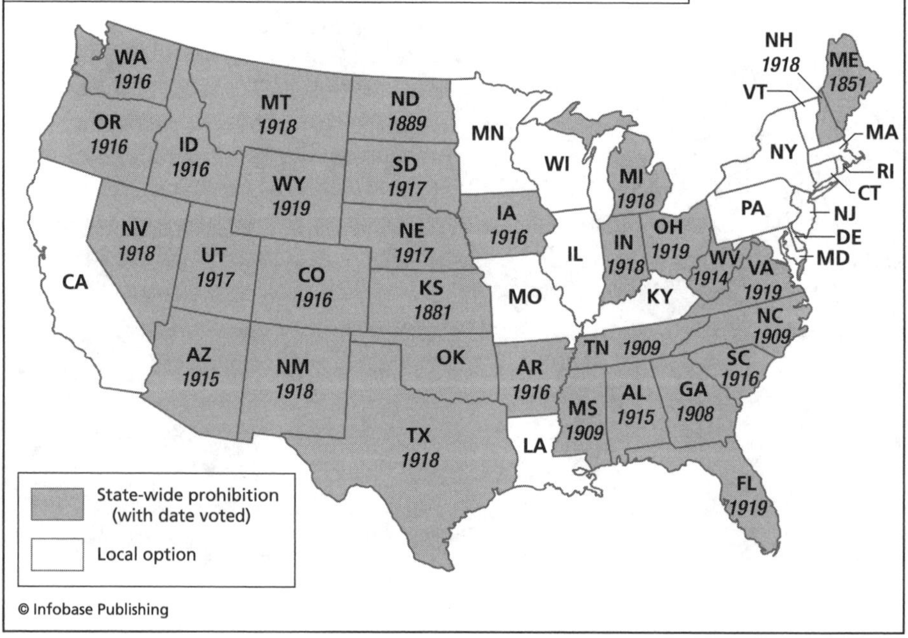

St. Valentine's Day Massacre

Gangsterism gained power and even prestige in the 1920s in ways never before imagined. Its emergence tore at the moral fabric and undercut social order and propriety. Although the Thompson sub-machine gun gave the roar to the Roaring Twenties, it was Prohibition that made all things possible. Bootlegging provided the social lubricant for society and filled criminal coffers with unheard of millions. The immorality and illegality of alcohol consumption influenced only a dwindling portion of the population, and the percentage declined as the decade progressed with illegality becoming accepted by the public at large.

Speakeasies became the distribution centers for the illegal trade and their cover charges allowed Jazz Age entertainment to flourish and furnished a front for other illegal activities such as gambling and prostitution. Profits were such that gangs often warred over boundaries for their trade and this meant disputes were often settled in blood. Al "Scarface" Capone's control of Chicago's bootlegging and vice made him an icon of the era. His gang of thousands of soldiers supported the many speakeasies that bought exclusively from him and helped bring in a reported $100 million annual income.

There were rivals who were willing to risk it all and challenge Capone's monopoly; one such upstart was the North Side's George "Bugs" Moran (1891–1957). To meet this threat, Capone, who was at his Florida retreat, planned a Valentine's Day gift for Bugs. It was hoped that Moran could be induced to come to the SMC Cartage Company at 2122 North Clarke Street on February 14, 1929, in order to buy some hijacked liquor and then be ambushed. Seven of his gang along with some associates did show up. They were: James Clark, Frank and Pete Gusenberg, Adam Heyer, John May, optometrist Reinhardt Schwimmer, and Al Weinshank. The Capone plot was organized by Jack "Machine Gun" McGurn and carried out by Fred "Killer" Burke and a small team of outside hit men dressed as either policemen or detectives to avoid suspicion. Acting as if they were raiding the garage, Capone's men had Moran's gang line up against a brick wall, where they were shot dead under a hail of shotgun and machine gun bullets.

Moran, the intended victim, was saved by his late arrival but his influence was broken. He reportedly commented that "only Capone kills like that." There were never any convictions for this crime, which remains a sensational landmark of the era.

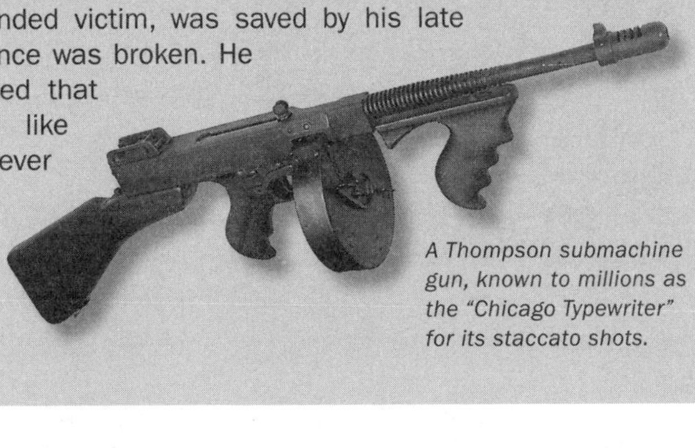

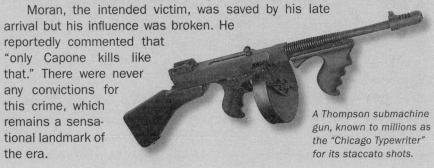

A Thompson submachine gun, known to millions as the "Chicago Typewriter" for its staccato shots.

Flappers: Lifestyle and Fashion

The women who emerged in the 1920s were often called flappers to indicate a style and approach to life that met the demands of the modern era. They were independent in spirit and looking for good times and self expression. Such a quest could take many forms from their fashion sense to their use of alcohol and cigarettes. The name itself appeared even before World War I, when independent women were compared to young birds flapping their wings to be free. During the war, with many males mobilized for the conflict, women had assumed a wide range of occupations previously thought the preserves of men. With the coming of the vote in 1920, women felt that this spirit of freedom and possibility could continue. Although women were but 20 percent of the workforce, the doors were opening for a change in status.

The fashion of the period reflected this changing sense of self. Flapper style offered a different look, stressing a boyish and youthful appearance. The corset was forgotten, and hair was shortened into a "bob," which had even more extreme varieties such as the short, pressed down "Eaton" or "shingle" that curled around the ears. To maintain this more androgynous look, busts were flattened and dresses were worn loose, with a low waist and bare arms. As the era progressed, hemlines rose; starting just below the knee, they rose to above the knee by the end of the decade. With the addition of cosmetics, the modern flapper look was distinctly different, as were their more provocative dances: the Charleston, Shimmy, and Black Bottom.

The new personal freedoms also increased the opportunities for the sexes to mix in cars, parties, and clubs, raising sexual impulses. Old taboos were challenged and more public displays were possible. Petting with the opposite sex became a major recreation that often led to full sexual encounters called "bamey-mugging." With sex becoming more commonplace, birth control discussion soon followed with the establishment in 1921 of Margaret Sanger's (1879–1966) American Birth Control League, then the first birth control clinic in 1923, as well as the development of birth control techniques such as the rhythm method. Sexuality was starting to be an area of scientific inquiry.

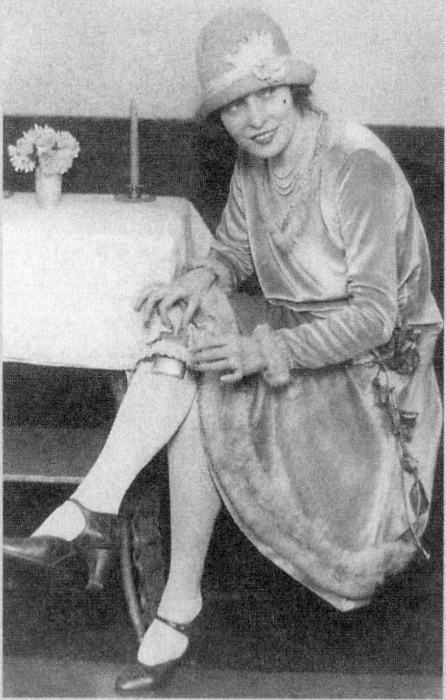

A flapper in 1926 shows off the latest risqué fad, a flask hidden in a garter.

more ways than crime; impure illegal liquor could blind and maim as well as addle the brain. Although quality liquor was still available, it had to be smuggled from the West Indies, Canada, and Great Britain, and was still the province of the bootleggers. The prices demanded for the imported drink generally made it a product reserved for those who were better off financially.

Prohibition contributed to an acceptance in American society of criminality as one of life's norms. In a climate that argued for core American values and Christian virtues, Prohibition produced a reality that challenged these very virtues. Bribery became a way of doing business, tax avoidance became a goal, and influence was there to be peddled, undercutting access and fairness in public life. In addition, Prohibition made the Mafia a national organization far removed from other immigrant communities. The sale of illegal alcohol had become a $3.5 billion yearly business and all profits were tax free. Further, bootlegging provided the profits for criminal expansion into other areas of American life. Many used their Prohibition know-how to become part of the legitimate liquor trade once Prohibition ended. Infamous criminals such as Meyer Lansky (1902–83), Lucky Luciano (1897–1962), and Bugsy Siegel (1906–47) established Capitol Wine and Spirits, becoming substantial wine merchants. Joe Kennedy (1888–1969), the father of President John F. Kennedy, built upon his fortune by controlling Haig and Haig, Pinchbottle, and Gordon's gin imports after Prohibition. Prohibition's impact upon American justice and morality is still being felt with a public sense that justice comes to those who can afford it, and to those who have the necessary connections to avoid prison.

PROTESTANT FUNDAMENTALISM AND THE CRISIS OF EVOLUTION

Besides the divide between the temperate and the intemperate members of American society, other clashes occurred during the 1920s as a result of societal change and the collision between conservative tradition and modern life. Immigration introduced millions of Catholics and Jews into American society, and some saw their presence as a challenge to the hegemony of American Protestantism as the dominant religious belief system. Yet it was science that provoked the most serious arguments of the era. The most dramatic threat to established beliefs, at least from the standpoint of fundamentalist Christians, was the scientific attack on religion posed by Darwinism.

Although the issue was first raised following the publication of Charles Darwin's *Origin of the Species* in 1859, it reached a crisis point in the 1925 Scopes Monkey Trial. The theory of evolution undercut certain literal biblical concepts regarding the creation of man. Prohibition fundamentalists waged a crusade, this time against the teaching of Darwinism in the schools. When a Tennessee teacher, John T. Scopes (1900–70), challenged this ban, he found himself in court facing charges. The case took on a national focus, when the well-known Chicago attorney, Clarence Darrow (1857–1938), came to Scopes's defense. He was opposed by a prosecution team led by William

Jennings Bryan (1860–1925), a fundamentalist politician, former secretary of state, and frequent presidential candidate. Hampered by the court, Darrow nevertheless succeeded in discrediting Bryan's handling of the fundamentalist cause. Although Scopes was convicted and lost the battle, fundamentalism suffered serious embarrassment and loss of face with the public at large. The result remains a lingering issue affecting religious debates in some quarters even today.

Social issues continued to ferment in other areas of American life outside of religion. There were changing social viewpoints and a more relaxed morality. The family, church, and communities had to meet the world of the 1920s and this adjustment could be painful. Urbanization made resistance to change even more difficult as social classes mixed more readily than ever before.

An expanding economy after the initial post-war recession saw new jobs created and better pay for workers, sometimes as much as $5 a day. This greater disposable income provided money for more goods, roads, tourism, holidays, and created real estate booms in the suburbs and elsewhere. Electricity had reached two-thirds of American homes, and this generated a drive for all sorts of new electrical goods that stimulated demand for consumer goods at levels never previously seen. This rising standard of living increased the demands for more freedom and provided greater opportunities to sample material pleasures.

Much as with past religious taboos, the old traditions though vigorously defended were being challenged daily, particularly among members of the younger generation who were looking for fun and amusements in an age that seemed to offer every possible indulgence as long as you could afford it. Pleasure was becoming a legitimate principle in everyday life. It was with this background in mind that the era became known as the Jazz Age, embracing the new freedoms associated with the emerging music form. With the movement of African-American musicians northward, where they found work in the many speakeasies that dotted the urban landscape, their music came with them. Jazz was a liberating style of music, and with its black origins it seemed to challenge the more traditional aspects of white middle-class existence.

BEHAVIOR AND SEXUALITY

Prosperity allowed older ideas of proper behavior to be discarded and replaced with a more riotous

John T. Scopes, the Tennessee teacher whose 1925 case drew national attention.

approach to life often fueled by illegal alcohol. Life became more socially liberated and less restrictive sexually. The dances of the era were sexually more suggestive and the fashions of the times reflected this assault on past social mores. "Flappers" was the name given to the fashion conscious young women of the 1920s who enjoyed more personal independence than ever before, and became symbols of the era. Flappers wore makeup, had short bobbed hair, and dressed in knee-length fringed skirts and stockings. They shocked the older generation through their rebellious behavior. They were un-chaperoned and they drank and mixed freely with men.

In many circles sex was no longer a taboo subject. It was discussed more openly, and premarital sex became more common. Sexually transmitted diseases were on the rise as were unwanted pregnancies. The advocacy and practice of birth control was not only difficult, but illegal. Therefore its promotion could bring about prosecution. Birth control did find supporters in the eugenics movement, which had a considerable following in the 1920s. Particularly alarmed by immigration from what they deemed the weaker races, believers in eugenics wanted to reduce impaired hereditary traits. One method to combat these supposed traits was through the sterilization of those deemed genetically tainted. Subsequently sterilization practices became law in many states.

The assault on traditional moral concepts also found support through the arrival of Freudian theories, which seemed to give a scientific foundation to the challenges being played out in everyday life. The individual and his or her id, ego, and superego became the determinants for explaining behavior. Freudianism supported the new-found individualism of the era and was largely passive in implementation. Ambivalence in terms of absolutes became an accepted feature of the new era, and perhaps a lasting definition of modernism.

TECHNOLOGY AND CHANGE

The new freedom in social attitudes gained an additional boost from technological changes that mirrored the expanding consumerism of the 1920s. Of critical importance in creating different attitudes was the increasing public availability of the motor car. Roads and highways were built to accommodate rising demand. Mass production reduced costs and pumped money into the economy, feeding its expansion. In the end millions of automobiles were produced in this decade and by 1928, the Ford Model T cost an affordable $295. The car became the means for fun and amusement. Destinations were now within easy reach and and cheap motoring was accessible for many people. In the process the automobile reduced even further the more obvious status differences between rich and poor. For some the car became the great enabler for social mobility and it was a conduit to vice, described by some as "prostitution on wheels."

Along with the automobile, the radio and phonograph became transforming media in these times of changing social circumstances. Listening to the

Langston Hughes, one of the most prominent writers of the Harlem Renaissance.

radio and phonograph spread Jazz Age music and brought entertainment into almost every home in the country, helping to shape mass culture and creating the beginnings of a celebrity society. Bessie Smith (1892–1937), King Oliver (1885–1938), Louis Armstrong (1901–71), Fletcher Henderson (1897–1952), Ma Rainey (1882–1939), and more became household names. Radio stations mushroomed across the country and important broadcasters, such as NBC, started operations in 1926. CBS followed in 1928. By 1929 there were over 10 million radios in circulation and radio sales totaled $426 million. In addition five million phonographs were sold in 1929 alone.

Besides the radio, social attitudes were being shaped by the growth of the motion picture industry, whose stars became the idols of millions. By the 1920s the film industry had moved to Hollywood where the climate was more conducive to filming and hundreds of films were produced each year. The films were primarily silent black-and-whites throughout most of the decade, yet cinema attendance was huge. Stars such as Harold Lloyd (1893–1971), Buster Keaton (1895–1966), Douglas Fairbanks (1883–1939), Mary Pickford (1892–1979), John Barrymore (1882–1942), Clara Bow (1905–65), Rudolph Valentino (1895–1926), and Rudy Vallee (1901–86) were nationally known and exercised a great influence on style and social perceptions. The Oscar awards for the best motion pictures began in 1927. Sound pictures soon followed with the *Jazz Singer* being the first commercially successful example. After 1929 sound pictures dominated the market. American culture was taking its modern form.

In response to the impersonal nature of urban society, the freewheeling social attitudes of the period made sports a principal recreational outlet, and sports became home to a new group of heroes. Sports became the personification of the era's individualism and its appeal crossed gender, ethnic, and racial lines. In some eyes the 1920s represented the Golden Age of American Sports. It was the era of Babe Ruth (1895–1948) in baseball, Harold Edward "Red" Grange (1903–91) in American college and later professional football, Jack Dempsey (1895–1983) in boxing, Johnny Weissmuller (1904–84) in swimming, and Bill Tilden (1893–1953) and Helen Wills (1905–98) in tennis.

The Harlem Renaissance

The Harlem Renaissance, also known as the New Negro Movement or the Negro Renaissance, began in New York City at the end of World War I in a 15-block section containing African-American movie theaters, night clubs, cabarets, libraries, schools, and churches. It reached its heyday in the 1920s before declining in popularity during the Great Depression. The Harlem Renaissance was of major importance to American literature, music, politics, and the arts because it incorporated African Americans into the mainstream for the first time.

Because of segregated housing, Harlem had become home to most African Americans who had migrated to Manhattan from other areas of the country. Two-thirds of New York's African-American population lived in Harlem. African-American writers, musicians, artists, and intellectuals became the most visible figures of the renaissance. Between 1923 and 1930, both blacks and whites gathered in the area to participate in intellectual and entertaining pursuits. It was in Harlem that the groundwork for the civil rights movement of the 1950s and 1960s was laid.

Thumbing their noses at Prohibition, so-called "black and tan" clubs attracted both black and white audiences. However, at the well-known Cotton Club, black musicians entertained all-white audiences. Jazz was popular with both black and white Americans, partly because its emphasis on improvisation suited the mood of rebellion that defined the 1920s. Renaissance writers who had a major social and literary impact both through their own works and on other African-American writers included poets Langston Hughes (1902–67) and Claude McKay (1890–1948), novelist and folklorist Zora Neale Hurston (1891–1960), and novelist Jessie Fauset (1882–1962).

The Harlem Renaissance also produced great painters, sculptors, actors, and dancers. Vocalists such as Ethel Waters (1896–1977) achieved major recognition. There was also a darker criminal side to Harlem in the 1920s. Gambling was a major attraction, and organized crime was quick to take advantage of the opening it provided.

Zora Neale Hurston in 1938, the year after her novel Their Eyes Were Watching God *was published.*

Store no. 10 in the People's Drug Store chain in Washington, D.C., in 1922. Chain stores spread across the country in the 1920s.

Sports enthusiasm was backed by the creation of mass audiences who supported local teams usually associated with state universities or particular cities. Newspapers developed sports pages that fed the newfound interest, and radio commentary brought sports coverage into millions of American homes. The ballparks grew in size to accommodate huge crowds of spectators, and team sports emerged on both high school and college campuses as a highlight of the academic life.

The fascination with individual exploits and triumphs was a key feature of the social attitudes of the age. Mass circulation magazines such as *Reader's Digest* and *Time* appeared on the scene in the early 1920s to chronicle the day's important events. They carried portraits of important personalities, as did other specialized magazines catering to glamour and entertainment. Perhaps the most famous example of heroic triumph was the flight of Charles. A. Lindbergh (1902–74). In 1927 Lindbergh flew non-stop from New York to Paris in 33.5 hours. His success set new standards of bravery and endurance and made him a symbol of the era's adventurous culture.

Society craved excitement and it looked for entertainment and individual exploits everywhere. Fads and crazes caught the popular imagination in the form of dance marathons, barnstorming flying stunts, flagpole sitting, and many other physical exploits. The dangerous escapes of Harry Houdini (1874–1926) from various chained predicaments made him a famous show man who seemingly could overcome all odds. In such changing times, with old social norms and old securities challenged on a daily basis, the public sought reassurance in the mystique of the individual who could overcome the odds and succeed, showing that bravery could win out even in the worst circumstances.

CULTURE AND SOCIETY

Social attitudes were also shaped by the flowering of African-American culture across a broad spectrum of the arts such as literature, painting, sculpture and music. The name given to this newfound appreciation of African-American culture was the Harlem Renaissance. It represented another aspect of black urban migration to cities like New York. Writers such as James Weldon Johnson (1871–1938), Charles W. Chesnutt (1858–1932), Claude McKay (1890–1948), and Langston Hughes (1902–67) were drawn to New York to develop their craft, and in so doing redefined African-American contributions to and understanding of American society.

The climate of the times also produced voices that had lost confidence, often in reaction to the losses of World War I. Members of the so-called Lost Generation represented still another aspect of the era's social attitudes. The newly discovered consumerism and prosperity did not satisfy everyone. It was in rebellion against such a society that some artists sought meaning and purpose in a less materially-dominated world. Many took their search to Europe, particularly to Paris. This scene drew writers such as Ernest Hemingway (1899–1961), F. Scott Fitzgerald (1896–1940), Gertrude Stein (1874–1946), and Ezra Pound (1885–1972). Other writers closer to home, such as Sinclair Lewis (1885–1951), challenged the shallow middle-class culture that had elevated conformity to a social art. Humorists, like H.L. Mencken, ridiculed the ignorance of the politicians and of the middle class who defined the morality of the time.

However for most Americans their social attitudes were not consciously or significantly shaped by the discontent of literary elites. Nevertheless change undoubtedly created tensions in living, and numerous contradictions in coping with the many aspects of an increasingly modern and technological life. The modern urban existence offered both opportunities and frustrations. In particular, for women the era transformed not only their appearance and styles but also the substance of many women's lives. The right to vote gave them greater influence, as did their religious and moral crusades. Many women even defined smoking in public as "the torch of freedom." The nature of work changed as well, for now more women could be found in medicine, social services, law, and in a variety of other service jobs including office work and hairdressing. Occupational changes increased social independence and personal liberation. The availability of more labor-saving devices made greater choices possible and freed time for other activities.

The general prosperity of the decade made Americans optimistic about the future and raised expectations in all areas of life. Consumerism was born and installment buying, stimulated by the arrival of a scientifically designed advertising industry, created insatiable demands for more of everything. Management itself was becoming scientific, and it seemed possible to organize for success. Chain stores expanded across the country, changing the nature of retail shopping for millions.

The concept of continuous debt became a part of many people's lives. Everything seemed possible and obtainable, especially with a steady growth in GNP of 4.2 percent annually. Federal tax cuts, budget surpluses, and rising levels of disposable income, along with impressive increases in corporate profits of 62 percent between 1923 and 1929, all made the economy seem strong, limited only by the depressed agricultural sector. With 40 percent of the work force earning $2,000 per annum, the general attitude was bright and self-congratulatory, yet inequalities in income distribution and a reliance on speculation made for economic uncertainties that would contribute to the Wall Street crash of October 1929. The coming of economic depression brought the spree to an end, and eventually doused the spirit of optimism that shaped so many lives and attitudes during the 1920s. However social attitudes had changed forever.

Research done by Robert and Helen Lynd and published as *Middletown* in 1929 still provides a lasting insight into the fundamental shift that occurred in American attitudes during the era. The Lynds found that old values and customs were transformed even in the heartland of Indiana. Even in small town America, people saw the world differently. Society's attitudes had changed so much that now the automobile was no longer seen as a luxury or novelty, but one of the necessities of modern life.

THEODORE W. EVERSOLE

Further Readings

Allen, Frederick Lewis. *Only Yesterday: An Informal History of the Nineteen-Twenties*. New York: Harper Row, 1931.

Behr, Edward. *Prohibition: The 13 Years that Changed America*. London: BBC Books, 1997.

Best, Gary Dean. *The Dollar Decade: Mammon and the Machine in 1920s America*. Westport, CT: Praeger Publishers, 2003.

Coben, Stanley. *Rebellion Against Victorianism: The Impetus for Cultural Change in 1920s America*. New York: Oxford University Press, 1991.

Dumenil, Lynn. *The Modern Temper: American Culture and Society in the 1920s*. New York: Hill and Wang, 1995.

Fass, Paula S. *The Damned and the Beautiful: American Youth in the 1920s*. New York: Oxford University Press, 1978.

Gertzman, Jay A. *Bootleggers and Smuthounds: The Trade in Erotica, 1920–1940*. Philadelphia, PA: University of Pennsylvania Press, 1999.

Higham, John. *Strangers in the Land: Patterns of American Nativism, 1860–1925*. Piscataway, NJ: Rutgers University Press, 1955.

Huggins, Nathan Irwin., ed., *Voices from the Harlem Renaissance*. New York: Oxford University Press, 1995.

Leuchtenburg, William. *The Perils of Prosperity, 1914–1932*. Chicago, IL: University of Chicago Press, 1955.

Lynd, Robert S., and Helen Merrill Lynd. *Middletown: A Study in Modern American Culture*. New York: Harcourt, Brace and World, 1929.

O'Neal, Michael J. *America in the 1920s*. New York: Facts On File, 2005.

Ware, Caroline. *Greenwich Village, 1920–1930: A Commentary on American Civilization in the Post-war Years*. Berkeley, CA: University of California Press, 1994.

Chapter 5

Cities and Urban Life

"I like people . . . to ask themselves now and then: "What can I do for my city?"
—President Warren G. Harding

THE 1920 U.S. Federal Census documented a fundamental change in American life. For the first time, the majority of the population lived in places designated as urban, rather than in the agricultural areas and small towns that had traditionally been considered central to the nation's identity. Anxieties about this transition to an urban society were reflected in the era's popular culture. For example, the Hollywood silent film *Sunrise* (1927), directed by F. W. Murnau, starkly portrayed the dichotomy between country and city, telling the fable-like story of a young farm couple nearly destroyed by an urban temptress, who coaxes the husband to contemplate murdering his wife. The expressionist film depicted the city as sleek and frenzied, a kind of phantasmagoric theme park of modernity, where people shed their inhibitions amid the depersonalizing surroundings. *The Crowd* (1928), directed by King Vidor, took a documentary-like, workaday approach to urban life. The film dealt with the frustrations of a young couple trying to make their way in New York City: a tiny apartment by the elevated tracks, stifling crowds at Coney Island, the tedious routines of a dead-end job. The film's critique of the conformity of mass society was neatly encapsulated by a scene set in a company bathroom at the end of a business day: while the protagonist washes his hands, his co-workers brush past him, one after another, every one of them asking a variation on the same friendly, but empty question—"Washin' 'em up, eh?"

Many Americans during the 1920s thought of the country and city in the manner exemplified by these movies, as antithetical environments, "country" meaning pastoral and perhaps backward, "city" meaning worldly, striving, and soulless. But urban historians today recognize that such distinctions were becoming moot during the decade, which saw the burgeoning of the American metropolitan area. City populations grew rapidly—25 percent in Chicago, 35 percent in Atlanta, 55 percent in Detroit—but most of the growth occurred in the residential and industrial suburbs that stretched out from the urban core. The expanding metropolis exerted its influence over outlying small towns and far into the agricultural hinterlands. Urban America was evolving into a new kind of social and economic entity, one that encompassed "city" and "country," characterized by decentralization, suburbanization, and high mobility.

Los Angeles was the nation's preeminent example. In 1900 it had been a relatively modest small city, surrounded by lemon groves; according to the chamber of commerce, the city's major selling point was its healthful sunshine. By 1930 the Los Angeles metropolitan area had a population of 3.3 million, serving as the world's motion picture capital and a major center for petroleum production, aviation, and manufacturing. The city annexed 45 adjacent communities during the 1920s, expanding its spatial area by 80 sq. mi. The widely dispersed population lived primarily in suburban single-family bungalows, commuting on an extensive network of roadways to their jobs in the scattered business districts. By the mid-1920s Los Angeles had the highest ratio of automobiles per capita in the world, with an estimated 262,000 cars congesting the downtown daily.

Indeed, the automobile profoundly affected urban life across America. By 1920 Americans owned nine million automobiles, and this figure catapulted to 27 million by decade's end. The automobile remade the city landscape.

A detail from a panoramic view of Beverly Hills in 1929 that shows new development extending into the open land in the distance toward the hills.

The Urban Ku Klux Klan

During the early 1920s, the Ku Klux Klan, preaching "one hundred percent Americanism," attracted more than a million members in cities across the United States, ranging from Buffalo to Dayton to Houston to Portland, Oregon. This urban membership was drawn primarily from lower middle-class men with a tenuous grip on their socioeconomic status: low-paid office clerks, struggling proprietors and salesmen, factory and railroad workers. Klansmen felt threatened by the newcomers that had flooded into American cities during the previous two decades, especially African Americans and eastern and southern European immigrants, who were predominantly Catholic or Jewish. The Klan insisted that only ardent patriotism and traditional morality could preserve what they perceived to be the nation's white, gentile, and Protestant heritage. Unlike their rural counterparts who sometimes engaged in violent vigilantism, urban Klansmen were interested primarily in social and political activities, during which they vented their scorn for a variety of "enemies."

The Klan established a significant presence in some cities. In Detroit, home to 35,000 members, newsboys hawked copies of the Klan publication *The Fiery Cross*. At the city's Cadillac Square Park in 1923, a hooded Santa Claus presided over a Christmas Eve ceremony before a large crowd. In Chicago, with an estimated membership in 1922 of 55,000, Klansmen made dramatic appearances on Sunday mornings at selected churches, silently marching past the congregation to drop offerings in the collection plate. In Dallas, where a slate of Klan-backed candidates nearly swept local elections in 1922, thousands of members held a celebratory demonstration outside the city's two newspaper buildings, accusing (incorrectly) the owners of being Catholic. The Klan dominated politics in Indianapolis for several years, maintaining their public image with carnivals and charitable activities, and parading through the city's black neighborhoods. Small businesses in Indianapolis were eager to advertise in Klan publications; a typical ad boasted that a cleaning service "Kleans Klothes Klean."

The Klan was a common topic of discussion in urban America during the early 1920s due to widespread media coverage. Anti-Klan sentiment was strong in many cities, and the organization made headlines when denounced by prominent leaders. An ironic byproduct of this publicity was that the Klan sometimes gained recruits. In 1921 an extensive *New York World* exposé, reprinted throughout the country, led to a U.S. House of Representatives investigation of Klan violence and financial chicanery. A few newspapers in cities where the Klan had aggregated local power, such as *The Commercial Appeal* in Memphis and *The Dallas Morning News*, waged brave journalistic anti-Klan crusades. African-American, Catholic, and foreign language newspapers across the country were also vocal in their opposition. In the mid-1920s the Klan plunged in membership, damaged by well-publicized scandals and internal rivalries.

Automobiles parked on the roof of an urban Buick sales and service center in December 1925. By the end of the 1920s Americans owned 27 million automobiles.

Traffic signals and parking meters sprouted along streets. Most downtowns featured "automobile rows," city blocks lined with dealer showrooms, body shops, and tire stores. One such row in Chicago offered 116 different makes of cars. Urban areas were crosscut by parkways and other "express" streets, funded by newly implemented gasoline taxes. In their daily lives, car owners benefited from a sense of greater personal mobility and control. They could decide exactly where they went and when, no longer dependent on public transit schedules (although they were often frustrated by traffic jams, another ubiquitous urban feature). Motor vehicles made the periphery of cities readily accessible, which enabled decentralization.

People were eager to move to established "streetcar" suburbs, which enjoyed explosive growth during the 1920s. For example, Elmwood Park outside Chicago grew 716 percent, Shaker Heights near Cleveland grew 1,000 percent, and Beverly Hills in Los Angeles grew 2,485 percent. Banks, movie theaters, and chain stores such as J.C. Penney and Walgreens followed the new suburbanites. The first suburban shopping center in America, the Country Club Shopping Center in Kansas City, opened in 1922. Taking advantage of the brand-new trucking industry, manufacturers also began to

The Chicago School of Sociology

During the 1920s progressive sociologists at the University of Chicago undertook the first intensive academic study of American urban life, using the city they lived in as their laboratory. The "Chicago School" approach was empirical and pragmatic, rather than macroscopic and theoretical, relying on firsthand ethnographic observations of urban neighborhoods and subcultures. As founding sociologist Robert E. Park urged his graduate students: "Go and sit in the lounges of luxury hotels and on the doorsteps of the flophouses; sit on the Gold Coast settees and on the slum shakedowns; sit in the Orchestra Hall and in the Star and Garter Burlesque. In short go and get the seat of your pants dirty in real research."

The Chicago School conceived of the city as a series of unique "social worlds" or "milieus." This model held that urban life was richly variegated, enabling likeminded people with particular cultural proclivities to find their own niche. Thus, the sociologists studied divergent groups within the city: Sicilian immigrants, gang members, and settlement house dwellers. Each group was analyzed for its shared vocabulary, activities, and values.

One drawback to the approach was that it viewed groups as essentially isolated and "closed," ignoring homogenizing influences. The resulting portrait of the city was skewed, favoring the marginal over the mainstream. But the Chicago School produced several ethnographic classics that offer vivid and valuable depictions of 1920s urban life. One is Paul G. Cressey's *The Taxi-Dance Hall: A Sociological Study in Commercialized Recreation and City Life*, published in 1932, which is particularly interesting for its exploration of the limited possibilities available to nonconformist young women from working-class backgrounds.

The book describes females who broke with their families and left home, in the process often quitting tedious factory jobs, to find work as "taxi-dancers"—employed to dance, at the cost of a $.10 ticket per song, with male patrons at commercial dance halls in the city. Many were attracted to the glamour of taxi-dancing, drawn by the good pay and a sense of romantic adventure, taking on stage names with their new urban identities.

Cressey charted the racially charged life cycle of the Chicago dance hall: after initially enjoying popularity as new girls, paired with the most exclusive white customers, the taxi-dancers eventually lost their status, relegated to dancing with all willing customers, including men from different races and ethnicities. Cressey found that some of the women finally descended into prostitution. But others genuinely thrived as nonconformists, moving from dance hall to dance hall, enjoying the independence and mobility provided by the city.

decentralize, relocating from their cramped five-story factories downtown to fringe areas where they could build horizontal plants necessary for assembly-line production.

Daily urban life was also influenced by national trends regarding home-building and home ownership. Under the guidance of Secretary of Commerce Herbert Hoover, associations of realtors, architects, contractors, and city planners encouraged a variety of "Own Your Own Home" initiatives. The rationale was that home ownership was "the best insurance in the world against social unrest." The 1920s witnessed a record number of single-family housing starts in urban areas, averaging around 400,000 per year. Savings and loan associations readily provided mortgage financing, including for modest-salaried earners. The result was that single-family home ownership in metropolitan areas increased 40 percent during the decade. By 1924 every major American city had established zoning regulations—typically controlling land use, density, and the height and bulk of buildings—that helped to ensure the regularity and stability of residential neighborhoods. This also had the effect of enforcing economic and racial homogeneity, as a variety of structures deemed undesirable—apartments, factories, "blighted" homes—could be eliminated from areas, along with the sort of people who typically utilized them. By the end of the decade,

The current Market Street Bridge in Harrisburg, Pennsylvania, was finished in 1928 and serves as the symbolic entryway to Pennsylvania's capital city.

The Century Hotel on Ocean Drive is one of many Art Deco landmarks built in Miami Beach in the 1920s and 1930s.

The Miami Real Estate Boom

On January 1, 1920, a brand-new automobile causeway opened across Biscayne Bay, connecting the small city of Miami, with a population of 30,000 people, to Miami Beach, a barrier island that had recently been cleared of thick mangrove swamps, rattlesnakes, and raccoons. Over the next decade the population of Miami increased almost 400 percent, to more than 110,000. Miami Beach real estate, with an assessed total value of $224,000 in 1916, was selling at $33 million for a 400-acre tract in 1925. Aggressively marketed as the American Riviera, the Miami boom epitomized 1920s speculative excess and hucksterism. In 1925 7,500 Miamians were issued a real estate license; across the state, 174,530 land deeds were officially filed, and 481 new hotels and apartment buildings were hastily thrown up.

That summer a single issue of the Miami *Daily Herald*, crammed with real estate ads, ran to 504 pages. "Binder boys" became a common sight in the city: men dressed jauntily in caps and knickerbockers (as opposed to the sober business suit), who carried around portfolios of land options, selling lots to speculators for a low down payment with the understanding that they could be quickly sold again for a profit. Miami lots were "flipped" as many as six times per day. Some widely advertised subdivisions were platted on swampland that remained undeveloped. Federal investigators looked into cases of mail fraud where brochures, with faked photographs, were distributed across the country—and buyers made purchases sight unseen.

The Miami boom ended abruptly in 1926, when a hurricane smashed into the city, wiping away much of the recent development. The speculative mania had drawn investors from across the country who had hoped to make a killing from Miami's vacant lots. During the boom, 20 million such lots were plotted in Florida, enough to potentially house the entire U.S. population.

three-fifths of the nation's urban residents lived in neighborhoods that were zoning controlled. Middle-class homeowners were thus usually guaranteed to dwell among others of similar backgrounds. Their suburbs were stylistically eclectic, although the simple, efficient bungalow became a favorite design. Owners increasingly stocked their new houses with the latest time-saving gadgets. For example, among city houses wired for electricity in 1926, 80 percent had an electric iron, while 37 percent had a vacuum cleaner.

Even with the increasing decentralization of American cities, the downtown retained its symbolic importance as an economic and cultural center. Blue-collar manufacturing relocated to the periphery, but white-collar offices remained downtown, where corporations and their attendant professions—banks, law offices, accounting firms—were concentrated. The 1920s witnessed a mania for building skyscrapers, which served as monumental advertisements for the corporations. By 1929 urban America featured 377 skyscrapers, more than 100 of them erected in New York City during the decade, including such famous structures as the Chrysler Building. New York's newly implemented zoning regulations, which encouraged large bases, pyramidal setbacks, and thin central towers, directly contributed to the city's "wedding cake" skyline. Downtown remained the primary location for consumer retail services and entertainment, such as restaurants, specialty shops, movie theaters, nightclubs, museums, hotels, and department stores. Perhaps a third of the people living in metropolitan areas visited the central business district on a typical day, such as the approximately 875,000 people who poured daily into Boston's downtown. As a result, city centers were bursting with crowds, vehicular traffic, and noise. In New York City, gaudy neon signs, first introduced in

A street clock from the 1920s manufactured by the Seth Thomas Co. of Thomaston, Connecticut.

1923, advertised Packard automobiles and chewing gum. Up to 200 commuters were routinely wedged into subway and elevated cars meant to carry 125 passengers. People constantly "hustled," one British observer noted, looking neither to their left nor right, so that "an earthquake in the next street would scarcely stop [their] progress."

MASS CULTURE AND NEW OPPORTUNITIES

American cities were the locus for the explosion of mass culture during the 1920s, which was generated by new means of communication such as the radio, and by an aggressive advertising industry. Middle-class urban Americans consumed the same standard-brand products (Rice Krispies, Jolly Green Giant canned vegetables, and Betty Crocker cake mixes were all introduced in the 1920s), shopped at the same chain and department stores, and purchased their automobiles and washing machines—since they could not really afford them—on the same installment plans. They consumed the same forms of leisure and entertainment. Sporting events in the cities drew enormous crowds. For instance, 300,000 fans attended the 1923 baseball World Series, and 130,000 saw Gene Tunney defeat Jack Dempsey for the heavyweight boxing championship in 1926. By 1927 movie attendance in the United States reached 110 million customers weekly—at a time when the national population was approximately 120 million people. Contemporary social critics deplored metropolitan America as the "titanic city" (in the words of urban planner Lewis Mumford), a dehumanizing place given over to commerce and conformity, threatening the nation's core values of individualism and democracy.

However, historians who have looked closely at American urban populations during the decade find much evidence that cities also fostered diverse experiences and opportunities; daily life was hardly a matter of marching in lockstep. For instance, historian Lizabeth Cohen has examined the cultural practices of ethnic workers in Chicago, who were able to adapt mass-culture goods to their own particular social needs. These workers typically attended movies in small neighborhood theaters, not the grandiose "movie palaces" found downtown. The theaters played pictures that catered to local interests; the experience of attending a movie included constant crowd interactions with the silent screen, audiences yelling "getem" and "catchem" as the good guys chased the bad guys. Similarly, listening to the radio was oriented around the family and the neighborhood, a communal rather than an atomizing experience, with four or five people typically listening together. In Chicago there were several radio stations intended explicitly for ethnic audiences, broadcasting "nationality hours," local church services, and favorite music from the home country. Ethnic workers tended to patronize independent rather than chain stores, so they could haggle over prices. While Chicago's workers partook in the new mass culture during the 1920s, they brought their own idiosyncrasies to the act of consumption, fusing the heterodox with the "mass" in their daily lives.

Urban nightlife challenged American social norms in the Prohibition Era. In New York City a nightclub circuit, largely financed and operated by bootleggers and gamblers, developed in Manhattan, tying together "respectable" midtown with African-American Harlem and bohemian Greenwich Village. These establishments, with cosmopolitan names such as the Café de Paris and the Club El Fey, attracted perhaps 20,000 visitors nightly during the mid-1920s. They served as congregating places where people from disparate walks of life rubbed elbows. Businessmen and their dates mingled with college students and tourists, waiters and bellhops, black and Jewish entertainers, chorus girls, homosexuals, and a colorful assortment of underworld figures. A contemporary reporter described the typical scene as follows: "the beer and alky runner, the junk pusher, the cannon mob and the booster...the tat-man and the hijacker," along with prostitutes and con artists, all out to take advantage of "the half-smart egg who thinks he is three jumps ahead of Broadway." The nightclub was thus a site where conventional social boundaries were relaxed. Women pursued pleasure along with men, imbibing alcohol, dancing the Charleston or the shimmy, ignoring traditional prescriptions for femininity. White club-goers sampled from African-American culture; the "primitive" stereotypes on display in nightclubs, conflating jazz and the jungle, enabled whites to fantasize about the "naturalness" of black life in a manner that was both condescending and envious.

For African Americans, daily life in northern industrial cities promised unprecedented opportunities. A half-million black southerners migrated to the north during World War I, attracted by a labor market facing manpower shortages due to military mobilization and immigration restrictions. This trend continued during the 1920s, as a million more blacks left the south. Their primary incentive was economic. In the south, blacks working in agriculture typically earned $1 a day in 1920, while in the northern steel industry they could earn five times as much for an eight-hour workday. African Americans also expected to be treated better in the north, assured by black newspapers and labor recruiting agents that racial strictures were not as pronounced as in the south. "I want to make a livelihood, and to educate my children," one man from Georgia explained in a letter to the Pittsburgh Urban League, succinctly summarizing migrant hopes.

But the realities of life in the northern city only partly met these expectations. Although blacks earned more money than they had in the south, their overall standard of living was either marginally improved—or worsened. In Chicago, migrants were packed into the confines of the South Side "Black Belt," an area of dilapidated, unsanitary housing. In Pittsburgh, they sometimes dwelled in shacks thrown up in ravines or in railroad cars and boathouses converted by realtors into "apartments." In Cincinnati in 1920, health investigators found 20 black migrants living in a three-room flat, and another 94 migrants sharing a 12-room tenement. African Americans inevitably paid high rents for this substandard housing, and home ownership was denied them by zoning laws. Available employment for black men, who had received inadequate education and job training in the south, was usually limited to the most dangerous and dirty industrial jobs: working on the killing floor at Chicago's meatpacking plants, or feeding blast furnaces in Pittsburgh's steel mills. Black workers were typically refused membership in labor unions, although companies would sometimes employ them as scabs during strikes. They were also frequently laid off, averaging two to four months of unemployment per year in some cities. Job prospects for African-American migrant women were

Los Angeles's "Borderland" Neighborhoods

As Los Angeles boomed during the early 1920s, a variety of populations moved into the city to fill the demand for labor, including Italians, Japanese, African Americans, and Russian Jews. The largest group to arrive was Mexican. Restrictive congressional immigration policies during the decade stopped the flow of southern and eastern Europeans into the United States, leaving Mexicans as the primary immigrant group legally permitted to enter the country.

Approximately 60,000 Chicanos settled in Los Angeles, making it the "Mexican capital" of the United States. But there was no segregated, distinctive Mexican section. Chicanos initially lived in almost every part of the city, mixing in with every population, including Anglo-Americans. Urban historians suggest that during this period of flux in Los Angeles, clear spatial lines could not be readily established between the dominant white society and other groups. For the most part, the city was comprised of multiethnic "borderlands," where residential transformation was almost continuous, and different cultures encountered each other on a daily basis.

As the decade progressed, real estate deeds were used to impose racial and religious restrictive covenants in predominantly white neighborhoods on the western side of the city, pushing the other groups out. Mexicans shifted to the eastern side, attracted by jobs, inexpensive housing, and community life. White Los Angeles tended to view Chicanos as a nomadic population of casual laborers, with no firm attachment to the city. But in East Los Angeles Mexicans quickly put down roots, exemplified by their high rate of home ownership, which ran to more than 60 percent in some areas.

However, this part of Los Angeles remained heterogeneous throughout the 1920s, as Mexicans, Europeans, Asians, and African Americans competed for jobs and housing in many of the same neighborhoods. The East Los Angeles "barrio" would not be established until after World War II.

Marcus Garvey and the United Negro Improvement Association established 700 branches in 38 states by the early 1920s.

even worse. Most of them were relegated to domestic service jobs, and when faced with limited opportunities in places such as vice-ridden Detroit, some of them turned to prostitution.

Transplanted African Americans enjoyed more freedom of movement in their daily lives than they had in the south, but this was inconsistent from city to city. In Chicago they could ride side-by-side with white passengers on streetcars; in Cincinnati and Pittsburgh they were excluded from restaurants, hotels, and soda fountains.

Urban blacks responded to continued racial and economic discrimination with aggressive community-building measures. Organizations such as churches, political leagues, fraternal orders, and women's clubs were highly visible in black life, helping southern migrants to assimilate with existing black northern populations. The Detroit Urban League encouraged young African-American women to participate in Dress Well Clubs and baby clinics. The Chicago Urban League, which provided a variety of employment and social services, reported assisting 20,000 newcomers in 1920. Marcus Garvey's United Negro Improvement Association held mass marches on the streets of many northern cities, and storefront Spiritualist churches were established in the vice districts, preaching clean living to residents who were ignored by mainstream black denominations. Black self-help measures reaped impressive results in Louisville, where by mid-decade black-owned institutions included two banks, four insurance firms, four newspapers, and six real estate companies. African-American assertiveness was evident even in the face of the worst racial violence. In 1921 in Tulsa, a race riot began after a group of blacks, attempting to protect a prisoner accused of an improbable sexual assault, exchanged gunfire with a white lynch mob. During the ensuing violence that torched the city's black district and killed at least 75 people, several black former World War I soldiers, dressed in their military uniforms, engaged in an hours-long standoff with white attackers before finally succumbing.

Writing during the 1920s, Lewis Mumford observed that the modern city was the place where man could "enter most fully into his social heritage," but also the place that launched a thousand daily assaults upon his spirit. When whites "slummed" in Harlem nightclubs, they were being culturally condescending—but also culturally transgressive. When African Americans shopped at a metropolitan chain store, it was an act of mass consumption—but also an act of hard-won self-assertion. In ways like these, urban life during the 1920s was both oppressive and disruptive.

TOM COLLINS

Further Readings

Brophy, Alfred L. *Reconstructing the Dreamland: The Tulsa Riot of 1921: Race, Reparations, and Reconciliation.* New York: Oxford University Press, 2002.

Brownell, Blaine. *The Urban Ethos in the South, 1920–1930.* Baton Rouge, LA: Louisiana State University Press, 1975.

Cohen, Lizabeth. *Making a New Deal: Industrial Workers in Chicago, 1919–1939.* New York: Cambridge University Press, 1990.

Cressey, Paul G. *The Taxi-Dance Hall: A Sociological Study in Commercialized Recreation and City Life.* New York: Greenwood Press, 1932.

Erenberg, Lewis A. *Steppin' Out: New York Nightlife and the Transformation of American Culture, 1890–1930.* Westport, CT: Greenwood Press, 1981.

Fogelson, Robert M. *The Fragmented Metropolis: Los Angeles, 1850–1930.* Cambridge, MA: Harvard University Press, 1967.

Gottlieb, Peter, *Making Their Own Way: Southern Blacks' Migration to Pittsburgh, 1916–30.* Urbana, IL: University of Illinois Press, 1987.

Grossman, James R. *Land of Hope: Chicago, Black Southerners, and the Great Migration.* Chicago, IL: University of Chicago Press, 1989.

Jackson, Kenneth T. *Crabgrass Frontier: The Suburbanization of the United States.* New York: Oxford University Press, 1985.

———. *The Ku Klux Klan in the City, 1915–1930.* New York: Oxford University Press, 1967.

Kyvig, David E. *Daily Life in the United States, 1920–1939: Decades of Promise and Pain.* Westport, CT: Greenwood Press, 2002.

Loeb, Carolyn S. *Entrepreneurial Vernacular: Developers' Subdivisions in the 1920s.* Baltimore, MD: Johns Hopkins University Press, 2001.

Monroy, Douglas. *Rebirth: Mexican Los Angeles from the Great Migration to the Great Depression.* Berkeley, CA: University of California Press, 1999.

Peretti, Burton, *Nightclub City: Politics and Amusement in Manhattan.* Philadelphia, PA: University of Pennsylvania Press, 2007.

Rae, John B. *The Road and the Car in American Life.* Cambridge, MA: MIT Press, 1971.

Revell, Keith D. *Building Gotham: Civic Culture and Public Policy in New York City, 1898–1938.* Baltimore, MD: Johns Hopkins University Press, 2003.

Sitton, Tom and William Deverell, eds. *Metropolis in the Making: Los Angeles in the 1920s.* Berkeley, CA: University of California Press, 2001.

Trotter, Joe William, Jr. *River of Jordan: African American Urban Life in the Ohio Valley.* Lexington, KY: University of Kentucky Press, 1998.

Wolcott, Victoria W. *Remaking Respectability: African American Women in Interwar Detroit.* Chapel Hill, NC: University of North Carolina Press, 2001.

Chapter 6

Rural Life

"My long scythe whispered and left the hay to make."
—Robert Frost

IT MAY HAVE been a boom decade for most of the country, but the 1920s were not a good time for increasingly marginalized farmers. A year after World War I ended, commodity prices plummeted. The drop-off was not as severe as the Great Depression that ended the 1920s, and prices remained flat after the initial fall. However, farmers throughout the decade certainly did not enjoy the prosperity that so enriched the urban centers of the country. In 1929—before the stock market crash—the prices for wheat, potatoes, and cotton were all half of what they had been in 1919, largely due to that 1920 drop.

The war had inflated demand, but European postwar recovery slashed it. As the United States made the shift from a debtor nation (owing money to European countries) to a creditor nation (one to which European nations owed money), the trade balance shifted as well. European nations now needed to sell to the United States, not buy from it, in order to earn the money to pay off their debts. Many agricultural goods once shipped to Europe from American farms were now bought in Canada and Australia. Meat exports dropped a staggering 85 percent in the 10 years after World War I.

While those factors did not directly affect domestic consumption, others did. Fewer Americans were manual laborers with laborers' appetites, and they ate fewer starches, reducing the demand for potatoes and grains. Synthetic fabrics, Prohibition (most alcohol was made from grain), and the declining

Automobiles, such as this Model T stopped at a general store, allowed farm families to participate more in the life of nearby towns, and even take trips to the city.

numbers of hay- and oat-eating horses (thanks to automobiles and farm equipment) all affected farms, and improvements in commercial canning, food transportation, and refrigeration meant less waste on the consumer end. It is particularly important that these were effects on purchasing habits that were not solved by price reductions or other enticements: no one trades in his automobile for a horse-drawn carriage just because oats are on sale.

In the meantime, rural standards of living had risen, and the institutions of the day all encouraged rural citizens to try to aspire to those standards. Having become accustomed a couple generations earlier to a greater tax burden because of government funding of compulsory public schools, farmers were now encouraged to think of sending their children to college. Higher education may have been cheaper than it used to be, thanks in large part to the congressionally-created land-grant colleges of the late 19th century, but it was still a substantial financial expectation for a group of people who for so long had depended on their children for labor to help out on the farm. Also, the growing national popular culture—the world of magazines, radio, movies, and books—encouraged rural Americans to buy labor-saving devices and appliances on credit. On top of those optional expenses—though they may not have felt optional, just as owning a cellular phone in the 21st century may feel like something that is expected of you—this was the first

Boon to Farmers: Tractors

In the early and mid-1920s, tractors began to replace draft animals at a greater rate than they had previously, as various technical problems with earlier designs were fixed. This was a huge boon to farmers, a promise of the Industrial Revolution finally realized—a single hard-working horse consumed six acres of oats and hay a year, and for obvious reasons, draft animals were subject to a number of problems and limitations that machinery was not. Over the course of the 1920s, thanks to new innovations—and despite the low cash-flow of American farms—the number of tractors more than tripled. But once again, this made farms more dependent on cash and unable to be self-sufficient. Oats and hay may have taken up a lot of space now usable for marketable crops, but at least they could be produced on the farm, which gasoline could not. While farmers had always been dependent on outside sources for fuel—lamp oil, if nothing else—nothing had ever consumed it as fast as petroleum-burning engines.

So it is important to note that, while tractors skyrocketed in popularity, they still were not common. The cost of purchasing and operating one and the slim profit margins of farming meant that by U.S. Department of Agriculture estimates, a farm needed at least 130 acres in order to generate enough income to pay for a tractor—which was true of only 40 percent of American farms. While some mid-sized farms attempted to expand in order to afford mechanization, many had to mortgage their lands in order to do so. Over the course of the decade, the number of small farms and large farms both increased, along with the average acreage—but the total number of farms declined. Mid-sized farms, big enough to be difficult to manage, but not big enough to afford significant improvements like tractors, slowly phased out, and have continued to do so up through the present time.

These Fordson tractors served a large farm in 1922. Only 40 percent of American farms could afford a tractor.

major decline in agricultural income since federal income tax had been instituted in 1913.

In some cases, the drops in agricultural profits were simply an adjustment as the boom of the war years faded away. However, while the incomes farmers took in diminished, the costs they paid out did not decline accordingly, either in their business or personal expenses. Whether or not this was a "real" agricultural depression or not, the effect on American farmers was the same. While American farms had never been fully self-sufficient, their cash dependency was greater in the early 20th century than it had ever been, and they very suddenly had much less of it.

Government assistance, demanded by the political base farmers had spent the last 50 years building in response to the urbanization of America, was little more than a trickle. The Farmer-Labor Party formed in 1920 had little impact except in Minnesota. In 1921 a bipartisan group of congressional representatives and senators called the Farm Bloc formed at the behest of the major farming organizations such as the Grange, the Farmers Union, and the Farm Bureau. They worked fairly quickly to pass acts that protected meat sellers from price manipulation and exempted agricultural cooperatives from antitrust prosecution. The Republicans in the Farm Bloc passed the Fordney-McCuber Tariff to dramatically increase the tax on imported agricultural

This spiral-bladed plow was made for towing behind a tractor. It was estimated that a farm in the 1920s needed at least 130 acres in order to generate enough income to pay for a tractor.

products in order to remove them from competition with their domestic counterparts. This had little effect, though. Imported goods were already more expensive, and their availability had little or nothing to do with the declining demand that had driven farmers' prices and profits down.

Branded orange crates from the 1920s. The names of several fruit and dairy coops created in the 1920s are still used today.

George Peek, an Illinois businessman, proposed a plan to help farmers: the parity price. The federal government, the Peek Plan suggested, should buy excess commodities from farmers (whatever could not be sold) at a price derived from their production and consumption, using as a baseline the prices and values established before the wartime boom. The government would then resell those goods internationally, and if they did so at a loss, they would charge farmers a fee. The main idea was, by guaranteeing that sales would always meet production capacity, farmers could charge more than the low demand would otherwise dictate. The Farm Bloc introduced a series of bills beginning in 1924, applying the Peek Plan on a crop-by-crop basis to cotton, corn, pork, rice, tobacco, and wheat. The bills faced considerable opposition because of the bureaucracy they required and the fear that, rather than helping farmers in need who were caught up short by the post-war decline, the Peek Plan would actively encourage poorly-planned agriculture and thus prolong the problem. That complaint should be familiar to anyone familiar with the New Deal. Throughout the 20th century, the tension between temporary solutions and their long-term consequences has been fundamental to the development of federal law.

In this case, the opposition won, if narrowly. While some of the bills were defeated in Congress, others had to be vetoed by President Coolidge. Farm cooperatives were formed in the meantime so that producers of the same crop could pool their products and resources, sell as a unit, and so avoid competing with each other or sharing profits with middlemen. The U.S. Department of Agriculture (USDA) strongly supported agricultural coops, and Congress protected them from antitrust laws. Fruit and dairy coops became especially successful, and many of their names are well-known today—Ocean Spray (cranberries), Sunkist (oranges), and Land O'Lakes (butter), among others.

Route 66 and the U.S. Highways

In the 1910s, the federal government had begun providing financial aid to construct and maintain interstate highways and other major roads. Throughout the early 1920s, this led to federal discussion of a planned system of marked and numbered U.S. highways, which would be so designated regardless of funding. That is to say, in addition to funding interstate roads, the federal government would also provide its designation to existing routes that did not need to be funded, if they were the best choice to be added to the system.

The idea was to make as much of the country accessible by as few routes as possible, to encourage cross-country travel not only among private citizens, but also by commercial drivers, as commercial trucking and overland delivery began to supplement the railways just as horse and carriage travel across the old roads had supplemented the waterways. Making this cross-country travel easier—eventually all these roads were paved, long before that was true of the majority of roads in general—meant many things for rural Americans.

It eased the creation of tourist industries in towns with historic or picturesque attractions, whether that meant ghost towns in Wyoming or Monument Valley in Utah. It meant families who had been separated generations earlier by the westward settlement of one branch could now be more easily reunited. And it meant commerce for all those little towns along the way between one destination and another, as those drivers—whether tourist, commercial, or just getting from one place to the next—would need places to stop, eat, sleep, and refuel.

After various plans were discussed, the U.S. highways were laid out with routes given a two-digit number (except in the cases of routes 1, 2, and 101) and interconnecting roads given a three-digit designation. The famous Route 66 was one of those first routes, incorporating a number of old private auto roads, running from Chicago to Los Angeles (though ending before the coast). Along the way it passed through Missouri, Kansas, Oklahoma, Texas, New Mexico, and Arizona, and it soon became home to the memorable sights of those businesses and communities that served the great highways—motor courts and motels, bingo parlors, laundromats, restaurants (and eventually diners and fast food joints), and so on. The route was predominantly flat, and popular with both commercial and private drivers for its ease and comfort. Until it was paved in the 1930s, Route 66 was mostly graded dirt and gravel.

The number of farms began to decline significantly, especially among mid-sized farms—larger mechanized farms with high yields and small near-self-sufficient family farms were better able to survive because they had more or needed less, but the average farmer was hit hard. The fact that the 1920s are remembered as a prosperous decade underscores the fact that the average farmer was no longer the average American—the agricultural nation of the 18th century was long in the past.

The rural population dwindled as a result of migration to urban centers; 6.25 million people in the 1920s moved from the country to the city or suburbs. Many of them were young, moving to the city before starting a family, or with young children to enter into the (often better-funded) urban schools. One reason so many rural dwellers loved the radio so much is because it provided them with a sort of contact, a community connection, that they were swiftly losing as the pews emptied in their churches.

Small schools and churches in rural areas tended to consolidate in the 1920s in order to conserve resources, and the spread of the telephone slowed almost to a stop, with many homes canceling telephone service until long after the Depression. But the radio, like the automobile, had practical utility. Indeed, in the 1920s the federal government considered there to be three kinds of radio stations—government-owned, entertainment, and weather/crop reports. Radio enjoyed enormous popularity on the Great Plains, where weather could change suddenly with punishing effects, and people tended to live further from their neighbors than in other rural parts of the country.

HILLBILLY MUSIC AND RURAL RADIO

There was something reassuring about the radio's entertainments as well, though. One of the most popular radio programs of the decade was the *Grand Ole Opry,* a music program broadcast on WSM ("We Shield Millions," the slogan of network owner National Life and Accident Insurance Company) beginning in 1925. WSM was—and still is—a Nashville-based clear channel station. The "clear channels" are a regulatory category of radio station, and were key to rural America in the first decades of radio. Particular medium-wave frequencies were designated for use by only one station each, broadcasting at night to both a primary and secondary service area. Clear channel stations are the only stations with a protected secondary service area, which means that federal law guarantees that their signal won't be interfered with.

For instance, there may be dozens of radio stations with the 107.9 FM frequency—that is not a clear channel and is not protected. WSM broadcasts on 650 AM, and at night its signal can be picked up throughout most of the eastern half of the United States. Other clear channels—all of them with powerful transmitters—covered similarly large areas, and clear channel stations were often the only stations that would come in at all in rural parts of the country, especially west of the Mississippi. In some cases, the same frequency was

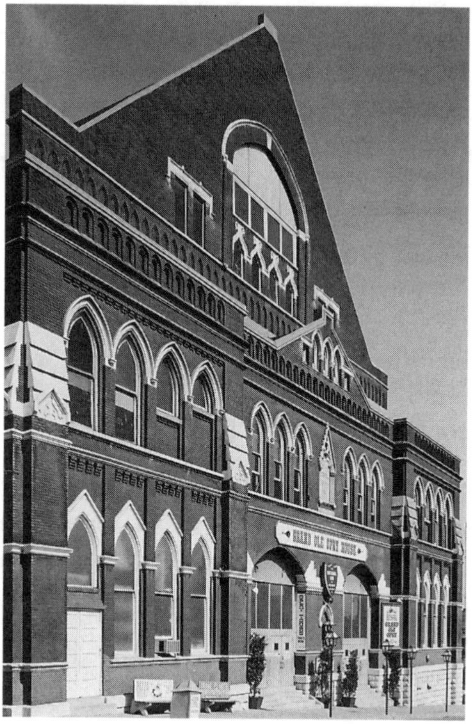

The Ryman Auditorium in Nashville, Tennessee, was the home of WSM's broadcasts of the Grand Ole Opry *for over three decades.*

used by a clear channel station on the east coast and another in the west—far enough apart that transmitters were simply not powerful enough for their signals to interfere with one another. The novelty and appeal of radio cannot be overstated. In the country's many remote and sparsely settled areas, the radio might bring more voices into the house each night than had been encountered throughout the day, and unlike the movies, the entertainment was free once you bought the radio itself. Nor were there fragile vinyl records that needed to be purchased, as there were for phonographs.

WSM began operation in 1925 and was mainly associated with its music program the WSM *Barn Dance.* In December of 1927, the *Barn Dance* took on a new name. It followed NBC's *Music Appreciation Hour,* which was decidedly upscale in its approach. The *Music Appreciation Hour* broadcast primarily classical music with a heavy dose of opera, and on that night the closing piece was an orchestral interpretation of a locomotive. The *Barn Dance*'s announcer and emcee, George Hay—who called himself "the Solemn Old Judge"—responded to that by announcing at the start of his show, "Friends, the program which just came to a close was devoted to the classics. [That program] told us that there is no place in the classics for realism. However, from here on out for the next three hours, we will present nothing but realism. It will be down to earth for the 'earthy.'" He then introduced DeFord Bailey, the Harmonica Wizard, whose performance of "The Pan American Blues," a traditional song about the Louisville & Nashville Railroad, provided a fine counterpoint to the airs put on by the *Music Appreciation Hour.*

"For the past hour," Hay said when Bailey was done, "we have been listening to music largely from the Grand Opera. Well, from now on we will present the Grand Ole Opry." The name stuck, and delineation had been drawn: the music of the *Grand Ole Opry* was "earthy" music, down to earth, unpretentious, and unassuming. It was in many cases not much different from the music people sang at home, the music the man of the house might play on the porch with a few simple instruments, his daughters accompanying him on the harmonies. In some cases it was the music people had grown up with, but in many cases it was new—or had a new spin thrown on it. All of this developed into what we call country music today, but that term was not used until World War II, and modern country music is a good deal closer to pop music than what the *Grand Ole Opry* was broadcasting in 1927. That music—which was called hillbilly music at the time, and sometimes referred to as "old timey"—had developed mainly in the Appalachians and Texas, as various fiddle styles blended with the instruments

Honky Tonks

What the juke joint was to the urban African American, the honky tonk was to the white rural American throughout the south and the American west. The etymology is a mystery and little more than a list of possibilities, but it definitely entered into use sometime after the word "honky," meaning a white person—so the racial connotation of a honky tonk may have always been there. But etymology is tricky—it is just as possible that it is a coincidence.

From the late 19th century on, honky tonks were bars with music. Everything else varied from place to place—they might double as brothels or simply attract prostitutes who hung around looking for customers. For music, there might be a steady piano player or house band, a player piano, or simply a juke box (though they were not called that until the 1930s). They might serve food, but usually did not; they often had room for dancing; there might be gambling, but usually just informal games of cards; and they were often considered tough establishments. The 19th-century honky tonks had been theaters, like a rowdier vaudeville house, but by the 1920s music and room to dance to it replaced other forms of entertainment. They were a staple fixture in towns with mostly male populations, like mining towns, military bases, and so on.

"Honky tonk music" has referred to various things since the early 20th century, but its contemporary meaning as the majority subgenre of country music, a slickly produced blend of Nashville-inflected pop, rock, and western swing, has little to do with its origins. The first honky tonk music was a sort of white ragtime, piano-based music played on typically out of tune pianos that might be missing a key or two—a limitation that required a loose approach to the melodies and a willingness to improvise, two things easily accepted by the drunken crowd. Honky tonk songs tended to be about drinking, women, cheating, and cheating women, and when the music was performed live, the singer might be as drunk as the patrons.

and traditions of immigrant groups. The Spanish guitar sometimes replaced or augmented the fiddle, as did the Italian mandolin and accordion.

The first hillbilly music was recorded in 1923, not long before the *Barn Dance* went on the air. The first major hillbilly hit showed the genre's interest in rural history: Vernon Dalhart, a Texan who moved to New York City, recorded "Wreck of the Old 97," a traditional ballad about the infamous train wreck of the Southern Railway train at the Stillhouse Trestle outside Danville, Virginia, in 1903. The record sold seven million copies—not just an enormous amount for the time, but the best-selling non-holiday song until the 1970s. The record companies and radio stations realized quickly that the public was hungry for more. Dalhart had a string of other hits, and a huge number of hillbilly musicians were recruited as recording artists.

THE RISE OF COUNTRY MUSIC

Charlie Poole and the North Carolina Ramblers played fiddle, banjo, and guitar music that later inspired both the bluegrass of Bill Monroe and the country music of Hank Williams, relying on Poole's unique fingerpicking style to render old classics. The Skillet Lickers played fiddle music on Atlanta-based radio station WSB, with blind Riley Puckett contributing vocals. Mississippi native Jimmie Rodgers, often called the father of country music and certainly the biggest star of the era, quit his job as a brakeman on the New Orleans & Northeastern Railroad in 1924 when tuberculosis made the manual labor too difficult for him, and turned to a singing career instead. He only lived another nine years, but spent almost all of it recording and performing music. The Carter Family, whose music continues to be influential especially to alt country, got their start in recording when A.P. Carter talked his wife Sara and brother's wife Maybelle into making the trip with him from southwestern Virginia to Bristol, Tennessee, where they auditioned in 1927 for a record producer who was paying $50 for every song he recorded.

Hillbilly music was only one flavor of the music being played and performed in rural America. West of the Mississippi, especially in the American southwest where Mexican music was a bigger influence than that of European immigrants encountered by Appalachians, the native folk music was "western music" (from whence came the term "Country and western," recently fallen out of favor). Sometimes called "cowboy songs," western music shared with hillbilly/country music its roots in English, Scottish, and Irish fiddle music and its reflection of the music sung at home by its listeners. Western music tended toward ballads, especially ballads for solo performers—the idea of the cowboy song as something sung by a lonesome cowboy out on the range, astride his horse with a harmonica or guitar, was an enduring one, even though the age of the cowboy had passed. The music had stayed alive in the former frontier territories, especially Oklahoma, New Mexico, Arizona, Arkansas, and the Texas Panhandle. It was music westerners could relate to.

There were no standout stars of western music in the 1920s—the true stars would come in the next decade, when the advent of sound films meant the birth of the "singing cowboy" movie—but many of the popular songs of the genre are still familiar today: "Home on the Range," "Don't Take Your Guns To Town," "Clementine," "Bury Me Not On The Lone Prairie," and "Tumbling Tumbleweeds," among others. At the time, many claims were made by music historians about the close relationship between western music ballads and European ballads, as though a musical tradition had been carried unchanged across the Atlantic, across the prairies, and across the generations. These claims were exaggerated, and mostly reflect the fact that western music lacked the blues influence that so much hillbilly music had.

Like hillbilly music, like western music, the blues were the music of "the people," not the music of professional songwriters. In the early 20th century, there was no clear distinction between the blues and hillbilly music, except for the race of the performer—and even that wasn't always an indicator, since a small number of musical groups were integrated. Though the blues tended to adopt elements from the old plantation spirituals to a greater degree than did hillbilly music, the biggest difference was simply that hillbilly music was

Two African-American musicians playing a guitar, a cello-like bowed instrument, and kazoos outdoors on a farm around 1920.

This unidentified band and their leader assembled to perform together around 1920, possibly for a radio program of popular dance music.

played in the country, while the blues were played both in the country and the city. Urban blues music, the blues played in nightclubs and closely related to ragtime and jazz, the blues of Harlem and St. Louis, was foreign and invasive to rural white ears.

CONCLUSION

For Americans living on farms, in small towns, and in isolated mining and lumber villages, many aspects of life in the 1920s remained little changed from the previous two decades. Electricity had not reached many such regions because of the high cost of building power lines for the sparse numbers of customers. With no linkage to electricity or gas pipelines, heating, cooking, and lighting usually relied on fuels such as wood, coal, or oil, with technologies little changed since the 1870s.

Farm life remained strenuous, both for men and women, as ordinary tasks such as gardening, cleaning, preserving food, cooking, and caring for clothing were carried out with the same equipment, methods, and processes used by households four or five decades earlier. While tractors made fieldwork somewhat less arduous for those farmers who could afford them, many still plowed, harrowed, and harvested with horse- or mule-drawn gear. In the home, in barns, in automobiles, and on tractors, of course, air conditioning was unheard of, adding to the drudgery of all work in the heat of summer. On the other hand, life in the country largely remained free of the pollution, noise, and congested traffic of the cities.

For those who could afford automobiles or trucks, access to market towns, to railroad stations, and even to urban areas gave hints of the transformations at work. Newspapers and magazines brought word of the growing sophistication and materialism of urban areas, accentuating the cultural clash between "city slickers" and "country bumpkins." The press, movies, and radio brought a growing sense that American culture was being homogenized, often in ways that the more traditional folk found disturbing. Defensively, many in rural regions believed that their lifestyles represented the true American way of life, corrupted in the cities by modernism, irreligion, immorality, foreign ideas, and crime. Rather than seeing the members of F. Scott Fitzgerald's generation as young and liberated, more conservative country people regarded the "flaming youth" and the "flapper" as symptoms of the growing corruption of values.

Support for Prohibition, for immigration restriction, and even for the revived Ku Klux Klan was much stronger in rural areas, symptoms of what urban intellectuals saw as a "reactionary" trend. The legendary show trial of high school teacher John T. Scopes for teaching evolution was presented by city journalists such as H.L. Mencken as a ludicrous example of the backward ways of country people.

The reaction found milder forms in music, of course. With battery-powered radios, hand-cranked phonographs, and widely distributed sheet music, country music in its several varieties gave a form of expression to rural values that became a more benign, and in some cases, lasting, contribution to the tapestry of American life.

BILL KTE'PI

Further Readings

Abbott, E.C. *We Pointed Them North*. Norman, OK: University of Oklahoma Press, 1955.

Boyd, Jean. *The Jazz of the Southwest*. Austin, TX: University of Texas Press, 1998.

Dary, David. *Cowboy Culture*. Lawrence, KS: University Press of Kansas, 1989.

Dawidoff, Nicholas. *In the Country of Country: A Journey to the Roots of American Music*. London: Vintage, 1998.

Escott, Colin. *Roadkill on the Three-Chord Highway*. New York: Routledge, 2002.

Kienzle, Richard. *Southwest Shuffle*. New York: Routledge, 2003.
Kyvig, David. *Daily Life in the United States, 1920–1940: How Americans Lived Through The Roaring Twenties and the Great Depression*. New York: Ivan R. Dee, 2004.
Latham, Angela. *Posing a Threat: Flappers, Chorus Girls, and Other Brazen Performers of the American 1920s*. Middletown, CT: Wesleyan University Press, 2000.
Malone, Bill. *Don't Get above Your Raisin'*. Urbana, IL: University of Illinois Press, 2002.
O'Neal, Bill and Fred Goodwin. *The Sons of the Pioneers*. Austin, TX: Eakin Press, 2001.
White, John I. *Git Along Little Dogies: Songs and Songmakers of the American West*. Chicago, IL: University of Illinois Press, 1989.
Zeitz, Joshua. *Flapper: A Madcap Story of Sex, Style, Celebrity, and the Women Who Made America Modern*. New York: Three Rivers Press, 2007.

Chapter 7

Religion

"Religion in its humility restores man to his only dignity, the courage to live by grace."
—George Santayana

LIKE THE 1920S as a whole, American religion of the period is the maturation of events put in motion in the previous decades, a sort of coming of age. The Progressive Era had seen the widespread marriage of religion with social activism, the response of Christianity and Judaism to modernity, and the enormous success of revivalists like Billy Sunday. All of those would come into play to different effect in the 1920s, and all of them fed into the two principal events of the decade: the inception of Fundamentalism and the trial of John T. Scopes.

The term "fundamentalist" has grown to refer to many sorts of religious movements that seek a return to the fundamentals of their faith, and is sometimes used synonymously with "Biblical literalist." Here, the capitalized term Fundamentalist refers exclusively to members of the informal Protestant movement associated with a series of books on Protestant beliefs called *The Fundamentals: A Testimony To The Truth*. For years, conservative Christians had been increasingly uncomfortable with the trends in their faith, such as the growing number of Catholic immigrants, the rise of atheism, and the secularizing of many religious groups. They were also alarmed by new faiths like the Latter Day Saints and Christian Scientists, the mysticism of Victorian spiritualism and popularization of Eastern beliefs, the conclusions of modern Biblical scholarship (especially Julius Wellhausen's documentary hypothesis), and Darwinian

The evangelist Aimee Semple McPherson, who could draw crowds of over 25,000, in 1927.

theories of evolution. The concerns of these Christians mirror those of the conservative Jews dismayed by Reform Judaism. Taken individually, these things were bad enough, but for all of them to be happening in such a short time span was alarming. Unlike the conservative Jews, the conservative Christians—members of the religion that had been demographically dominant throughout American history—were more alarmed by developments outside the world of their faith, and the possibility of being marginalized, or at least losing that dominance.

Just as conservative Jews worried that Reform Judaism was stripping away all the Jewishness—as indeed it sometimes strove to do—these conservative Christians saw the erosion of an essential Christianness in American Christianity. Even when they agreed with the aims of the Social Gospel, for instance, or other liberal/progressive Christian movements, they disagreed with the emphasis on Christian ethics at the expense of Christian supernaturalism. Jesus was not just a philosopher or a prophet—he was the Son of God. The Bible was not simply a historical document—it was the revealed word of God. An early Presbyterian conference identified as indispensable and endangered five Christian points of belief: Biblical inerrancy; the reality of miracles as attested in the Bible; and the virgin birth, sacrifice, and bodily resurrection of Christ.

During World War I, Congregationalist minister Reuben Torrey, a student of Dwight Moody, edited *The Fundamentals* books, which defined fundamental Protestantism in exclusionary terms, by what it was not: it was not liberal, it was not Catholic, it was not atheistic or spiritualistic or mystical. The books included essays by a variety of writers and theologians and—key to the development of Fundamentalism—were distributed for free to clergy, missionaries, and influential church workers. Combined with the Scofield Reference Bible, they set the intellectual stage for Christianity in the 1920s. The goals of Fundamentalism also appealed to the adherents of Landmark Baptism, because of its emphasis on an unchanging church.

Aimee Semple McPherson

The most famous female evangelist, Aimee Semple McPherson, was born in 1890 in Canada, and had converted from agnosticism to Pentecostal Christianity after falling in love with her future husband, a Pentecostal missionary. His mission work took them around the globe, and after his death, she moved, pregnant, to the United States. Semple eventually remarried and took work with the Salvation Army, and like Mary Baker Eddy, felt a reconnection with God after a prolonged illness.

She began to travel across the United States as an itinerant evangelist, and her popularity soared quickly. Her tent revivals were always filled to capacity, and on multiple occasions the National Guard and other services were required in order to organize crowds of over 25,000. People showed up hours early and waited in lines that streamed more than a block in order to get a good seat. Without fail, her audience always included members of the local clergy, regardless of denomination. Eventually she settled down in Los Angeles where she founded the Angelus Temple in Echo Park, with a seating capacity of about 5,000.

She proved more able than Billy Sunday at retaining her popularity through the 1920s, and was the first woman in any country to preach on the radio, as well as the first woman granted a broadcast license, which she used (beginning in 1924) for a regular radio show. It was huge news when, in 1926, she disappeared at the beach, presumed drowned. The search for her body in the water cost two lives, and a month later, a ransom note was sent to her mother threatening to sell McPherson into white slavery if they were not given $500,000. Her mother assumed it was a cruel joke.

On June 23, days after the note, McPherson was found wandering the desert on the Mexican border of Arizona. She said she had been kidnapped and tortured in Mexico, and after escaping had walked 13 hours before finding help.

From the start, though, her story was questioned—her shoes showed little sign of wear other than grass stains a desert could not account for, and she was wearing her own clothes, an outfit and watch that she had not been wearing when she disappeared. Witnesses stated she had been seen in the company of a married man, and when indicted by a grand jury, she refused to elaborate on her relationship with him.

Popular theories suggested that the disappearance had been arranged to conceal an abortion, but the matter was never settled. Toward the end of the decade, McPherson's sunny disposition and public persona had faltered during struggles for control of her church (both her mother and her now-grown daughter jockeyed for position), and she suffered a nervous breakdown in 1930. She would go on to be active in charity throughout the Great Depression, and died of a barbiturate overdose in 1944.

THE FUNDAMENTALIST-MODERNIST CONFLICT

The term "Fundamentalist" was adopted in 1920 and saw increasing use through the decade—and, critically, could be applied regardless of denomination. Though the first Fundamentalists were largely Presbyterians, the movement encompassed Baptists, Methodists, and the whole of American Protestantism. The liberal and progressive Christians, in contrast, were referred to as Modernists, and the Fundamentalist-Modernist conflict recurred throughout the 20th century. The proponents of Fundamentalism insisted that the recent developments in Protestantism were radical enough to constitute, in essence, a new divergent religion—that Fundamentalism preserved authentic Christianity, while others moved away from it. For this reason, it was not enough to simply pursue their practices. They had to actively fight for and defend them, treating Modernists as invaders of a sort. The Baptists formed three organizations in as many years to seek the expulsion of Modernists from their churches, perhaps still feeling the sting of the decline of Landmark Baptism. Other denominations followed suit.

Among the Presbyterians, Charles Macartney and Gresham Machen were the leaders of the Fundamentalist faction. Machen was a professor at Princeton Seminary, where he became the face of the resistance against Modernist innovations in the school's theological teachings, taking them on their own terms. His book *The Origin of Paul's Religion* challenged the notion that Pauline Christianity owed an intellectual debt to Greek philosophy, while Christianity and Liberalism made the fight explicit. Christianity's biggest enemy, Machen said, was Christianity itself, as the true church fought off rebellion from within. He also opposed the evangelical beliefs popularized by the Scofield Reference Bible, though, which was as widespread as *The Fundamentals*, rejecting premillennialism and the notion of a Rapture, along with contemporary interpretations of prophecy that claimed the End Times were imminent.

Macartney had been raised in the Reformed Presbyterian Church, in which his father was a pastor, but converted to the more conservative Presbyterian Church (USA), and challenged liberal Harry Fosdick's contention that soldiers returning from World War I would be unable to acclimate to an unchanging church. The church, Macartney and Machen both argued, was by nature unchanging and its righteousness meant that it did not need to adapt to the times. Fosdick's challenge set off the Fundamentalist-Modernist battle in the Presbyterian Church that until then had only been simmering, as Modernists prepared to fight back against the Fundamentalists who had been condemning them. "Shall the Fundamentalists Win?" Fosdick asked in a widely-disseminated sermon. Modernists, Fosdick argued, were no less pious than Fundamentalists, no less invested in their faith—they sought only to reconcile new discoveries in history and science with their religion, rather than ignore them. "Shall Unbelief Win?" Macartney countered, accusing the liberals and

In smaller churches throughout the country, a portable upright organ like this one, powered by foot pedals, would be used to provide accompaniment for hymns sung by the whole congregation.

Fosdick of secularizing the church and turning it into little more than a social fellowship, "a Christianity of opinions, a Christianity without worship."

The Fundamentalists' early victory had been in pressuring the Presbyterian Church into those five affirmations of faith, which it announced at repeated conferences. In 1923 a group of Presbyterian clergy signed the Auburn Affirmation, declaring that the affirmation of the Five Fundamentals was an unnecessary innovation in Presbyterian practice, and that individual churches and clergymen should be free to interpret the message of God as they saw fit, without having it impressed upon them. Macartney and Machen were outraged, especially after the 1926 ordination in New York (Fosdick's home) of

The Dispute Over Comma Johanneum

An interesting area of overlap between modern Catholicism, Biblical textual criticism, and Fundamentalism is the passage referred to as the "Comma Johanneum" (CJ), meaning "the short clause of John," from the First Epistle of John:

For there are three that bear record [in Heaven, the Father, the Word, and the Holy Ghost: and these three are one. And there are three that bear witness in Earth], the Spirit, and the water, and the blood: and these three agree in one.

The bracketed portion is the CJ: without it, the "three that bear record" are the spirit, water, and blood. With it, the passage is one of the only explicit references to the Trinity in the Bible. Trinitarianism mostly developed among second- and third-generation Christians in the days leading up to the Council of Nicaea.

The CJ does not appear in the oldest copies of the Epistle, nor in the first translations or the original Latin Vulgate. If it were in the original Epistle, we would expect to find it quoted in those early debates about trinitarianism, as it is the strongest Scriptural evidence for it. It originates in an early Latin text, and later appears in a subsequent edition of the Latin Vulgate and the "Textus Receptus" (TR) edition of the Greek text of the New Testament, from the 16th century. From the TR, it was translated into the various languages of the Protestant denominations.

In 1927, after a long period of support, Pope Pius XI decreed that the CJ was disputable, that it was appropriate for theologians to question its authenticity. Biblical scholars, meanwhile, in both Germany and the United States, had investigated the matter of Johannine authorship and come to the conclusion that the CJ was probably added much later, in support of trinitarian debates—and further, that the Epistles and Gospel of John probably did not share an author, and that Revelation was written by some other John altogether.

It was exactly these conclusions that Fundamentalists abhorred, and so by permitting them, the Catholic Church simply demonstrated its inappropriate modernity. It is for this reason that when Fundamentalist groups who supported the inerrancy of the Bible selected an edition, they nearly always chose the King James Version—which had been translated centuries earlier, and included the CJ long before anyone questioned it. If the King James Version were divinely guided, then it did not matter which older texts did or did not include the CJ—because God clearly meant it to be there.

ministers who denied the reality of the virgin birth of Christ. When Princeton Seminary officially reorganized as a more liberal institution, after generations as a conservative outpost, Machen resigned and founded the Westminster Theological Seminary to safeguard Fundamentalist theology, eventually convincing Macartney to join him.

Over the course of the decade, these fights were waged in all the major Protestant denominations, to one extent or another. While the Modernists sometimes downplayed the need for a conflict, to the Fundamentalists it was very clear. The issue was what beliefs would be required of anyone ordained as a minister, what theology would be taught in seminaries, and what beliefs would be passed on overseas through missionary efforts. It was, metaphorically, a fight over genes. The Modernists protested that the Fundamentalists were not being threatened, but the Fundamentalists perceived that there was a risk of their "genes" not being passed on to future generations, making them the only and last of their kind. Phrased like this, it was a fight for survival.

By the end of the decade, Fundamentalists had failed to win, though they had not been defeated exactly. Modernists, in the main, saw no need to remove them, so they were allowed to remain in the church bodies and continue their worship as they saw fit—but that was not enough for them. In numbers that would increase in the coming decades, Fundamentalists removed themselves

The Princeton Theological Seminary in Princeton, New Jersey, moved in a more liberal direction in the 1920s, becoming the epicenter of the Fundamentalist-Modernist conflict.

to their own churches, with varying degrees of formality. Unaligned churches, not part of any ecclesiastical body but sympathetic to evangelical and Pentecostal concerns, began to become more common.

FUNDAMENTALIST BELIEFS

One of the important issues debated between Fundamentalists and Modernists is the treatment of Scripture. Some Modernists would hold that much of the Bible is to be taken metaphorically or symbolically—that it is not important if there really was a King David of Israel, if an actual Flood occurred, if Jesus performed miracles. The message of the Bible does not require these facts, many Modernists would say. This became particularly important with the rise of modern geology and biology, as the scientifically derived age of the Earth conflicted with a literal six-day Creation.

Fundamentalism is not the same as literalism. Literalists are a minor voice, believing that the whole of the Bible is literally true, despite its occasional internal contradictions—the dual Creation story of Genesis, the attribution of Goliath's death to both David and Elhanan, and so on. Literalists acknowledge the use of parable and metaphor in contextually obvious ways—when Jesus says the Kingdom of God is a mustard seed, he does not mean an actual seed, and his parables do not need to be read as accounts of events that happened to real people—but underscores the need for that contextual obviousness. Anything that would have been taken literally by ancient readers, such as the six-day Creation and the Flood, must be accepted as Biblical fact.

True literalism generally exists only as a strawman. People unfamiliar with Christianity, or those raised as Christians without practicing it actively themselves, have since the 19th century tended to assume that "true believers" are literalists. For about that length of time, many lay people have believed that literalism was an original Christianity from which the modern world had deviated, but nothing could be further from the truth: even before the birth of Jesus, many Jewish scholars had ceased to treat the Old Testament as a purely historical account, while treating as historical everything that presents itself that way, for instance the accounts of Judges and Chronicles, and the genealogies, and Christian thinkers from the very beginning did likewise. Augustine's understanding of Genesis was highly figurative, and the tendency to demonstrate Genesis's agreement with scientific findings has, through the ages, been one that depends on non-literal readings of the book.

More common than literalism is the belief in Biblical inerrancy, which states that the Bible is correct. It contains metaphors and figurative language, it contains prophecies that require interpretation, but it is not wrong. This is the explicit pillar of Fundamentalism, erected in protest against Modernists' discussions of the influence of Mesopotamian mythology on the writing of

In response to increased Catholic populations, a diocese would authorize the construction of new parish churches. This St. Joan of Arc Catholic Church, built in Hershey, Pennsylvania, in 1921, was sold to a Protestant denomination when the Catholic parish opened a larger church in 1962.

the Old Testament, or the possibility of monotheism having been developed by the Egyptians, or Jesus being mythical. Supporters of inerrancy believe that the writing of the Bible was divinely guided—a belief feasible even within source criticism—and so may not believe that every translation of the Bible is inerrant. Indeed, in more recent times, Fundamentalists have encouraged the learning of Biblical languages in order to study the books of the Bible with as

Fundamentalists and Catholicism

In the 19th century, Catholicism had adopted two doctrines that moved it further from Protestantism, increasing its alienation from American Protestants: papal infallibility and the Immaculate Conception. The Immaculate Conception is widely misunderstood—the term refers not to the conception of Jesus but to that of Mary, who according to this doctrine was conceived without original sin and lived a life free of sin, keeping her body pure as a vessel in which the body of Christ could gestate. The belief had been popularly held by lay Catholics since before the inception of Protestantism, but was only made dogma in 1854. Papal infallibility was made a point of dogma 16 years later, declaring that in certain contexts (which have occurred only once since the dogma's introduction), the Pope has the ability to declare a dogmatic teaching without the possibility of being in error.

The reverence of the Virgin Mary and the rulership of the Pope had always been the two areas in which Catholicism was the most different from Protestantism, and so enhancing those two areas in the same generation made the Catholic immigrants who arrived in the United States in the following decades seem even stranger in their practices and beliefs. The 20th-century revival of the Ku Klux Klan was primarily anti-Catholic and anti-immigrant, concerned with preserving a heroic view of American religio-ethnic identity more than with white supremacy. While Fundamentalists did not commonly agree with the Klan or advocate violence or unfair treatment of Catholics, they did want to distance themselves—and much of their country and fellow Protestants—from "Romanism," as they disparagingly called it.

few filters of translation as possible. Other groups have chosen one translation or another to view as inerrant—often the King James Bible, with more modern translations suspect.

In time, as Fundamentalist groups separated from their churches, other beliefs became common, beliefs that do not pertain directly to the Fundamentals. Creationism is the biggest and earliest of these. Fundamentalist groups also, as they overlapped with Pentecostal and evangelical groups, became increasingly interested in prophecy, especially prophecy about the End Times and debates about the validity of the Rapture, and whether it would come before or after a period of tribulation. For some groups, the existence of a real and supernatural evil became important, as Modernist groups emphasized the idea of Satan less and less. The more alarmist groups publicly worried about the influence of Satan in the popularity of liberal Christianity, atheism and agnosticism, secularism, and socialism. In the south, Fundamentalist concerns also sometimes dovetailed with the lingering southern sentiments that painted the south as more pious than the Union, and so developed into a fear or distrust of the federal government as an agent of secularism, liberalism, or other bogeymen.

THE SCOPES TRIAL

Former presidential candidate and Secretary of State William Jennings Bryan had converted to evangelical Christianity after one of his presidential losses, and had included the evils of Darwinism in his lecture tours since the turn of the century. It was not until the aftermath of World War I that he came to see evolutionism as a serious threat to the Western world and American Christianity, though, and it was at that time that he began campaigning for states to pass laws against its teaching in public schools. Tennessee was one state where he succeeded, and on May 7, 1925, less than two months after the law was passed, John Scopes was arrested for violating it.

Both sides had planned the conflict. Bryan wanted the issue brought to national attention; he wanted a platform where he and his fellows could be heard. The American Civil Liberties Union needed a prosecution in order for the law to be challenged in court, and 24-year-old Scopes agreed to be the test case, having been talked into it by his friend George Rappleyea, a mine owner in the small town of Dayton who convinced the other men of the town that the publicity would bring in much-needed money. Every participant, in other words, was involved by choice, knowing that the trial was the goal. The prosecutors were friends of Scopes, and Rappleyea tried to talk science fiction writer H.G. Wells—neither American nor an attorney—into serving on the defense.

Bryan joined the prosecution team as a special consultant, to try his first case in nearly four decades. Clarence Darrow joined the defense team, essentially guaranteeing a national spotlight even brighter than the one Bryan would have drawn alone. The 67-year-old Darrow was perhaps the most famous practicing attorney in the nation, having defended Nietzschean sociopaths Nathan Leopold and Richard Loeb a year earlier, in the murder of a 14-year-old boy.

The trial was, frankly, ridiculous. Scopes was virtually ignored. An all-star cast of expert witnesses meant to present their opinion that the theory of evolution did not contradict the Bible or Christian belief were instructed to deliver their testimony in writing, for use in an appeal if necessary. Bryan accused the teaching of evolution as partially responsible for Leopold and Loeb's murder, complained that evolution claimed humans descended from monkeys that were not even American monkeys, and volunteered to be a witness for the defense, testifying as an expert on the Bible. Darrow cross-examined Bryan on matters of Biblical literalism, asking if Jonah had really been swallowed by a large fish or if Joshua had made the sun stand still. The judge threw out most of the evidence and testimony, having excluded the jury from the defense's half of the trial so that it could be presented with cherry-picked testimony after the fact. Darrow and Bryan traded speeches, and the judge let them do so for hours before expunging it from the record.

In the end, Scopes was found guilty and ordered to pay a $100 fine—and that, the amount of the fine, was in the end what won his case for him. Legally, a judge could not set a fine of more than $50, and the Tennessee Court of Appeals overturned the decision on that basis and no other. Of course, the whole thing was a media circus. H.L. Mencken unfairly characterized the people of Dayton as "morons" and "yokels," and left town before Darrow's cross-examination of Bryan. The northern and midwestern press made Bryan out to be a raging holy warrior past his intellectual prime, while the southern press focused on Darrow, still the object of contempt for many conservative Americans since he succeeded in avoiding the death penalty for the unrepentant Leopold and Loeb.

What was meant to be a test case unfortunately did irreparable damage to the discussion of evolution and religion, a discussion which arguably has yet to be held in reasonable terms in the United States. In the long run, however you look at it, both sides failed their mandate. By presenting the matter as a trial between opposing sides, the participants had unfairly and inaccurately oversimplified the matter. The truth was that it was only recently that Christians saw it as a black-and-white issue. Evolution was a new discovery, and rather than dismiss it out of hand or blindly embrace it, most waited for science to say more about the matter. After all, unlike many scientific discoveries, it had no real bearing on everyday life. There was no evolution serum you could give a monkey to turn him into a human, nor did evolution yet have any particular effect on human medicine. Medical discoveries were far more important. The age of Darwin was also the age of Pasteur, and in the 1920s Americans still looked forward to the great race for the polio vaccine.

Essentially, the Scopes Trial conflict forced the discussion into a two-party situation rather than looking for synthesis or common ground, to the extent

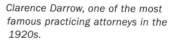

Clarence Darrow, one of the most famous practicing attorneys in the 1920s.

that even liberal Christians and the non-religious often speak and act as though evolution and Christianity are anathema to each other. But that was not the case in the 1920s, especially before the trial. Catholicism taught that an allegorical reading of Genesis was acceptable, and many Protestant denominations (even before the Progressive reforms of the late 19th century) actively promoted it.

The clash between traditional values and new social and intellectual trends in the 1920s had lasting effects. Religious ferment and the rise of fundamentalism in the 1920s split churches along fine lines and set up both real and perceived cultural divides that are still with us today. Even if they were exaggerated by the media, divisions in American culture that were made sharper by the Scopes Trial contributed to a lasting impression of vastly different values and cultures in rural and urban areas.

Bill Kte'pi

Further Readings

Appleby, R. Scott, Gabriel Abraham Almond, and Emmanuel Sivan. *Strong Religion*. Chicago, IL: University of Chicago Press, 2003.

Armstrong, Karen. *The Battle for God: A History of Fundamentalism*. New York: Ballantine Books, 2001.

Barr, James. *Fundamentalism*. London: SCM Press, 1977.

Beale, David O. *In Pursuit of Purity: American Fundamentalism Since 1850*. Greenville, SC: Unusual Publications, 1986.

Carpenter, Joel A. *Revive Us Again: The Reawakening of American Fundamentalism*. Oxford: Oxford University Press, 1999.

Harris, Harriet A. *Fundamentalism and Evangelicals*. Oxford: Oxford University, 1998.

Hart, D.G. *Defending the Faith: J. Gresham Machen and the Crisis of Conservative Protestantism in Modern America*. Phillipsburg, NJ: P&R Publishing, 2003.

Kazin, Michael. *A Godly Hero: The Life of William Jennings Bryan*. New York: Knopf, 2006.

Larson, Edward J. *Summer of the Gods: The Scopes Trial and America's Continuing Debate Over Science and Religion*. New York: Basic Books, 1997.

Lawrence, Bruce B. *Defenders of God: The Fundamentalist Revolt Against the Modern Age*. San Francisco, CA: Harper and Row, 1989.

Longfield, Bradley J. *The Presbyterian Controversy: Fundamentalists, Modernists, and Moderates*. Oxford: Oxford University Press, 1993.

Miller, Kenneth R. *Finding Darwin's God: A Scientist's Search for the Common Ground Between God and Evolution*. New York: Harper, 2000.

Sandeen, Ernest Robert. *The Roots of Fundamentalism: British and American Millenarianism 1800–1930*. Chicago, IL: University of Chicago Press, 1970.
Scopes, John T. and James Presley. *Center of the Storm: the Memoirs of John T. Scopes*. New York: Henry Holt, 1967.
Sutton, Matthew Avery. *Aimee Semple McPherson and the Resurrection of Christian America*. Cambridge, MA: Harvard University Press, 2005.
Torrey, R.A. *The Fundamentals: A Testimony to the Truth*. Los Angeles, CA: The Bible Institute of Los Angeles, 1917.

Chapter 8

Education

"Education is a kind of continuing dialogue, and a dialogue assumes . . . different points of view."
—Robert Hutchins

IN THE 1920S teacher education continued the march toward professionalism. Teachers also began to organize to win certain rights by unionizing around matters of salaries, curriculum control, and job benefits. Teachers' unions faced unique conditions in collective bargaining efforts. Since public school teachers' salaries were largely dependent on local and state tax dollars, bargaining was difficult. Most school administrators had little control over the size of their budgets, only over the allocation of the budgets. Gender discrimination continued in matters of hiring, pay, and promotion, in spite of the unions' best efforts.

In 1920 women won the vote after 72 years of campaigning for suffrage. The new political powers of women were slow to result in meaningful change regarding educational and career opportunities, although the number of schools opening their doors to women continued to increase throughout the decade. The "new woman," as epitomized by the flapper, scandalized older generations, but the cultural shifts in acceptable dress and behavior for women did not immediately result in legal changes protecting and codifying their employment rights.

The membership composition of the National Education Association (NEA), however, did begin to change during this time. The ratio of teachers to administrators became more balanced. In the years between the world wars, a major recruitment effort sharply increased the number of elementary and secondary teachers who became members. In 1928 Cornelia S. Adair became the first classroom teacher to be elected president of the NEA. Meanwhile, the number of college and university professors and administrators in the NEA declined, due in part to competition from other emerging associations focused solely on higher education issues.

Parent-teacher associations sprung up across the country in the first two decades of the century to provide support for local public schools. The roots of a national Parent-Teacher Association began in 1897 with the first National Congress of Mothers, but it took until 1925 for all 48 states to create state-level congresses. These state organizations spawned local networks of mothers who raised funds for new school buildings and school districts, advocated improved teacher wages, shared the latest educational research, and influenced classroom reform. By the mid-1920s district administrators grew concerned about the power of maternal involvement in schools. Women's organizations had the ability to transform educational policy because they controlled a sizable portion of school funds, and the local administrators had no direct control over them because they were not employees. Administrators responded by limiting the roles of mothers' organizations to supplementary classroom activity and school-approved fundraisers. By 1929 parent-teacher organizations turned their focus from classroom reform to filling educational volunteer roles such as classroom aides.

SCHOOL DAYS

In Cannelton, Indiana, during this decade, a typical school day at Myers Grade School began at 8 A.M. Classes met until 11 A.M., when students walked home for lunch. They came back to school in the afternoon from 1 to 4 P.M. Morning and afternoon recesses gave the students a chance to play outside. The school building contained grades one through eight, each with its own classroom. Boys and girls were not allowed to play together at recess. Subjects taught included reading, spelling, penmanship, math, science, geography, and art.

To get a sense of what later elementary education was like, consider this sample curriculum, described in a history of Warren G. Harding Middle School

These cursive letters illustrate the Palmer Method, which was taught in school penmanship classes beginning in the early 1900s.

Montessori Education

Maria Montessori was born in Ancona, Italy, in 1870. She showed unusual promise as a young child, developing language skills early and keeping up easily with older children. When she was five, her family moved to Rome as a result of her father's government career. They wanted their daughter to have access to a good urban education. Maria's mother, Renide, supported her against her father's wishes, and allowed Maria to enter technical school at the age of 13. She first studied engineering, but found her school's teaching methods poorly suited to many of its students. She began to develop educational theories based on her experience at the technical school, using it as a model of education that she considered unsuccessful.

After her graduation in 1886, she left the pursuit of engineering, focusing instead on the natural sciences at the Regio Instituto Tecnico Leonardo da Vinci until 1890. After several years of unsuccessful petitioning, she was the first woman admitted to the University of Rome's medical school in 1892. (Some researchers believe that Pope Leo XIII intervened to gain her admission.) She received her medical degree in 1896 and became the first female doctor in Italy. At that time, Italian hospitals refused to hire a female doctor, so she worked as a surgical assistant instead, at the Hospital of Santo Spirito. Her medical work made it necessary for her to visit insane asylums. During these visits, she saw a number of children with various mental illnesses whose families did not know how to care for them. She began to think about types of schools that might be able to help these children. In 1901 she returned to the University of Rome with the goal of learning more about the human mind, and studied anthropology. She was offered a teaching position there in 1904, which she took for two years.

In 1906 she opened the Children's House in San Lorenzo, Rome. Here she taught the young children of 60 working families, and developed teaching methods that enabled learning-disabled children to excel in classrooms. She observed how children absorbed knowledge from their surroundings, and developed pedagogies based around motor education, sensory education, and language skills. Children began in her classes as young as two and a half years of age, and learned at first through exploration and manipulation of interesting classroom materials; order and repetition were also key. For the seven- to 12-year-old age group, abstract concepts and communication were emphasized in addition to the other four learning methods. Teachers were trained as guides to assist children in learning experiences, rather than as authorities who provided instruction.

Over the next two decades, Maria Montessori wrote three books outlining her system of education: *The Absorbent Mind, The Child in the Family,* and *The Montessori Method*. Her system gained international popularity and spawned numerous schools across the world. As of 2007 over 8,000 Montessori schools operate on six continents.

in Philadelphia: "Harding was originally built not only to provide liberal arts education and basic skills, but also to develop skills that could be useful once students entered the work force. Reading, math, social studies, science, wood shop, metal shop, sewing, cooking, drafting, choir, orchestra, and athletics were all considered important studies in 1925 and for much of Harding's history." Harding was a junior high school for seventh, eighth, and ninth graders in East Philadelphia. This urban junior high had a curriculum that incorporated both vocational training and classical liberal arts courses, similar to the curriculum proposed in the early 1900s by the NEA Committee of Ten.

In 1921 the book *Manners and Conduct In School and Out* appeared in print. This book, written by a group of "deans for girls" from across the Chicago public high school system, set forth a code of conduct for all secondary students. This code covered many aspects of student behavior, including politeness, cleanliness, interactions with the opposite sex, behavior at school dances, and how to properly address teachers. Male students were to avoid spitting, boisterous behavior, and chewing gum in public, while a female was expected to keep herself "physically fit, her thinking on a high plane, and her manners gentle and winsome." This guide provides one indication that by the 1920s, social training was considered a part of the educational process and a duty of schools, not only of parents.

HIGHER EDUCATION

In March 1921, two organizations—the Southern Association of College Women and the Association of Collegiate Alumnae—merged to form the American Association of University Women (AAUW). The merger meant this organization of college-educated women had local chapters across the country. One of the AAUW's goals was to improve the quality of public education. Local chapters raised funds for adequate female student support, researched the financial problems facing public schools, and educated the public regarding public school needs. The AAUW continues its work to the present day, providing scholarships, commissioning research, and encouraging young women to participate in a broad range of educational opportunities.

The "organized curriculum" movement of the 1920s, led by Franklin Bobbitt, reexamined the public school curriculum through the lens of task analysis. Bobbitt proposed that the goal of education was to prepare children for adult life as citizens. He proceeded to analyze the major life activities common to functioning societal members, and then broke down these activities into a series of tasks for children to complete over time. Because Bobbitt believed that schools were an inherently social enterprise, he proposed that curriculum should be controlled at the local level, as only local communities would be able to determine the skills of their pupils and the demands placed on adults within each community. Bobbitt taught a course on "The Curriculum" at the University of Chicago, and was one of the first to approach curriculum development through empirical reasoning from social needs. His work is indicative of the interest that colleges and universities took in reforming public education at the time.

CHILD AND ADOLESCENT PSYCHOLOGY

The 1920s was a decade of notable work in the emerging field of child psychology. Researchers such as Jean Piaget, Max Wertheimer, and Lev Vygotsky revolutionized understanding of how children thought and learned. Jean Piaget (1896–1980) was a psychologist who studied child development. His theories revolutionized the understanding of the cognitive processes of children. Born in Switzerland, Piaget published his first paper at the age of 11. His early passion for science led to a career in human psychology.

After receiving his doctorate from the University of Neuchatel, he studied in Zurich for a brief time before moving to France to work with Alfred Binet. While Binet developed intelligence tests, Piaget noticed patterns in the test responses of the children. He noticed that young children made types of errors that adolescents and adults did not, regardless of their overall test scores. This led Piaget to hypothesize that young children had different ways of thinking, not undeveloped adult processes. They had uniquely coherent systems

This large urban high school, which was named for colonial settler William Penn, was built in 1928 in the city of Harrisburg, Pennsylvania.

An illustrated classroom dictionary from the early 20th century. In the 1920s, important changes were made to the public school curriculum.

for organizing their experience. Albert Einstein called Piaget's idea "so simple that only a genius could have thought of it." He continued to develop this hypothesis while working at the University of Geneva and raising three children with his wife, Valentine.

Wertheimer's Gestalt theory, first put forth in 1924, posited that some processes must be understood in terms of the whole, rather than by breaking them down into their composing elements. Wertheimer's basic proposition laid the groundwork for educational research regarding children's concept formation. He described human problem-solving as involving a process of interaction with a given situation. Concepts are reformed and reorganized when interactions cause cognitive dissonance. For example, suppose a child believes that big objects sink in water, while small ones float. The child will be surprised to see a sponge float and a penny sink, and will categorize objects differently afterward to avoid dissonance between mental belief structures and experienced reality. The theory that children learn problem-solving through insight continues to shape classroom methods in several academic fields, including mathematics and physical sciences.

Lev Vygotsky (1896–1934) was a Russian psychologist interested in the social aspects of children's learning. He posited the idea of a zone of proximal development. This learning zone describes the range of knowledge from a child's current level of understanding to their potential level of understand-

Piaget's Four-Stage Model

Piaget's four-stage model was first put forth in 1929 in *The Child's Conception of the World*, and then developed in great detail over the rest of his lifetime. The first three stages reflect incomplete versions of reality. Piaget posited the theory that children at each age would interact with their environment in a way that harmonized with their views of the world. Eventually children within one of the first three stages receive enough error messages that they reorganize their thought processes. The model describes four stages of human cognitive development: the sensorimotor stage (infants); preoperational stage (toddlers and young children); concrete operational stage (children); and the formal operational stage (adolescents and adults).

In the sensorimotor stage, very young children interact with the world through their senses. They begin by repeating basic reflexes such as sucking and applying them to new objects such as rattles and stuffed animals. Eventually they grow to understand object permanence, the idea that objects still exist when they are out of sight. By the end of this stage, children love to play peek-a-boo and can solve simple multiple-step problems such as putting down one object to grasp another.

The preoperational stage involves the understanding of symbols and mental manipulation of objects. Most children learn to read and write during this stage. They approach problems by centering on a single dimension of understanding. When Piaget studied children taking intelligence tests, for example, they often erred in estimating a container's volume. Tests with coins demonstrated the same type of error; children in the preoperational stage selected a nickel as being worth more than a dime because the nickel was the larger coin.

Concrete operations involve the application of logic to the world. Children in this stage begin to understand ideas such as conservation of matter. They focus on classification (identifying types of objects) and seriation (putting objects in order) during this stage of cognitive development. Many children in this stage possess collections of objects, such as rocks, that they constantly reorganize according to identifying characteristics.

Formal operations is the final stage, and involves abstract thinking. Some humans never develop to this stage, and most adults operate cognitively in this way only part of the time. Formal operational abilities enable us to solve logic problems and hypothesize about the world around us.

Piaget explained human knowledge as being constructed from within each child, rather than imposed from without. This constructivist philosophy supports educational models for young children that emphasize experiential education. His work opened many new paths in educational psychology, especially for those interested in early childhood education.

ing. Vygotsky believed that children learned from collaborating with their peers, as well as from adult instruction. He studied the interactions within children's peer groups to monitor a range of activities including language and speech development. His theory of language development suggested that children begin to learn language by developing audible speech, and that their "inner speech" or metacognitive abilities developed more slowly. Vygotsky also worked with "abnormal children," those with mental and learning disabilities, to study how their development differed from typical children.

While some psychologists focused on child development, others focused on means of evaluation of their potential. Princeton psychologist Carl Brigham developed a test in the mid-1920s to evaluate secondary school students' academic abilities. First publicly administered to high school students in 1926, the Scholastic Aptitude Test (SAT) is still in use today. This standardized test was designed to allow college admissions administrators to evaluate students coming from many different secondary schools in order to choose the highest-achieving students. The test was first used by Ivy League schools such as Princeton, Harvard, and Yale to evaluate the academic aptitude of their incoming students. Today many colleges and universities across the country use SAT scores as one factor in making their admissions decisions.

CHILD LABOR

The battle to end child labor had moved from the Congress to the courts and back again by the 1920s. A 1916 federal child labor law was declared unconstitutional by the Supreme Court in 1918. The National Child Labor Committee urged Congress to draft new legislation, which passed in 1919. When that law successfully passed the test of the courts, the organization turned its attention to the states, demanding child labor reforms at the state and local levels in order to comply with the new federal laws. By 1921 17 states had put significant legal reforms in place to protect children, mandating school attendance and restricting work hours.

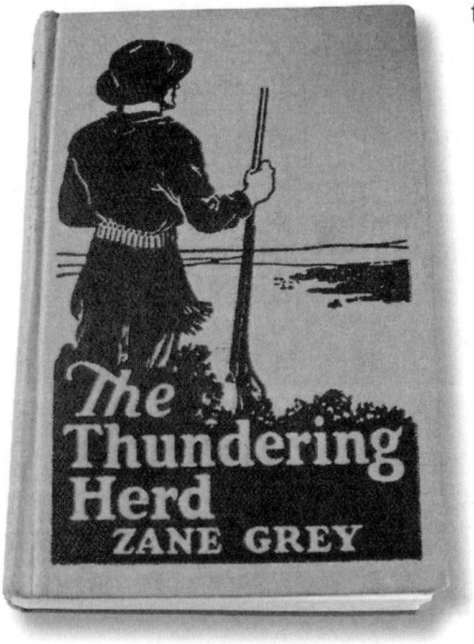

A 1925 western adventure by the popular novelist Zane Grey.

In 1922 the anti-child-labor movement received a fresh setback. The Supreme Court declared the 1919 federal law unconstitutional. Unbowed by this defeat, women's organization leaders worked with the National Consumers' League and Women's Joint Congressional Committee to pass a Child Labor Amendment to the U.S. Constitution in 1924. Although this amendment easily passed in Congress, it was rati-

Scenes like this one of a boy working in a cotton mill in Augusta, Georgia, in 1909 grew less common in the 1920s as the battle to end child labor had some success at the state level.

fied by only six states, and so failed to become law. By the mid-1920s, though, almost half of the states had ratified some kind of child labor protections and mandatory school attendance laws due to pressure from local organizations. It would take until the 1930s for child labor laws to pass at the federal level.

EDUCATIONAL ACCESS AND AFRICAN AMERICANS

In the southern United States between 1890 and 1910, school districts concentrated resources and funding in schools for white children, resulting in large class sizes, poor educational materials, and lower quality of instruction for African-American students. By the 1920s, decades of boll weevil infestations of cotton crops resulted in mass migrations to the northern United States within the African-American population. Workers migrated as opportunities for agricultural and industrial labor opened in the north. Because northern public schools were less likely to be segregated, migrating African Americans had opportunities to access a higher quality of education. Literacy rates and graduation rates among African Americans briefly began to recover from the lows of the 1910s.

As the mass migration continued, though, African-American population concentrations within urban areas led to schools effectively segregated by race in parts of cities like Chicago and Detroit. Although such segregation was not made formal, the economic and geographic reality was that certain neighborhoods created impoverished schools. Meanwhile, in the southern United States, the National Association for the Advancement of Colored People (NAACP) began a major effort to improve the quality of education for African-American children.

Philanthropists such as Anna Jeanes and Julius Rosenwald led campaigns to build new schools for black children. Their efforts aided in fundraising for schools, but the money raised came primarily from black citizens, in addition to the taxes they already paid to support whites-only public schools. It would take until the 1950s for educational reforms to end public-school segregation and to begin equalizing opportunities for ethnic minorities in the south.

MANDATORY ATTENDANCE

Mandatory school attendance laws were on the books in many states by the 1920s. In Oregon, this set of laws was known as the Compulsory Education Act. In its original form, the act mandated public education for children between the ages of eight and 16. It also included a list of exceptions, among which were children who attended private schools. In 1922 Oregon voters passed a referendum that eliminated the exception for private school students. In effect, if the law was upheld, two kinds of schools would have to close. The first were elite nonsectarian private schools; the second were religious schools.

Two schools brought their cases before Oregon courts by suing the governor, Walter Pierce, and other legal officials whose duty would be to enforce the new law. The schools proclaimed that the new law was unconstitutional. Prosecutors for the nonsectarian school, Hill Military Academy, argued that the law violated the Fourteenth Amendment by violating the school's property rights. Prosecutors for the religious school, run by the Society of Sisters, argued that the law violated the First Amendment rights of parents by preventing them from free practice of their religion. The schools won their case at the state level, and the matter was appealed to the U.S. Supreme Court in 1925.

When the case reached the Supreme Court, the court considered the obligation of the state with regard to children's education. The defense, on the side of the state of Oregon, argued that the state had significant interest in the education of its young citizens.

They attempted to prove that the state's interest in maintaining consistent educational standards, and its need to implement controls over education providers, overrode individual parents' desires for educational choice. The defense also argued that since the schools were corporations and not individuals, they did not fall under the legal protection of the Fourteenth Amendment.

In its unanimous ruling, the Supreme Court declared the Compulsory Education Act unconstitutional. The court did retain the rights of the state "reasonably to regulate all schools, to inspect, supervise and examine them, their teachers and pupils; to require that all children of proper age attend some school, that teachers shall be of good moral character and patriotic disposition, that certain studies plainly essential to good citizenship must be taught, and that nothing be taught which is manifestly inimical to the public welfare."

However, the court determined that the exercise of the above rights did not mean that the state could standardize its children by standardizing their education and restricting it to a public educational system. From Justice McReynolds' opinion: "The fundamental theory of liberty upon which all governments in this Union repose excludes any general power of the state to standardize its children by forcing them to accept instruction from public teachers only. The child is not the mere creature of the state; those who nurture him and direct his destiny have the right, coupled with the high duty, to recognize and prepare him for additional obligations."

Pierce v. Society of Sisters is important not only for its impacts on the U.S. educational system, but also for its implications regarding the concept of due process. The wording of the Fourteenth Amendment states that "No State

This class of 75 African-American sixth-graders in Muskogee, Oklahoma, was packed into one small room with a single teacher.

shall make or enforce any law which shall abridge the privileges or immunities of citizens of the United States; nor shall any State deprive any person of life, liberty, or property, without due process of law; nor deny to any person within its jurisdiction the equal protection of the laws." By extending the protections of this amendment to apply to corporations, not only individuals, the Supreme Court entered a period of broad legal interpretation regarding the application and protection of individual freedoms.

The battle over state control of education contributed to the growing modernization of education in the 1920s. Administrators and educational associations continued to become more professional and organized, while educators developed new methods of analyzing learning processes. Child labor declined from its peak in the 1910s and was controlled in half of the states, but it was still not outlawed on the federal level. Other improvements in education in the 1920s affected women, who gained more access to and influence in education in the same era in which they finally won the vote. African Americans were not as fortunate, and de facto school segregation in the northern cities to which many had moved worsened, setting the stage for some of the most important educational reforms of the 20th century, which were still to come.

HEATHER A. BEASLEY

Further Readings

American Association of Community Colleges. *America's Community Colleges: A Century of Innovation.* Washington, D.C.: Community College Press, 2001.

Anderson, James D. *The Education of Blacks in the South, 1860–1935.* Chapel Hill, NC: University of North Carolina Press, 1988.

Bjork, Robert. "The Schoolteacher as 'Economic Man.'" *Peabody Journal of Education* (v.34/3, 1956).

Carter, Susan B., et al. "Race and Ethnicity: Population, Vital Processes, and Education." In *Historical Statistics of the United States, Millennial Edition.* New York: Cambridge University Press, 2004.

Fitzgerald, Stephanie. *The Scopes Trial: The Battle Over Teaching Evolution.* Minneapolis, MN: Compass Point Books, 2006.

Goble, Joan. "Myers Grade School: A Proud Past and a Fabulous Future." Available online: http://www.siec.k12.in.us/cannelton/myers/. Accessed May 2007.

Leinwand, Gerald. *William Jennings Bryan: An Uncertain Trumpet.* Lanham, MD: Rowman and Littlefield, 2007.

Lemons, J. Stanley. "Social Feminism in the 1920s: Progressive Women and Industrial Legislation." *Labor History* (v.14/1, 1973).

Linder, Douglas. "The Scopes Trial: An Introduction," University of Missouri at Kansas City Law School. Available online: http://www.law.umkc.edu/faculty/projects/ftrials/scopes/scopes.htm. Accessed May 2007.

Montessori, Maria. *The Montessori Method.* New York: Cosimo, 2006.

Pass, Susan. *Parallel Paths to Constructivism: Jean Piaget and Lev Vygotsky.* Greenwich, CT: Information Age Publishers, 2004.

Piaget, Jean. *The Child's Conception of the World.* Lanham, MD: Jason Aronson, 2007.

Smith, Fanny R. *Manners and Conduct In School and Out.* Chicago, IL: Allyn and Bacon, 1921.

Standing, E. M. *Maria Montessori: Her Life and Work.* New York: Penguin (Plume), 1998.

"Warren G. Harding Middle School History." Available online: http://www.phila.k12.pa.us/schools/harding/hardinghistory.html. Accessed May 2007.

Wertheimer, Michael, and Brett King. *Max Wertheimer and Gestalt Theory.* New Brunswick: Transaction Publishers, 2005.

Chapter 9

Science and Technology

"The advancement of science and our increasing population require constantly new standards of conduct."
—Herbert Hoover

THE DECADE IMMEDIATELY following World War I marked an unprecedented movement of technological devices into the homes of ordinary citizens. While previously such devices as automobiles, telephones, and household appliances had been strictly the preserve of the wealthy, the sudden expansion of wealth that distinguished the Jazz Age made it possible for ordinary working people to afford them. However, this prosperity did not begin immediately after the armistice. The nation's economy was still on a wartime footing, and it took time to retool for consumer goods. In addition, large numbers of men were still in uniform. Demobilization was often frustratingly uneven, with large numbers of unskilled laborers flooding the job market, while desirable skilled workers were retained by the military.

The shift back to a peacetime economy was further hindered by the Red Scare. This period of intense fear of Communist infiltration of labor movements was largely the result of the successful Communist revolution in Russia. Such events as the Palmer Raids and the brutal crushing of the Steel Strike of 1919 ensured that the prosperity of the 1920s would be capitalistic. Yet there would be no return to the excesses of the Gilded Age. Instead, the great captains of industry found their best hope in keeping their workers happy with the material goods higher wages could buy. Thus they could teach their employees to see the capitalist not as an enemy, but as a provider of prosperity and well-being.

ELECTRICITY

One of the key technologies of the Jazz Age was electricity. Modern public electric distribution systems had taken shape in the 1890s, but for the next decade and a half the penetration of integrated electrification was slow. Heavy industry was almost entirely electrified, and whole industries such as aluminum refining had developed because of cheap electricity. But bringing electricity to individual homes was a slower process, and only in 1920 did it reach a tipping point at which domestic electrification became so common that it began to significantly restructure everyday life.

However, when broad electrification occurred, the effect of electricity on the lives of ordinary people was pervasive. The pre-electrical home was dominated by the use of combustion for both heat and light. As a result, rooms were small and were closed off from one another to prevent drafts that could blow out a candle or lamp. Decorating tended to be in dark tones that would better hide soot that accumulated in the vicinity of oil or gas lamps. Electricity made it possible to open up the home, allowing rooms to flow into one another. Instead of a clearly defined kitchen, dining room, living room, and formal parlor separated by doors, the new style of house had a range of less clearly-defined spaces separated only by partial walls and joined by archways. Architects such as Frank Lloyd Wright also used light colors to emphasize the airiness and spaciousness created by the open-plan home, in which only private spaces such as bathrooms and bedrooms were closed off with doors.

Hand-cranked ice cream churns such as this one were used in rural homes before electrification.

Electricity also made possible a wide variety of household appliances. Some had pre-electric counterparts, but the icebox was dependent upon deliveries of ice from a central icehouse, and the supply of ice was in turn dependent upon the weather. An unusually warm winter would mean that supplying lakes did not form thick layers of ice, and a hot summer could cause the stored ice to melt prematurely. Once ice was acquired, its use required the continual disposal of meltwater in the drip pan. By

The Tivoli Theater in Chattanooga, Tennessee, finished in the early 1920s, was one of the first buildings in the United States to be air conditioned.

The Rise of Comfort Air Conditioning

Air conditioning was originally invented to regulate humidity and temperature for industrial processes. However, by the 1920s air conditioning began to move beyond industrial applications. The first comfort air conditioning installation took place in 1924, when the J.L. Hudson department store in Detroit was having customers in their bargain basement collapse from heat prostration due to the sheer number of warm bodies in a confined space. The company bought three centrifugal air conditioning units from inventor Willis Carrier, and was so satisfied it decided to air condition the upper floors as well.

The cinema was the venue in which air conditioning became a cultural phenomenon. Previously movie theaters had run at a loss or shut down altogether in the hot summer months. In 1925 the Rivoli in New York City became the first movie theater equipped with air conditioning. On opening night, a number of motion picture executives came in from Hollywood to see this new phenomenon.

As the feature began, the audience fanned themselves, much to Carrier's horror. But it was in fact a gesture born of habit, and as the reality of cool air sank in, the hand fans dropped one by one into laps and people settled in to enjoy the show. The value of air conditioning so proved itself that word of mouth soon brought sellout crowds to the Rivoli. Other movie theaters, not wanting to lose out on this new market, hurried to acquire this new technological wonder. By the close of the 1920s Carrier had installed air conditioning in over 300 movie theaters, and its presence had rapidly become a selling point in advertising.

contrast, a refrigerator needed only access to a steady supply of current to keep foods cold and fresh. Similarly, washing machines had existed before electricity, but they were crude and generally powered by a small gasoline engine, which had to be located on the porch or another well-ventilated area to prevent the buildup of deadly carbon monoxide gas. The electric washing machine could be located wherever one had both power and water. Electricity also made possible thermostatically controlled heating appliances, which provided safer and more controllable heating. The cook no longer needed to stick her arm into the oven to check the temperature, and it could be set to a precise temperature instead of an approximation. The pop-up toaster eliminated the guesswork of making toast. No longer was it necessary to watch the bread closely to prevent burning. Instead, one simply dropped two slices into the slots, pressed down the lever, and the toast popped back up when done.

Widespread domestic electrification also transformed the way Americans spent their time. Even before the advent of widespread domestic electrification, the electrification of factories and office buildings had steadily divorced the rhythms of the urban workday from the rising and setting of the sun. White-collar and blue-collar workers often had noticeably different schedules, since it was no longer essential to begin the day as close to dawn as possible to take advantage of natural light. But as electricity in the home became steadily more common, it became possible to carry on recreational activities that required ample light well into the evening. For instance, recreational reading increased greatly with the spread of electric illumination, crowding out such optically less-demanding activities as the playing of charades and singing around the piano.

THE WONDER OF RADIO

The spread of domestic electrification made possible the spread of an even more important technological wonder into the homes of ordinary Americans. The radio receiver, an extraordinary invention, enabled people across the nation to hear plays, concerts, popular music, and news in the comfort and privacy of their homes.

The technology to broadcast and receive Hertzian waves, as radio waves were first called, had been invented at the turn of the century. As early as 1898, the eccentric Serbian-American inventor Nikola Tesla had demonstrated a radio-controlled boat. However, it was Guglielmo Marconi whose focused and businesslike approach enabled him to permanently associate his name with the invention of radio in the public mind. But Marconi thought of radio in terms of a wireless telegraph, sending business messages in code to specific recipients. Even after Reginald Fessenden successfully created a carrier wave upon which complex modulations could be imposed, Marconi's company deemed it a curiosity.

These AT&T radio broadcasters were testing a radio system before the broadcast of Herbert Hoover's inauguration in 1929.

One far-sighted young executive of the company did not think it a curiosity, however. David Sarnoff, a rising star in the Marconi Company's American branch, had come a long way since he taught himself code and worked as a radio operator. In 1915 he wrote a memorandum describing a device that would use the new system of radiotelephony not as a point-to-point communications device, but for a central transmitter to send to receivers throughout a wide area. Because the concept was so new, he made it comprehensible by comparing it to the known technology of the phonograph. His "magic music box" would be like a phonograph with an infinite number of records. Even more important, the device would require no technical expertise to use. It would be an appliance.

His dream was delayed while the United States became involved in World War I. During this period, the government seized control of American Marconi and its patent pool, not wanting such a vital technology as radio to be controlled by a foreign-owned company, even one in the hands of an ally such as the United Kingdom. Although it was assumed at the time that this measure would be for the duration only and after the peace everything would be returned to *status quo ante*, it was subsequently decided to form a new, wholly American company, the Radio Corporation of America (RCA), with Sarnoff as its executive director.

Although the original founders still thought of RCA primarily in terms of a purveyor of wireless telegrams, Sarnoff saw a vast and untapped market in the realization of his magical music box. But to realize that vision, he had to provide a grand spectacle that would grab the imagination of the populace at large. On July 2, 1921, he set about broadcasting the boxing match between Jack Dempsey and Georges Carpentier. It was already a heavily hyped fight, since Dempsey had gained notoriety for refusing to set aside his boxing career to serve in the war, while his French opponent had been wounded at the front. Broadcasting the fight via radio made it possible for an estimated 300,000 listeners to join in all over the New York City area. Luckily for Sarnoff, Dempsey was quick about defeating Carpentier, for shortly after the fourth-round knock-out, the transmitter catastrophically overheated, reducing itself to a mass of slag.

With the concept proven, America went wild about radio. Soon the airwaves were crackling with news, sports, and music, including that daring music known as jazz. While new stations sprung up all across the nation, hobbyists put together their own crystal detector sets, an often frustrating process that involved jiggling finicky and often unreliable parts to bring in a signal. In an era before semiconductor theory, nobody understood exactly why a germanium crystal should be able to capture radio waves and translate them into audible sound, making it impossible to produce a crystal radio set that would work reliably. As a result, vacuum tubes such as the Audion triode created by Lee De Forest soon became the gold standard of receiver technology. Because so many of the key patents for tube receivers were owned by RCA, the radio boom meant enormous profits for its shareholders. RCA stock, often referred to simply as "Radio" by those who touted it, was further inflated by speculation.

Wooden cabinet-style home radios appeared in living rooms across the country in the 1920s.

The quality and affordability of home cameras, such as these Kodak models from the early 20th century, continued to improve in the 1920s.

The Golden Age of Radio also meant the development of a receiver industry. Although some radio receivers were housed in fine cabinets of wood, many companies turned to Bakelite and other early plastics to fabricate cases quickly and cheaply. The 1920s marked the appearance of a large number of these new materials, including phenolic plastics and urea formaldehyde. Unlike Bakelite, they could be produced in a variety of colors, and unlike the even older celluloid, they enjoyed relatively low flammability.

EXPERIMENTS WITH TELEVISION

Even as the Jazz Age was becoming the Golden Age of Radio, inventors were considering the possibility of the new technology to transmit visual information. If the radio could be a "magic music box" with an infinite supply of records, could it also become a magic movie theater, allowing people to view cinematic productions from home?

In order to make this technology viable, it was first necessary to determine a way to encode the information onto a carrier wave, and then decode it at the receiving end. With voice, the problem was relatively simple, due to the close parallels between the radio carrier wave and the sound wave. With visual information, it was necessary to break down the picture into small elements for which brightness (and later color) information could be transmitted sequentially, a process known as scanning.

As it turned out, a simple method of scanning an image had been described in 1883 by a German inventor, Paul Nipkow. His device involved a disc with a spiral of holes cut along its rim. When the disc was spun, each hole would successively pass over a section of the image, allowing a detection device to measure the brightness of the light coming from it. Although Nipkow had envisioned a device similar to a modern facsimile machine, transmitting photographs via telephone, its potential was quickly seized upon by the earliest television inventors.

In England, Scottish inventor John Logie Baird demonstrated a primitive television system in 1925. Using a pair of lensed Nipkow disks, a photocell, and a neon light, he was able to create recognizable moving images in light and shade, although the image was no bigger than a postage stamp. Meanwhile, American inventor C.F. Jenkins used a variant of the Nipkow disk that involved a spiral prism, based upon the work he had done in cinematic shutters, but was only able to transmit shadow figures. In spite of the technical limitations of their apparatus, both men broadcast programs for an audience of hobbyists desiring to be on the cutting edge of the new science.

However interesting a proof-of-concept it might be, mechanical television was ultimately a dead end. Resolution was limited by the ability to machine the scanning apparatus to the necessary level of precision. Furthermore, mechanical television systems were notoriously prone to breakdown. Baird had one of his largest lensed discs go off balance, and he narrowly avoided being injured by the shower of glass lenses flying from their places.

In Idaho, a Mormon farmboy had already glimpsed the solution. After reading a cache of old science magazines found in an attic, Philo T. Farnsworth envisioned an entire television system using the only tool suitable to drawing the pictures, namely, the electron. However, he faced enormous hurdles in terms of funding, while his rival on the east coast had the vast and growing resources of RCA to put to the task. David Sarnoff was never a man to miss the main chance, and he too had seen that television was the wave of the future, and it must be all electronic. With fellow Russian émigré Vladimir Zworykin, he was building his own system of electronic television, and did not intend to endure competition.

UNIVERSALITY OF THE AUTOMOBILE

While domestic electrification and radio were changing the way people lived at home, the automobile was transforming the way people moved around. It too was by no means a new invention, having its roots in the closing decades of the 19th century. Even Henry Ford's famous Model T, by which he made the automobile accessible to ordinary people, first came out in 1908. He had spent the following decade assiduously finding every way humanly possible to increase the efficiency of its manufacture, and thus to steadily reduce its price.

However, the decade after World War I saw several social and economic changes that helped to make this technology almost universal. Most important was the growing prosperity of the Jazz Age, which gave more people the buying power to afford what was previously unimaginable luxury. In an era of

This well-preserved Ford Model A Tudor Sedan was built in 1930. Hundreds of thousands of Americans made down payments on the Model A sight unseen.

The Model A

In the early 1920s the Ford Motor Company manufactured half the world's automobiles, and the Model T was the source of this success. However, the Model T was also rapidly becoming antiquated as General Motors introduced various technical innovations to even their entry-level models. Thus, Henry Ford's son Edsel and several key engineers decided to produce a prototype of an improved Model T while the elder Ford was on a trip to Europe.

If they were expecting praise when the Henry Ford returned, they were sadly disappointed. Scowling, he began to demolish the vehicle with his bare hands. The Model T was perfection, he thus decreed, and was not to be changed. However, Henry Ford could no more stop the march of progress than King Canute could command the tide to stop. By 1926 Model T sales were declining to the point that something had to be done. The following year, all Ford factories were closed for retooling, and six months later the first Model A rolled off the assembly line. Although 300,000 advance orders had been taken during that period, the loss of momentum could never be made up, and General Motors took the lead in the automobile industry. Worse, Ford now had to fight for third place with a strong new rival, Chrysler.

A young Charles Lindbergh in the open cockpit of an airplane at Lambert Field in St. Louis, Missouri, in the mid-1920s.

prosperity, attitudes toward credit changed, making it acceptable to purchase chattel property over time. Since a car held its value over time, there was a reasonable expectation that a lender could recover the money from a defaulted loan by repossessing the car and reselling it on the used market.

Once General Motors created their lending division, GM Acceptance Corporation, the economics of automobile purchasing shifted. So long as one had to save the entire price of a car, there was a tendency to favor the cheapest possible option. But with the ability to make smaller payments over time, buyers became willing to pay a little extra every month to have features that previously were found only on high-end automobiles. General Motors thus was able to create an entire series of product lines, from the rock-bottom Chevrolet to the luxury Cadillac. Not only could people buy the best car they could afford, but as their circumstances improved, they could trade up, replacing their old car with one from the next model up the ladder.

The rise of automobile culture also meant changes in the oil industry. Petroleum had originally been developed as an alternative to whale oil for illumination in the new industrial cities. However, Thomas Edison's electric light bulb had relegated the kerosene lamp to a curiosity everywhere except rural

Lucky Lindy and the *Spirit of St. Louis*

Although military use of the airplane was one of the major factors in driving the development of aviation technology, another important factor was the challenge of prizes offered for being the first to accomplish a particular feat. Among those prizes was the $25,000 award offered by New York hotel manager Raymon Orteig in 1919 for the first pilot who could fly a heavier-than-air craft across the Atlantic Ocean from New York to Paris nonstop. Given the scope of this challenge, he broadened it to state that it was sufficient to reach the shores of France, and that European pilots could fly the route westward. During the middle of the 1920s a number of famed aviators made attempts at the prize. However, all relied upon large multi-engine aircraft operated by crews of two or three. Given the enormous amounts of fuel necessary for transatlantic flight, these aircraft proved too heavy to get off the ground.

Charles Lindbergh, a former barnstormer and airmail pilot, believed this approach was wrong-headed. His solution was to build a plane as light as possible and to fly solo, although it would mean having to stay awake for the entire 40-hour trip. With backing from important St. Louis business leaders, he approached the Ryan Aircraft Company to commission and build a special aircraft with maximized fuel capacity and range. The resulting plane was named the *Spirit of St. Louis* in honor of his financial supporters.

Early on the morning of May 20, 1927, Lindbergh took off from Curtiss Field on Long Island. Rather than going straight across the Atlantic, he followed what is known as a Great Circle route, which describes the shortest distance on a spherical surface. This route took him north past Cape Cod and Newfoundland and over the icy North Atlantic, then south across Ireland and Great Britain to France. To keep himself awake, he relied upon the extreme responsiveness of his plane, which would shake the moment his hand faltered on the stick. Even so, sleep deprivation took a toll on Lindbergh, to the point that he saw phantoms wandering in and out of his aircraft while he crossed miles of empty ocean.

On the evening of May 21, he reached Paris and circled the Eiffel Tower. From there he flew to Le Bourget Airfield, on the outskirts of the French capital, where he completed his historic flight. Vast crowds of Parisians were on hand to welcome him, and took him on an impromptu tour of their city. Only in the wee hours of the next morning did they finally allow him to collapse into an exhausted slumber.

Lindbergh became a hero throughout the Western world. However, his later years were stained with tragedy. His eldest son was kidnapped and murdered, and the trial of the accused kidnapper has often been suspect. As World War II approached, Lindbergh also became entangled in isolationist politics, which damaged his reputation in the eyes of many.

areas, leaving petroleum few roles. The rise of the automobile created a strong new demand for gasoline. Previously regarded as a troublesome contaminant that made cheap kerosene apt to explode, and sold primarily as an industrial solvent, gasoline rapidly became the most desirable fraction. In fact, there was so much demand for gasoline that it outstripped the amounts that could be distilled directly from crude oil.

Several technical advances enabled the oil companies to keep up with the growing demands of a nation on wheels. Geophysical surveying techniques took advantage of recent seismological discoveries to observe how sound waves from small explosions reflected off various subterranean strata, thus identifying those most likely to hold deposits of oil. As a result large reserves unconnected to surface seeps or mineral wells were located. In addition, better drilling, transportation, and refining techniques tightened up what had been a very wasteful industry, enabling more of every barrel of oil pumped to the ground to actually reach the consumer in useful form. One of the key developments was thermal cracking under pressure, which allowed refiners to break heavier petroleum fractions into useful gasoline.

THE FORDSON TRACTOR

While the automobile was changing life for people in the city, life on the farm was also changed by the internal combustion engine. The agricultural tractor was not a new invention, for steam engines had first come to the farm in the form of the steam traction engine in the last decade of the 19th century. However, the steam traction engine was a giant with a clumsy steering system that took an entire acre to turn, which meant it was useless for plowing on anything but a few of the giant spreads of the Great Plains. Even the earliest true tractors were not much smaller, and were likewise mostly relegated to stationary applications such as threshing.

The earliest small tractors were rickety disappointments such as the Little Bull, which rarely survived a single season of use and was notorious for tipping on slopes. But automobile giant Henry Ford was determined to change that situation. A farm boy himself, he had never forgotten the backbreaking labor farming entailed for humans and beasts alike, and was determined to lighten it. His first attempt at an agricultural tractor was a modified Model T designed to pull a plow. Although it was successful enough to do useful work, Ford could already see the advantages of a dedicated machine designed for agricultural work.

Actually producing a tractor that satisfied Ford's standards proved more difficult than previously thought. Only when the demands of World War I for soldiers made it essential to reduce the number of people working the land did Ford finally agree to compromise on a tractor that was good enough. Unfortunately for him, he could not simply produce it under the Ford name, as he did automobiles. A few years earlier, another tractor com-

Charles Lindbergh's Spirit of St. Louis, *which is now on display at the Smithsonian Institution's National Air and Space Museum in Washington, D.C.*

pany, eager to capture the associations of the Ford name, had simply hired an accountant with that common English surname and named their ill-designed offering after him. Although the company had since ceased to produce tractors, they still held the rights to the name on tractors. Never one to let an obstacle deter him, Henry Ford simply created a separate company with his son Edsel, named it Ford and Son, and brought out his tractors under the label Fordson.

Ford proudly proclaimed that his only competition was the horse, and it was not entirely egotism. Unlike the 20-ton behemoths, the Fordson was a nimble little tractor, suitable for plowing even small fields. Furthermore, it was a sturdy tractor that would last for years, unlike the earlier small tractors that had so badly disappointed farmers as to make many of them suspicious regarding the whole idea of replacing horses with horsepower.

THE AIRPLANE

The airplane was another technological innovation that had its roots in the previous decade, but really came of age in the 1920s. World War I proved the airplane's worth, first as a scouting device and then as a weapon of war. Men such as Manfred von Richthofen and Eddie Rickenbacker became folk heroes for their daring exploits as "knights of the air." However, there was still no clear idea what role the airplane could play in peacetime. The war had produced a large number of trained pilots of restless temperament who found it difficult to return to ordinary civilian employment. Furthermore, although American industry had been unable to produce militarily significant numbers of airplanes before the armistice, in the period shortly afterward large numbers of light, maneuverable, and easily maintained airplanes were produced.

The combination of the restless young aviator and the Curtiss Jenny led to the development of the traveling air show. Many of these young men would literally fly from one town to another, all their possessions fitting in a kit bag tossed into the cockpit of their plane. The shows by which these knights of the air earned their bread and fuel featured various acts of derring-do, including close-formation flying, aerobatics, and allowing teammates to move upon their wings as they flew. From a trick in which they flew through an open barn, sending chickens fleeing in panic, they got their common nickname of "barnstormers."

An aviator in a flight suit beside a Cleveland Pittsburgh Air Mail plane in the 1910s or 1920s. The needs of the air-mail service led to the establishment of permanent airfields.

Even as the barnstormers were firing imaginations about flight, the Post Office was putting the airplane to practical use delivering high-priority mail for a fee. The Air Mail Service, along with continued work in military aviation, brought the government into the development of aviation and ensured that the airplane would have a continuing role in society, not merely as a plaything, but as a workhorse. The Air Mail Service's regular routes led to the development of permanent airfields with signal lights and radio beacons. Government interest in aeronautical engineering led to the development of the modern airplane with its metal hull and enclosed cabin, which made regular passenger flight possible. In many ways, the 1920s were as revolutionary for aviation as those first years after the Wright brothers first demonstrated powered heavier-than-air flight.

The 1920s were a period of dizzying progress in the areas of science and technology. Most importantly, these years were a period in which technological devices came into the hands of ordinary people at an increasing rate as wealth expanded. After the economic crash of 1929, the Jazz Age was remembered somewhat ambiguously as a time of both great wealth and great excess.

LEIGH KIMMEL

Further Readings

Abramson, Albert. *Zworykin, Pioneer of Television*. Urbana, IL: University of Illinois Press, 1995.

Bak, Richard. *Henry and Edsel: The Creation of the Ford Empire*. Hoboken, NJ: Wiley, 2003.

Bray, John. *The Communications Miracle: The Telecommunication Pioneers from Morse to the Information Superhighway*. New York: Plenum Press, 1995.

Brinkley, Douglas. *Wheels for the World: Henry Ford, His Company and a Century of Progress*. New York: Viking, 2003.

Davies, L. J. *Fleet Fire: Thomas Edison and the Pioneers of the Electric Revolution*. New York: Arcade Publishing, 2003.

Dreher, Carl. *Sarnoff: An American Success*. New York: Quadrangle, 1977.

Fenichell, Stephen. *Plastic: The Making of a Synthetic Century*. New York: HarperBusiness, 1996.

Fisher, David E. and Marshall Jon Fisher. *Tube: the Invention of Television*. Washington, D.C.: Counterpoint, 1996.

Godfrey, Donald G. *Philo T. Farnsworth: The Father of Television*. Salt Lake City, UT: The University of Utah Press, 2001.

Kent, Zachary. *Charles Lindbergh and the Spirit of St. Louis*. Berkeley Heights, NJ: Enslow, 2001.

Leinwoll, Stanley. *From Spark to Satellite: A History of Radio Communication*. New York: Charles Scribner's Sons, 1979.
Lewis, Tom. *Empire of the Air: The Men Who Made Radio*. New York: Edward Burlingame, 1991.
Lyons, Eugene. *David Sarnoff*. New York: Harper and Row, 1966.
McCarthy, Pat. *Henry Ford: Building Cars for Everyone*. Berkeley Heights, NJ: Enslow Publishers, 2002.
Oslin, George P. *The Story of Telecommunications*. Macon, GA: Mercer University Press, 1992.
Schatzkin, Paul. *The Boy Who Invented Television: A Story of Inspiration, Persistence and Quiet Passion*. Silver Spring, MD: TeamCom Books, 2002.
Schwartz, Evan I. *The Last Lone Inventor: A Tale of Genius, Deceit and the Birth of Television*. New York: HarperCollins, 2002.
Stashower, Daniel. *The Boy Genius and the Mogul: The Untold Story of Television*. New York: Broadway Books, 2002.
Tilton, Rafael. *Henry Ford*. San Diego, CA: Lucent Books, 2003.
Williamson, Harold F. et al. *The American Petroleum Industry: 1899–1959, The Age of Energy*. Evanston, IL: Northwestern University Press, 1959.

Chapter 10

Entertainment and Sports

"Play as a ruling impulse is wholly modern and characteristically American."
—Robert L. Duffus

THE INVENTION OF amplifying vacuum tubes and the increasing shift of American identity and media to the national level both helped to power the radio revolution of the 1920s. The first commercial radio stations in the United States began broadcasting in 1920, after a 1919 broadcast by the University of Wisconsin at Madison. KDKA in Pittsburgh and WBL in Detroit were, like their early followers, broadcast for free and without commercials. KDKA was owned by the Westinghouse Electric Company, which used the station to encourage customers to buy radios. WBL was owned and operated by the Scripps newspaper company as a way to get an edge over other media companies.

Early radio broadcasts were mostly news reports. The first regularly scheduled entertainment programs began in 1922, and on the first day of the following year, the Rose Bowl was broadcast by Los Angeles station KHJ. Most programs were musical showcases bearing a sponsor's name in their title, such as the *Clicquot Club Eskimos*. Panel discussions, quiz shows, interview shows, sports coverage, talent shows, and dramatic programs would follow—though the heyday of the latter radio drama did not arrive until later decades.

The *Grand Ole Opry*, originally called the WSM *Barn Dance*, was a weekly country music program broadcast from Nashville. In the years when it first aired, it followed the NBC *Music Appreciation Hour*, which was devoted to classical music and opera. In contrast, the *Grand Ole Opry* declared itself

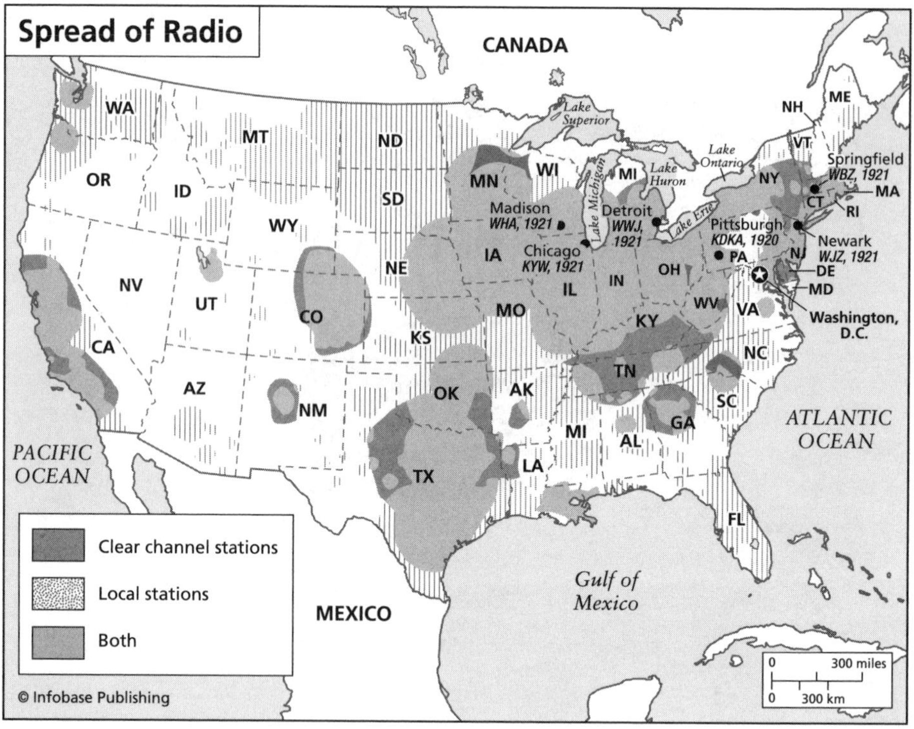

"earthy" and "realistic." The *Opry* was not just a noteworthy early radio program; it was an important force in 20th-century popular music.

Meanwhile, the *Eveready Hour*, the first sponsored variety program, began in late 1923 and continued as an NBC program until 1930. The aforementioned *Clicquot Club Eskimos* was a music program sponsored by Clicquot Club, a popular ginger ale that had an Eskimo as its advertising mascot. Though Clicquot Club may be long forgotten, their involvement is a good demonstration of the growing link between soft drinks and entertainment. Sodas soon became the default beverage of the moviegoer as well.

Other than the *Grand Ole Opry*, the early program best-known to modern audiences is the *Amos 'n' Andy Show*. It was written and voiced by Freeman Gosden and Charles Correll, white actors who had done minstrel-like routines on WGN in Chicago beginning in 1925. Those routines became the *Amos 'n' Andy Show*—casting the two men as black caricatures—in 1928 on rival station WMAQ. WGN had rejected Gosden and Correll's plans for a nationally syndicated show, which WMAQ was happy to pick up. The show introduced "Holy mackerel" to the country's vocabulary, a catchphrase spoken by the scheming Kingfish, whose plans often fueled the show's plots. The show was essentially a sort of audible blackface performance, with Gosden and Correll's exaggerated mannerisms serving the same purpose as makeup. Though well-written and long-lasting, the fundamental premise of the show is an unfortunate reminder of the tail end of what has been called the nadir of American race relations.

THE NEW ART FORM: MOVIES

In the 1920s movies were still a new and developing art form. Amusement parks and dime museums were still more popular for the working class, and most of the motion pictures they saw were in nickelodeons, the small neighborhood theaters that showed films about 15 minutes long. Movies in this day did not compete with television and DVD as they do now. The competition they faced came from the waning but still-extant vaudeville shows, boxing matches, and horse races. At the beginning of the decade, not everyone believed that movies (and their companion media, television) would one day be the dominant form of American entertainment.

Movies became more popular with middle- and upper-class audiences as they came to resemble plays more and more, with developed characters and plots instead of the simpler nickelodeon fare. Though there was a limit on how detailed the plot could be without sound to carry it (title and dialogue cards could only carry so much, and had to be used sparingly) movies had more visual potential than the stage. The premiere for *The Thief of Baghdad* took place in a theater decorated in an Arabian style, complete with censers of incense and ushers in Arabian costumes. Lavishness was a cinematic selling point: movies (at least the more expensive ones) could offer more elaborate sets than plays could, not to mention outdoor locations and chase scenes, neither of which suffered much from the lack of sound.

Many of the early movie stars were vaudevillians, and the silence of the medium made slapstick a naturally successful genre. Buster Keaton, Harold Lloyd, and Charlie Chaplin were the three biggest stars of slapstick, and all came to prominence in the 1920s, as film technique and quality allowed for more elaborate and better-constructed gags than in the previous decades of film. Keaton had taught himself to make movies by taking a camera apart, and succeeded with shorts in the first three years of the decade before turning to features. His most enduring features were *Sherlock Jr.*—notable also for being a movie about the movies, as Keaton portrays a projectionist daydreaming about being Sherlock Holmes in the mode of the dramatic silent stars of the day—and *The General,* which flopped at the time but is considered one of the greatest technical achievements of the decade.

While movies in the past decade had sometimes relied on special effects as simple as a toy boat hitting an ice cube (in an early movie about the *Titanic* disaster), *The General* not only showed Keaton doing a number of unprecedented stunts (most of which were performed on a moving train), it also portrayed a real bridge collapse. Because it was too expensive to salvage the wreckage, the ruins of the train in the Oregon river bed remained as a tourist attraction for decades.

This set from the Goldwyn Studios's 1923 silent film In the Palace of the King *shows the growing complexity of movie productions in the 1920s.*

Englishman Charlie Chaplin, meanwhile, had moved to the United States in 1912 (rooming with fellow countryman and future film star Stan Laurel) and made shorts about his Tramp character throughout that decade and into the 1920s. After the 1919 founding of United Artists with Mary Pickford, Douglas Fairbanks, and D.W. Griffith, Chaplin went on to make his strongest pictures. Like Keaton, after the first few years of the decade he shifted to features, which were becoming the cinematic standard. In contrast to the movies of the previous decade, which were rarely longer than 20 minutes and often no longer than a modern-day commercial break, the feature-length film of the 1920s was frequently an hour and a half long, which necessitated better (and more) sets, more developed plots and characters, and altogether a more involved and expensive production. Chaplin's *Gold Rush*, released in 1925, was the most memorable silent film of all time. Even 80 years later, scenes from this Little Tramp movie are well known to audiences, especially the house wobbling on the cliff, the Tramp carving up his boot on his plate to stave off hunger, and the "bread roll dance" the Tramp performs after stabbing two dinner rolls with his forks to make them look like feet. Seventeen years later, Chaplin actually rereleased the movie—with

Sound and Color

Color motion pictures had been produced in one form or another since the 1890s, but the 1920s saw major advances in film color technology. In 1922 Technicolor invented the subtractive color process (Technicolor Process 2), in which a special camera exposed two adjacent frames of film at the same time, one with a green filter and the other with a red filter. The green strip of film was toned red, and the red green, and the two were affixed together. While this created a compelling and sometimes beautiful sense of color and shading, the film had little longevity: it tended to bunch up and buckle in the hot projectors, and prints needed to be replaced frequently. A small number of Process 2 movies were made, notably Douglas Fairbanks's *Black Pirate* and *The Phantom of the Opera* (starring Lon Chaney).

Process 3 was developed to replace Process 2, and premiered in 1928 with *The Viking* (a synchronized score movie). Process 3 was essentially a refinement of Process 2, but instead of affixing the strips together, they were processed in gelatin baths so that they could be used to dye a new strip. Though Process 3 was time-consuming, the final product was less finicky and needed replacing much less frequently than the Process 2 reels. Further improvements would come in the next few decades.

Warner Brothers experimented with sound, meanwhile, releasing talkie shorts first, using the Vitaphone system. Movies with synchronized scores and sound effects had been released first. Dialogue was the hardest, because the slightest error in synchronizing the audio and video would be obvious when the dialogue did not match the movement of actors' mouths; minor errors in a score were much harder to detect. Finally *The Jazz Singer* was released in 1927, a mostly silent movie that included synchronized dialogue. A story of Jewish-American assimilation, *The Jazz Singer* starred Al Jolson, a blackface vaudevillian billed as "the World's Greatest Entertainer," whose first spoken dialogue in the movie not only repeats a catchphrase from his own well-known vaudeville act, it comments on the advent of the talkie itself: "Wait a minute, wait a minute, you ain't heard nothin' yet."

A 1922 poster for a silent black-and-white film.

sound added, mostly in the form of his voiceover narrating the film, since looping in dialogue would have been problematic.

Like Chaplin and Keaton, Harold Lloyd made movies with intricate slapstick sequences that depended on challenging stunts and careful pacing, over the simple sight gags of less enduring filmmakers. A conscious imitator of Chaplin, Lloyd shared his colleague's concern with modern life, and his most famous movie, 1923's *Safety Last!*, includes the memorable image of the strawboat-hatted actor hanging from the face of a clock tower amid a busy urban landscape.

Of course, the newly lengthened feature films provided a boost for drama, too, as more in-depth characterization was possible. Lon Chaney's career revolved around his roles in horror movies, always featuring the make-up that he applied himself, possessing a mad genius for it. He was best known as the Hunchback of Notre Dame and the Phantom of the Opera—and for his role in Tod Browning's lost movie *London After Midnight.* Browning went on to direct *Dracula* and *Freaks* in the early talkie era. John Barrymore was another famous portrayer of villains. The hard-drinking womanizer was the greatest stage actor of his generation and a member of a famous theatrical family (Drew Barrymore is his granddaughter), and after transitioning to movies, he portrayed Dr. Jekyll and Mr. Hyde, Captain Ahab, Beau Brummel, and Lord Byron's Don Juan.

A Keystone Moviegraph film projector from the 1920s.

But the most famous dramatic actor of the decade was Rudolph Valentino. If he was not the first male movie star, it was only because Douglas Fairbanks beat him to it by a few years, and the two played very different roles. He was an Italian actor who found fame in Hollywood after several years as a taxi dancer in New York. Despite occasional lighthearted complaints in the press about his contributions to the "feminization" of the American man, and his probable bisexuality, Valentino became the first true male sex symbol of the cinema—a romantic lead whose presence was enough to turn a movie into a blockbuster. The 1921 movie *The Four Horsemen of the Apocalypse* helped to further popularize the tango, and his follow-up hits *The Sheik* and *Son of The Sheik* proved enduring enough that more than 40 years later, Elvis Presley would parody them in his movie *Harum-Scarum.* The term "sheik" entered the Jazz Age lexicon to mean a charismatic man who aggressively pursued women, particularly for sex or other short-term pleasures.

Valentino died at the age of 31 in 1926, following complications from surgery for an ulcer. His funeral was attended by over 100,000 people, including four actors the funeral home hired to pose as a fascist honor guard sent by Italian leader Benito Mussolini. Rumors abounded that his body was replaced with a wax replica to protect it from manhandling, and for years after his death, a mysterious woman in a black veil brought flowers to his grave. With Valentino, the whole concept of celebrity in America had changed.

Rudolph Valentino's dashing Latin looks made him one of the earliest of many male screen idols to capture the hearts of American women.

Family movies, too, thrived in this era, such as the *Rin Tin Tin* series, which starred a shellshocked dog found by an American soldier in a French kennel at the end of World War I. Rin Tin Tin turned out to be unusually talented at performing tricks, and went on to star in a number of silent films through the 1920s—and even a radio show in the 1930s.

Sometimes better known as the *Little Rascals*, the *Our Gang* series comprised mostly shorts, starting in 1922 (and moving to sound in 1929). Unlike most portrayals of children in film, the *Our Gang* series showed children more or less realistically—often mischievous but not especially precocious. Both whites and blacks, girls and boys, were part of the group with no comment offered for the diversity. Although Buckwheat is the best-remembered black Rascal, Farina, Stymie, and Sunshine Sammy were regular black members of the cast; all played stereotypes typical of the time, speaking poor English and portrayed as the children of criminals. The child actors were generally not shown scripts, as few of them could read at an adult level. Instead, the director would explain the scene to them immediately before filming, and would encourage improvisation.

All during the decade, of course, experiments were made with adding sound to movies. Appropriately enough, talkies began to be introduced just as the 1920s ended—just the incentive a Great Depression audience needed to keep them coming to the theater. And as if in recognition of this, as if to acknowledge that the addition of the sound brought film out of its childhood and into its adolescence, the first Academy Awards were given in 1929.

THE RISE OF ANIMATION

The 1920s were one of the most important decades in the history of animation, and certainly the most important to that point. While live-action and animated movies share much of their history (they were shown in the same theaters, of course, and benefited from many of the same technological advances) they have also developed to a great extent independently, and in the 1920s there were few people who worked in both live-action and animation. It is no coincidence that the first name to come to the popular mind when thinking of early animation is still the best-known name in animation today: Walt Disney.

A midwestern animator, Disney founded the Iwerks-Disney Commercial Artists studio in 1920 with Frisian-American artist Ub Iwerks. They started out in Kansas City, but relocated to Hollywood within a few years. The studio's first significant work was the *Alice Comedies*, a series of shorts about a live-action Alice and her animated cat Julius, and their adventures in an animated world. The *Oswald the Lucky Rabbit* shorts soon followed, created in 1927 for Universal Studios. After more than 20 successful shorts about the rabbit over the next year, Disney asked for a budget increase. Instead, he was told the budget was going to be significantly cut, and that the studio had taken the precautionary measure of signing most of his employees to new contracts first, thinking that this would leave him with no choice.

Disney and Iwerks ended their relationship with Universal in disgust. An up-and-coming artist named Les Clark left Universal with them, and would go on to become the longest-employed staff member of the Walt Disney Company. Together, in shares that vary depending on whose account you read, the three created one of history's most iconic characters: Mickey Mouse. Walter Lantz, a screenwriter for Frank Capra and Mack Sennett, was meanwhile hired to continue the Oswald series for Universal (he would later be better known as the creator of Woody Woodpecker).

The first Mickey Mouse cartoons were riffs on popular movies of the day. "The Gallopin' Gaucho" takes Mickey down to Argentina and features the tango Valentino helped to popularize, in a parody of Douglas Fairbanks's "The Gaucho." And the third Mickey short—the first to use sound—parodied Keaton's "Steamboat Bill Junior," which these days is not nearly as famous as "Steamboat Willie." In these early shorts, Mickey is rougher than he'd become later. In his violence and mischievousness, he is more like the zany cartoon protagonists than the Everyman he became.

In 1929 the Mickey shorts were followed by the *Silly Symphonies* musical shorts, the first of which were almost entirely Iwerks' creation. At the end of the decade, frustrated with Disney's temperamental attitude and feeling he

Heavyweight Boxer Jack Dempsey

Jack Dempsey ready to fight in Jersey City, New Jersey, in 1921.

An Irish-Choctaw from Colorado, Jack Dempsey was a brawler who as a young man would famously enter a saloon and announce, "I can't sing or dance, but I can lick any son of a bitch in the house," and would earn money betting on himself in these barroom fights.

He reigned as the heavyweight champion in boxing from 1919 to 1926, one of the most successful athletes in the world thanks to exhibitions and prize purses.

In 1926, in a match attended by more than 120,000 people—the biggest sporting event in history and still the second-largest attendance to this day—Dempsey lost his title to Gene Tunney in 10 rounds, telling his wife afterward, "Honey, I forgot to duck" (a line repeated more than 50 years later by President Ronald Reagan, after being shot in an assassination attempt). The following year, the Dempsey-Tunney rematch was held at Soldier Field in Chicago, with more than 100,000 spectators in attendance and an unprecedented 50 million listening on NBC radio. Dempsey was losing on points when he knocked Tunney down in the seventh round, but failed to move to a neutral corner as the rules required, which delayed the referee's count—Tunney had been down for 14 seconds when he got up on the referee's count of nine and dropped Dempsey in the following round. The controversial fight is known as "The Battle of the Long Count" as a result. Tunney remained the heavyweight champion until 1928, when he retired undefeated.

had received too little credit for his contributions, Iwerks left to form his own studio. But with the one-two punch of Mickey and the *Silly Symphonies*, the Disney brand had been created.

"Steamboat Willie" was not the first talkie cartoon. A month earlier, Paul Terry's "Dinner Time" had been the first cartoon to include spoken dialogue. And from 1924 to 1926, the *Sound Car-Tunes* shorts from Max and Dave Fleischer had used soundtracks: the *Car-Tunes* are remembered for their "follow the bouncing ball" instruction, in which a ball bounced along

Consumer Culture

The public fascination with fame and glamour led to the age of the celebrity endorsement, as national magazines and newspaper chains carried ads announcing Babe Ruth's favorite running shoe and Jack Dempsey's preferred brand of toothpaste. Radio shows sponsored by Ovaltine or Red Man Chewing Tobacco featured commercial breaks in which the stars extolled the virtues of the product. Brand names became important, and the hedonistic Jazz Age especially prized the non-utility of consumer goods in a way past generations of Americans could not have fathomed.

It was one thing that by the end of the decade, most homes with electricity had an electric iron and more than a third had washing machines and vacuum cleaners—those were labor-saving devices, utilitarian and practical. But cosmetics, phonographs, and radios sold in incredible numbers considering how few Americans had owned them in the past, and the relative expense of a radio weighed against its absolute lack of practical purpose.

Nightclubs and amusement parks increased in popularity, too, and 20 to 30 million Americans went to the movies each week. More and more workers received paid vacation time thanks to the work of labor unions, and by the end of the decade, three times as much money was being spent on recreation as in 1919. With more money available to fight over, the advertising industry rose to prominence, and more stores offered installment plans for the purchase of more expensive items like washing machines and automobiles. More than 20 percent of Americans owned a car by the end of the decade, and some estimates have as many as half of the non-farming households in the country owning an automobile.

Meanwhile, much of the focus shifted from production and the great man heroes of the 19th century to the idea of realizing the self, adapting one's personality, and being aware of the perceptions of others. The Book of the Month Club formed in 1926 with the explicit promise to keep customers abreast of the latest interesting books that were providing party conversation.

the subtitled lyrics to the song syllable by syllable, encouraging the audience to sing along, while subtly underscoring the synchronicity of the music with the animation. The Fleischers had patented the rotoscope in the previous decade, bringing a new sense of realistic movement to animation, and were among its principal innovators in the 1920s. Max even made a 50-minute animated feature about the new theory of relativity in 1923, followed two years later by a feature combining live action with animation to explore Darwin's theory of evolution.

Another noteworthy innovator was Winsor McKay, the creator of the comic strip *Little Nemo in Slumberland*, whose cartoon *Gertie the Dinosaur* was the first combination of live action and animation. His *Dream of a Rarebit Fiend* series, based on his comic strip about dreams and nightmares, furthered the surrealism and expressionism of cartoons and are among the best cartoons of the decade.

The *Felix the Cat* shorts produced by Paramount Pictures (it remains a matter of controversy who exactly created the character) were the most popular cartoons in the world in the silent era. Felix was one of the first characters to be the subject of merchandising, including a spin-off comic strip, and his shorts often reflected recent events, such as the Bolshevik Revolution in Russia and the Charleston dance. Respected author Aldous Huxley cited Felix as an example of the potential of cinema, the potential to tell stories that could not be told with mere words or static images. In 1928 a Felix doll was the first image broadcast over television in an experimental demonstration of the new technology.

MARKETING MUSIC

Jazz Age or not, many of the most popular hits in the 1920s were still produced by Tin Pan Alley, including 1923's "Yes We Have No Bananas" and 1925's "Sweet Georgia Brown." The music industry began marketing music at specific ethnic groups—foreign folk music for immigrants, blues and jazz for blacks, and "hillbilly music" (the nascent country genre, especially Appalachian folk music) for rural southern whites. The radio and the phonograph helped to popularize jazz, which was the most popular form of live music in speakeasies, especially in affluent northern cities. Rudy Vallee and Leo Reisman were among the popular bandleaders. Paul W hiteman was instrumental in hiring white musicians to play intricately orchestrated jazz such as "Rhapsody in Blue," which he commissioned from George Gershwin in 1924. "Rhapsody in Blue" took classical music's approach and applied it to jazz styles and elements, eschewing the improvisation and "jamming" normally common to that genre. The result was a piece that far exceeded any brief-lived novelty value that might have been expected of it, a piece not quite like anything else, as modern as any of the avant-garde classical compositions coming out of Europe.

A Victrola record from Capitol Records that featured a blues singer and band.

The music industry, bolstered by radio and phonographs, began marketing music at specific American ethnic groups in the 1920s. The photo shows five unidentified musicians with piano, banjo, and guitars in 1921.

The blues reached white audiences primarily through the filter of Tin Pan Alley, where W.C. Handy combined them with elements of Cuban music and ragtime, focusing on uptempo music appropriate for dance venues. Night clubs in the northeast and industrial midwest, and juke joints in the rural southeast, began hiring blues performers, and soon Beale Street in Memphis was one of the prime locations for finding such music. Recorded blues were clearly divided into two subgenres—the country blues of Blind Lemon Jefferson and Charlie Patton, which included the Mississippi Delta blues style and the Piedmont blues of the Carolinas; and urban blues, which predominantly consisted of more refined vocals and arrangements, with debts to jazz and vaudeville.

Blind Willie Johnson, one of the greatest slide guitarists of all time, combined blues and gospel music into fiery religious-inflected music like "John the Revelator" and "Dark Was The Night, Cold Was The Ground," about the Crucifixion. He was one of the innovators who would prove to be a precursor for rock-and-roll music in later generations.

In earlier years, Sophie Tucker had begun her career as a "Coon Shouter," a white person performing in what was considered an African-American style, which she did in blackface. By the 1920s she had abandoned the gimmick in favor of her own persona. Her shows were racy and burlesque, with frequent reference both in the lyrics and in her stage patter to sex and her sexual appetites. In 1920 when Tucker was too sick to attend a planned recording session, Okeh Records brought in cabaret singer Mamie Smith. Her recording of "That Thing Called Love" was successful enough for her to move from cabaret performance into a recording career, and the popularity of "Crazy Blues" among African-American customers awakened the record industry to the potential in this market.

In 1923 Vernon Dalhart's "Wreck of the Old 97" became the first nationwide country music hit. Country music shared many of its origins with the blues, just as honky tonks and juke joints were essentially race-based mirrors of each other. Jimmie Rodgers, a brakeman on the New Orleans and Northeastern railroad, became a popular country musician when illness forced him to retire from railroad work. His music focused on the common man, often drawing on the form of traditional ballads and exploring dark material such as premature death, debilitating disease, alcoholism, and adultery. Meanwhile, the Carter Family—A.P. Carter, his wife Sara, and his brother's wife Maybelle—performed a mix of traditional hill country songs and original works. There is little, if any, country music that does not owe a debt to either Rodgers or the Carters, if not both.

ATHLETICS AND SPORTS

The most popular spectator sports in the 1920s were baseball, boxing, and college football. Golf and tennis grew in popularity as participatory sports, encouraging more country clubs and parks, but spectator sports saw the real boom in this decade, as the mass media contributed to their popularity and to the creation of sports heroes. In 1921 a Pirates-Phillies game was the first baseball game broadcast on the radio, on KDKA, and the sport would continue to be associated with radio for the rest of the century. Successful athletes, their photos carried in newspapers and magazines and their endeavors reported live in the radio, seemed like ordinary citizens who had achieved greatness through perseverance—a compelling notion in a decade when the whole country seemed to be thriving for that very reason.

In 1925 the American Legion started an athletics program as part of their initiative to encourage good citizenship and fight radicalism and unionism. By 1929 100,000 boys had joined the legion's Junior Baseball league. Eastern European immigrants—long one of the legion's targets—encouraged their children to play the game as a way to become less foreign and better-integrated to their birthplace. This was especially true of Jewish immigrants, who were twice-marked as different from the mainstream—and Jews would prove to be many of the heroes of the early decades of organized baseball. The concept of a home team began to acquire prominence, especially in baseball, in contrast to the newly-formed national identity of the Progressive Era. But the use of "home" is key there, as more than bringing the national identity down to the regional level, this was an echo of the "home and family" identity in the public sphere. In cities with multiple teams, team association came to be connected with ethnic or religious identity—as in Chicago, where Protestants tended to be Cubs fans, and Catholics were mostly White Sox fans.

BASEBALL AND THE "BLACK SOX"

Baseball began the decade with the revelation that several players on the Chicago White Sox had deliberately lost the 1919 World Series, in collaboration with an organized group of gamblers. Other players on other teams were suspected of similar corruption, and although a grand jury found the players innocent, the league appointed federal judge Kennesaw Mountain Landis as Commissioner of Baseball—a new position created just for this purpose. Landis banned 10 players from baseball for life. The so-called Black Sox have remained an important part of baseball lore.

That same year, the "deadball era" of baseball ended when trick pitches like the spitball were outlawed by a rules change, taking a significant advantage away from pitchers. Former pitcher Babe Ruth—recently traded to the New York Yankees by the Boston Red Sox in a move that would later be memorialized by the "Curse of the Bambino" that allegedly prevented Boston from winning a World Series for 86 years—was the first hitter to benefit from the new rule, as his extraordinary knack for power hitting transformed the home run from an occasional oddity to a regular feature of the game. Not only had he broken the home run record in 1919, he nearly doubled it in 1921 and broke his own record repeatedly until peaking in 1927 with 60 home runs. The game had never seen anyone like him before.

Blacks had long been barred from the white leagues. Three Negro Leagues formed in the 1920s, as baseball grew in prominence. The Negro National League and the Eastern Colored League competed against each other, while

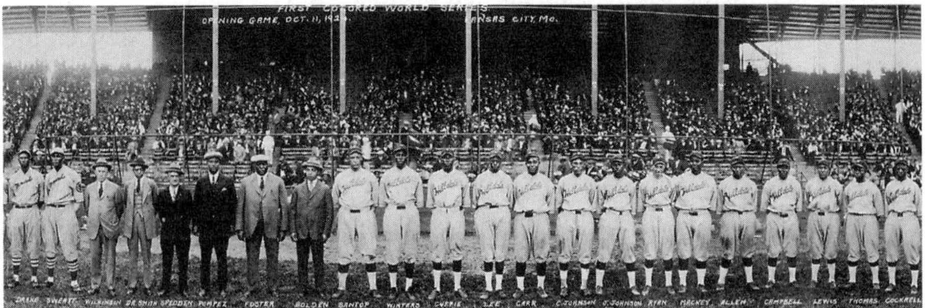

Players line up at the opening game for the first segregated Negro League World Series on October 11, 1924, in Kansas City, Missouri.

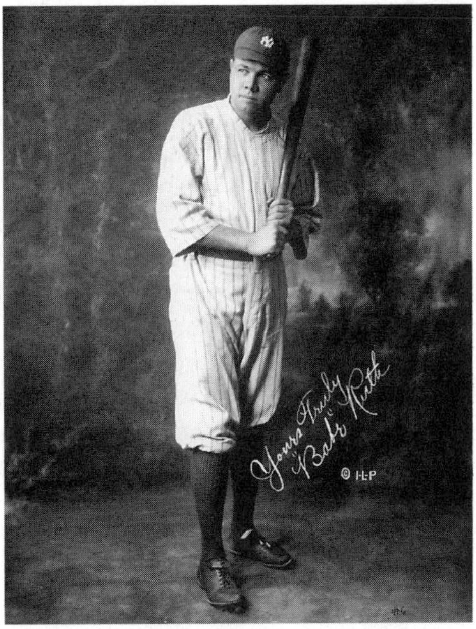

Babe Ruth, in a 1920 autographed portrait. Baseball players, like film idols, became familiar faces, part of the emerging new celebrity culture.

the Negro Southern League remained independent, far from the industrial centers of the other two. From 1924 to 1927 the Negro National League and the Eastern Colored League ended each season with the Negro League World Series, with the NNL winning three of the four series.

From time to time a sports historian would suggest that it is unfair to consider Babe Ruth the greatest player of his time, because he neither competed with Negro League players nor had to face their pitchers, which in the 1930s were especially formidable. Ruth himself called John Henry Lloyd, an aging African-American shortstop in the 1920s who soon moved to management, the greatest ballplayer of all time, an opinion he shared with many sportswriters and sports historians. Lloyd was a fiercely intelligent batter, expert at placing his hits in unreachable parts of the field, a classic technique known as "inside baseball," which had dominated the deadball era when most home runs had been the product of foiled fielding.

That said, Ruth was the first baseball superstar. He was the first athlete represented by a press agent, who started out by ghost-writing articles credited to Ruth, describing each of his home runs in turn. During the off-season Ruth toured the country making paid celebrity appearances, and he endorsed countless products. Though he was not the first to do so, he was probably the first to make considerable income from it. He even made a number of film appearances, usually as himself or as a player clearly meant to be him.

Ruth was at the center of Murderer's Row: the 1927 Yankees, with one of the best lineups in history. They had a combined batting average of .307 and a staggering 110-44 win-loss record. The Murderers were among the best hitters of the year and the era, and also included Lou "The Iron Horse" Gehrig. That year, Gehrig had one of the greatest seasons in baseball history: a .373 average, 52 doubles, 20 triples, and 47 home runs, amazing stats in every category of hitting. Gehrig's over-2,000 game streak had begun in 1925, and he showed no signs of slowing down.

FOOTBALL

In 1920 the first professional football league formed, the American Professional Football Association, consisting of 11 teams in the midwest and New York state. It changed its name to the National Football League (NFL) in 1922, but would not be taken seriously until after World War II, when college sports waned. In the 1920s interest in football was dominated by college teams. At the University of Illinois, Red Grange became a national sports hero with a four-touchdown first quarter against Michigan in 1924. He appeared on the cover of *Time* magazine the following year and later signed to the NFL's Chicago Bears for a barnstorming tour that paid him $100,000, about 50 times as much as the typical player.

Knute Rockne, meanwhile, coached the football team at Notre Dame, enjoying what was then the greatest winning percentage of all time, at nearly 90 percent. He introduced the "shift" to the Notre Dame playbook and helped establish that school's reputation as one of the best football schools in the country.

BASKETBALL

College basketball was also popular, and professional basketball enjoyed more popularity than professional football, with hundreds of teams—most of them barnstorming teams. High school basketball was widespread because of the modest cost and low risk of injuries compared to rugby, another low-cost sport.

Though they were formed in Chicago in 1927, the Harlem Globetrotters took their name because of the association of Harlem with the African-American community, and especially the modern developments therein. The original players all grew up on the South Side, and the team initially played local exhibition games—but was taken on the road as a touring team at the end of the decade. In these early days, they were a serious team with a flair for showmanship; only later would the showmanship take center stage, turning the sport into a performance.

CONCLUSION

The increased consumption and indulgence of the 1920s, while short-lived, allowed movies to blossom into a new art form and led to the birth of entire new fields of entertainment such as animation. The spread of radio and film transformed sports and was instrumental to the rise of celebrity culture as screen idols, pop musicians, and athletes became known nationwide. Despite the divisiveness of the 1920s in other areas, entertainment and sports helped contribute to the growth of a shared national culture that would only become more dominant with the upcoming arrival of television.

Bill Kte'pi

Further Readings

Crafton, Donald. *Before Mickey*. Chicago, IL: University of Chicago Press, 1993.

David, Ewen. *Panorama of American Popular Music*. Englewood Cliffs, NJ: Prentice Hall, 1957.

Dawidoff, Nicholas. *In the Country of Country: A Journey to the Roots of American Music*. London: Vintage, 1998.

Eig, Jonathan. *Luckiest Man: The Life and Death of Lou Gehrig*. New York: Simon and Schuster, 2006.

Ferris, Jean. *America's Musical Landscape*. Madison, WI: Brown & Benchmark, 1993.

Kyvig, David E. *Daily Life in the United States, 1920–1939: Decades of Promise and Pain.* Westport, CT: Greenwood Press, 2002.

Montville, Leigh. *The Big Bam: Life and Times of Babe Ruth*. New York: Broadway, 2007.

Oakley, Giles. *The Devil's Music*. London: British Broadcasting Corporation, 1976.

Peterson, Robert. *Only the Ball Was White*. Oxford: Oxford University Press, 1992.

Schuller, Gunther. *Early Jazz*. Oxford: Oxford University Press, 1986.

Titon, Jeff. *Early Downhome Blues*. Chapel Hill, NC: University of North Carolina Press, 1994.

Zwonitzer, Mark and Charles Hirshberg. *Will You Miss Me When I'm Gone? The Carter Family and Their Legacy in American Music*. New York: Simon and Schuster, 2002.

Chapter 11

Crime and Violence

"A holding company is a thing where you hand an accomplice the goods while the policeman searches you."
—Will Rogers

AS IN ALL eras of American history, crime and violence in the 1920s was related to events from the previous era. The pessimism with which the 1920s began was a backlash against the idealism and sacrifice of the Progressive Age and World War I. It was fueled by xenophobia and paranoia created by war, labor tension, and the Bolshevik revolution. In 1919 steelworkers, coal miners, and even Boston police officers went on strike, often with violent consequences. Radicals sent package bombs to business and government leaders; this was the nation's introduction to domestic terrorism. The emergence of Communism set off a frightened reaction among business, political, educational, and spiritual leaders. Attorney General A. Mitchell Palmer, the politically ambitious "Fighting Quaker," was applauded for taking advantage of still-existing wartime regulations to round up and deport hundreds of suspected Communists, including the fiery anarchist Emma Goldman, to the Soviet Union.

On New Year's Day 1920, Palmer launched a series of raids on Communist Party offices across the United States that had already been infiltrated by his agents. Everyone in the buildings—many branches were holding meetings—was taken to jail, without warrant, whether or not they were Communists. Everything in the buildings, including books, papers, and pictures on the wall, was taken as well. Palmer's men followed up these raids by storming the homes of suspected Communists. More than 6,000 Americans were put into jails and held for weeks without charges or arraignment. At least one American citizen was jailed for days without charges in a case of mistaken identity. In Detroit, more than 100 men were held in a bullpen measuring 24 x 30 ft. and kept there for a week. Anyone who came to visit those held in Hartford was also arrested as a fellow Communist. Palmer told the press that the Communists meeting that day were armed and preparing a revolution.

But as the weeks passed, it turned out that there were no plans for revolution beyond protests and angry rhetoric, and despite the massive raids only three handguns were produced. Nonetheless, there were few protests. Even college students called for professors suspected of radical ideas to be fired. The anti-Red hysteria spread in all directions. Business leaders denounced unions, racists fulminated against blacks and Jews, Fundamentalists blasted scientists, and Prohibition activists railed against liquor and saloons. Even comedians Charlie Chaplin and Will Rogers were denounced as Reds.

RACIAL VIOLENCE

Ultimately, the hysteria led to violence. Chicago had already had a vicious race riot in 1919 that began when a black swimmer floated to the white side of a segregated beach. The whites threw stones at him and he drowned. Angry blacks accused the whites of stoning him to death, and the ensuing week of violence left 15 whites and 23 blacks dead and 1,000 others homeless.

Racial violence rolled across America in the 1920s, as the Ku Klux Klan, energized by all the xenophobia, rocketed to historic heights, dominating Democratic Party politics, controlling whole states, and causing chaos everywhere they went. Thousands of Klan members paraded on Washington's Pennsylvania Avenue in their white hoods and robes. In Louisiana, they kidnapped five men, bound them with wire, and drowned them in a lake. Blacks who refused to sell land to white men for a fraction of its value faced beatings and found burning crosses on their lawns.

Whites were persecuted by the Klan as well: Jews, Catholics, and immigrants were subject to beatings, as were whites who taught or employed blacks. One immigrant was severely flogged for marrying a native-born American woman. The Klan's massive power began to decline in 1925 when David Stephenson, the Grand Dragon of the Indiana Klan, enticed Madge Oberholtzer, a schoolteacher, onto his private railroad car. He got her drunk and brutally raped her. Devastated, Oberholtzer tried to kill herself but failed. Stephenson and fellow Klansmen drove her back to Indianapolis where she made a deathbed statement to authorities. Stephenson was convicted for rape and second-degree murder, and drew a life term. Klan members across the nation were stunned by the incident and its depravity. Violence against blacks and Jews was one thing, but raping a Protestant female white schoolteacher was another. Klan membership in Indiana alone fell from 178,000 in 1925 to 4,000 in 1928.

Meanwhile, Palmer's war on radicals continued but ran into problems. Palmer declared that May Day 1920 would be the day selected by radicals for a general strike and a wave of assassinations. Across the country, police officers sat mobilized in their station houses, rifles ready, motors running in their trucks, but nothing happened. The press and public hooted at the spectacle. Palmer looked foolish, and his hopes to win the presidential nomination collapsed.

PROHIBITION

Despite all this political and racial violence, one word ultimately defined crime and violence in America in the 1920s: Prohibition. Designed to enhance morality in America, the Prohibition movement actually turned millions of Americans into criminals overnight, strengthened and glamorized the already growing organized crime movement, corrupted city governments and put them in the hands of gangsters, and brought new levels of violence to the streets of those cities.

The Prohibition movement had been growing in America in the early decades of the 20th century, motivated by an unlikely combination of forces—progressives, women's suffrage activists, and fundamentalist churches. Women's suffrage was a powerful force against liquor. Newly-enfranchised women saw drunken husbands and saloons as menaces to their lives and society. Carry

A large crowd, some in Ku Klux Klan robes and hoods, mills around a burning 80-foot cross on a summer night in August 1925.

When the Eighteenth Amendment went into effect in January 1920, the legal system was inundated with crimes connected to violations of liquor laws. Above, a jury "box" of the period.

Nation and her legendary hatchet was the visible symbol of a movement crisscrossing the United States, of angry men and women storming into saloons and bars, smashing the premises, denouncing "demon rum" as the cause of domestic abuse, poverty, and crime.

All three were certainly major problems, and booze was a stressor for all three conditions, but not the primary cause. However there was more to the dry movement than logical and justifiable opposition to drunken wife-battering. The alcohol industry was seen as a manifestation of the growing negative power of urban America and its factories, which were gaining political and economic power at the expense of rural America. Equally important, cities were seen as the source of the new innovations and immoralities that were frightening to rural and fundamentalist Americans.

Cities were home to teeming millions of immigrants who spoke virtually no English, took jobs for near-starvation wages, and brought Socialist ideas with them from Europe. The alcohol industry was seen as empowering immoral behaviors and activities, ranging from women using makeup (then only associated with prostitutes), to opium dens, bordellos, and crime rackets, all of which threatened the quality of life and profaned the Sabbath. America's response to these perceived menaces was a spate of blue laws to control these activities and ideas. New York, for example, banned Sunday baseball until the 1920s, to the

The Tulsa Race Riots

Tulsa, Oklahoma, exploded on Memorial Day 1920 when a black shoeshiner named Dick Rowland entered an elevator and apparently tripped, grabbing the arm of the operator, a white girl named Sarah Page. She screamed and Rowland fled the scene to his family's home in the black neighborhood of Greenwood. When a nearby clerk found Page in a distraught condition, the police were summoned to investigate the incident. The suggestion that a black man had assaulted a white girl set off the core fears of both Tulsa's white community—the fear of black lust for white women—and that of the black community—fear of false accusations and lynch-mob violence.

Rowland was arrested the next day, and taken to the courthouse. Soon a 1,000-person mob of whites converged around the courthouse. Some demanded that Rowland be lynched; a Jewish man had been lynched earlier that year in Tulsa for supposedly robbing a taxi driver. Others in the mob merely watched. At the same time, the black community massed in the streets of its neighborhood to discuss the situation. Ultimately, 25 black men went to the courthouse to offer their services to the police to help defend Rowland against the mob. The appearance of armed black men set off rumors and fear among the white crowd. The whites surrounded the National Guard Armory, demanding weapons as well. Police Chief Carl Gustafson called for tempers to cool and rejected the black offers of support.

By now, armed groups of blacks and whites were walking or driving around Tulsa, brandishing their weapons or firing them in the air. In this atmosphere, it was inevitable that fighting would break out. By 11 P.M., white mobs were chasing black mobs to Greenwood. As blacks and whites were killed, the remaining whites were adding to their supply of arms by looting stores. The National Guard was deployed to protect white neighborhoods from black rioters. They rounded up the blacks and herded them to the armory.

All night, whites and blacks exchanged gunfire in Tulsa while white mobs stormed into Greenwood, burning black-owned homes and businesses. By dawn, the white mob numbered more than 5,000 people in three separate groups. At 5 A.M., with the blast of a whistle they thought was the signal for a black revolt, the white mob swarmed into Greenwood, burning homes, shooting people, and looting stores. The violence lasted all day. Many blacks fled Tulsa; others were rounded up and held in temporary detention centers. By late afternoon, more National Guardsmen arrived from Oklahoma City to end the violence and enable firefighters to quell the blazes. Officially, 29 blacks and 19 whites were killed, but historians estimate the number of dead to be between 75 and 300. The 35-block Greenwood neighborhood, known as the "Negro Wall Street," was destroyed. It would take until 2001 for the Oklahoma State Legislature to pass a bill that would create a memorial to the riot's victims, provide 300 scholarships for descendants of Greenwood residents, and fund economic development of the still-blighted neighborhood.

The end result of a car chase with rumrunners in Washington, D.C., in 1922. During the 1920s, police departments made much more use of automobiles; the New York Police Department added over 500 cars to its fleet from 1919 to 1925.

annoyance of sandlotters and major leaguers. Many states banned fornication. Those caught in the act were pressured by the judge to marry each other. The 1920s also saw the state of Tennessee ban the teaching of evolution in its public schools, which set off the famous "Scopes Monkey Trial" in 1925.

The dry movement was also powered by the idealism of the Progressive Era that felt that men and women could, with government support, rise to their highest ideals as a matter of daily life. The dry movement was strong before the 1920s, and succeeded in imposing Prohibition at local and even statewide levels. There was little organized opposition to Prohibition. The chief antagonist, the alcohol industry, already had an unsavory reputation. Worse, faced with a growing outcry against the impact of liquor, the alcohol industry took little action to promote responsible drinking. American children as young as six years old were "rushing the growler" of beer from taverns to construction sites to provide workers with their 5 P.M. bottle of suds. Nor did the liquor industries band together in the face of Carry Nation—business organizations and professional lobby groups were a marvel yet to come.

In some ways, Prohibition was the ultimate blue law, although the stressor that put it into law was not the domestic threat of crime or violence, nor women gaining the vote, but the distant threat of Germany and Kaiser Wilhelm II. When the United States entered World War I in 1917, ordinary citizens and national leaders alike called for national mobilization and unity to defeat the Hun. Doing so called for a wide array of measures, including rationing and raising production of war material. It also called for Spartan idealism, and Prohibitionists seized on the opportunity.

The federal government called for food-saving programs that would end all grain production for liquor. As much of the brewery industry was dominated by German-Americans (based in heavily Germanic cities like Milwaukee, St. Louis, and Newark), public opinion turned against the liquor industry as being un-American. Liquor was also seen as a force that could weaken America's war effort: drunken soldiers, sailors, and factory workers would undermine victory. Prohibition moved from a moral demand to a necessary war measure.

There was little opposition. Most of the male beer-drinkers were in uniform or working double shifts in war plants. Even baseball players had been mobilized under the Work or Fight order. The American Federation of Labor complained about the amendment, and there were some scattered protests, but all were half-hearted. There was a war to be won, after all.

Large stills could produce 50 to 100 gallons of alcohol a day.

In 1917, the U.S. Senate passed the Eighteenth Amendment, which banned the sale, production, possession, or transportation of alcoholic beverages. The amendment was passed by a one-sided vote after only 13 hours of debate. A few months later, the House of Representatives ratified it after a single day. From there, the state legislatures ratified the amendment in short order. By January 1919, the necessary three-quarters of the states had ratified the amendment. Of all 48 states, only two would refuse to pass it: Connecticut and Rhode Island.

At the same time, Representative Andrew J. Volstead of Minnesota easily pushed through the law that would bear his name, the Volstead

A 1922 jail cell preserved at the Mount Dora History Museum in Mount Dora, Florida.

Act, designed to enforce the Eighteenth Amendment. The act followed a model developed by the Anti-Saloon League. The normally prim President Woodrow Wilson vetoed the act, but Congress overrode him. Amazingly, there was no public debate over the Volstead Act, but only over what a truly dry country would be like, and how national sobriety would affect the social order and the next generation. Prohibition merely seemed to a nation energized by waging and winning the "war to end all wars" to be a shortcut to a dry utopia, to be achieved as an adjunct to building a new world where peace and justice reigned through the Fourteen Points and the League of Nations.

The Armistice and the Treaty of Versailles burned off most of the idealism and enthusiasm, but Prohibition became law in January 1919. The first Prohibition Commissioner, John F. Kramer, told reporters, "This law will be obeyed in cities, large and small, and in villages, and where it is not obeyed it will be enforced... The law says that liquor to be used as a beverage must not be manufactured, nor hauled in anything on the surface of the earth or under the earth or in the air." The Anti-Saloon League estimated that Congress would only have to appropriate $5 million annually to enforce the Volstead Act.

With the issue put into law and the matter presumably settled, Prohibition went into operation at the stroke of midnight on January 16, 1920. An hour later, six men, led by Herschel Miller, the leader of a Jewish gang on Chicago's West Side, drove a truck into a railroad yard. There, armed with revolvers, they tied and gagged two yard watchmen, trapped six trainmen in a shack, and made off with $100,000 worth of medicinal whiskey (still legal) from two sealed freight cars. Simultaneously, another gang raided a warehouse, making off with four barrels of booze. Almost immediately, the law became a farce and a menace.

Prohibition had been demanded without thought for its consequences. The human drive for liquor could not be controlled through mere legislation. As soldiers came home and workers came off their shifts, finding their saloons and bars padlocked, they demanded a substitute for their beer. The upper classes who had bitterly complained that beer-drinking cut into the war effort and war profits now found they could not have their highballs, whiskey-sodas, or sundowners anymore. There were no more bottles of champagne to celebrate births, weddings, or even the launchings of ships. America had just fought and won a major war, America was thirsty, and America wanted a drink. But under the law, there was none to be had. So Americans started breaking the law, from the first hour of its imposition.

Alcohol remained legal for medicinal purposes, and breweries were still allowed to make that and near-beer, which required the distilleries to bleed off much of the alcohol. Industrial alcohol production was also still permitted. Despite the best efforts, there was no way that this vast production could be tightly controlled as it made its way down the production, distribution, and sales channels. Soon, alcohol bled off from near-beer was disappearing from inventories. Ingenious chemists could fiddle with industrial alcohol production to make it drinkable. And doctors across the nation happily wrote out numerous prescriptions for medicinal alcohol for all sorts of illnesses.

GIN IN THE BATHTUB

These were criminal activities, but if illicit alcohol production had remained at that level, it would have had little impact on crime and violence as a whole. But even hundreds of prescriptions for medicinal alcohol could not slake America's thirst. Americans soon became micro-brewers, re-learning basic chemistry, purchasing $500 stills, and setting them up in their basements, producing as many as 50 to 100 gallons a day. A one-gallon still for personal use could be bought for only $6 or $7. Soon, it seemed, every American had, or knew of, someone who was making gin in their bathtub.

Enforcement had not been seriously contemplated by the Prohibitionists. The U.S. border spanned 18,700 mi. In the days before radar, heat sensors, and X-ray baggage screening, it could not be as well-guarded as needed. Congress did not take the issue seriously, either. In 1920, the federal government assigned only 1,520 men to Prohibition enforcement, and by 1930, only 2,836 agents were detailed to the task. The Coast Guard, Customs Service, and Immigration Service were periodically assigned to the task, as was the Treasury Department, but even so, there was only one man to guard each 12 mi. of border or coast against rumrunners, leaving no one to pursue domestic stills and illicit breweries.

Worse, Prohibition agents were poorly paid: 1920 salaries ranged from $1,200 to $2,000 per year. By 1930, they had gone up to between $2,300 and $2,800. Agents paid $35 or $50 a week were not likely to be skilled detectives, but very likely to be susceptible to corruption and payoffs.

As matters developed, the most famous Prohibition agents would turn out to be two semi-comedians. Izzy Einstein and Moe Smith made numerous successful raids in a variety of disguises, but irritated authorities with their colorful personalities. State governments proved lackluster at enforcing the law, too. By 1927, state governments were allocating to Prohibition enforcement one-eighth of the money they spent to uphold fish and game laws.

Izzy and Moe, however, proved effective. Izzy, 5'5" and 225 lbs., was a postal clerk. He did not look the part of a cop, but he spoke English, Yiddish, German, Polish, and Hungarian, and could make himself understood in French, Italian, and Russian. Moe was a cigar store owner, taller and heavier than Izzy, but shrewd. Disguised as Park Avenue swells, poultry salesmen, football players, gravediggers, Democratic National Convention delegates, or even violinists, Izzy and Moe relied on their intelligence and sense of humor. Without carrying firearms, they raided speakeasies for five years, confiscating five million bottles of liquor worth $15 million, thousands of gallons of booze in barrels, and hundreds of stills. In one night, they raided 48 saloons. They made 4,392 arrests, which resulted in a 95 percent conviction rate. In 1925, however, the Prohibition Bureau dismissed the pair for "the good of the service."

Within a short time, the Volstead Act became a national joke. Saloon owners turned their establishments into speakeasies, camouflaging them in a variety of ways, usually as private homes or soda joints. In New York, Chumley's opened on Bedford Street, without any sign or menu posted, a tradition it has maintained ever since. Speakeasies sold home-brewed beer at $.75 per drink to customers, and free to police officers in order to prevent raids.

THE HYPOCRISY OF IT ALL

The hypocrisy of the situation became increasingly blatant. Everyone knew that President Warren G. Harding was drinking alcohol with his buddies at White House poker games. Congressmen showed up on the floor of the House of Representatives drunk. Future President Harry S. Truman complained bitterly about Prohibitionists who fulminated against demon rum on Sunday mornings in their churches in his neighborhood, then dashed into speakeasies after the service for a beer. U.S. Representative Fiorello La Guardia showed the silliness of the law by making liquor in his office for reporters and serving it to them without fear of prosecution.

Incredibly, the dry movement, having succeeded in forcing Prohibition on the country, took little action against these blatant acts of defiance. The most they could do was successfully pressure the federal government to expand the three-mi. limit on territorial waters to 12 mi., to enable Coast Guard cutters to pursue rumrunners. One Coast Guard cutter chased a Canadian rumrunner, the *I'm Alone*, for two and a half days, and finally sank her 215 mi. from the U.S. coastline, dismaying the Canadian government.

The illegal whiskey trade became huge business. The Bahamas, British Honduras, and Bermuda became centers for shipping Canadian whiskey and French champagne to America. St. Pierre, France's last foothold in North America,

Sacco and Vanzetti

Nicola Sacco (right) and Bartolomeo Vanzetti handcuffed together.

The climax of the battle between law enforcement and radicals came in May 1920, when Nicola Sacco and Bartolomeo Vanzetti, two Italian immigrants, were arrested near Boston. The two men were accused of robbing a store and murdering a paymaster and factory guard in connection with a payroll robbery that netted the crooks $16,000.

The evidence against Sacco and Vanzetti was thin, but they were foreigners and admitted anarchists, two negatives at the time. Worse, when the pair was arrested, they were carrying loaded pistols, and police claimed Sacco's gun was the murder weapon. The defense claimed that the bullet the ballistics expert studied was planted on Sacco by the prosecution.

The case was inflamed further when the defense produced 107 witnesses to alibi Sacco and Vanzetti, while the prosecution put 61 witnesses on the stand to place the pair at the crime scene. Judge Webster Thayer blatantly favored the prosecution, even in his instructions to the jury, who found Sacco and Vanzetti guilty. The case became an international sensation, with writers like Dorothy Parker, H.G. Wells, Edna St. Vincent Millay, George Bernard Shaw, and Upton Sinclair calling for a new trial. They got one—with Thayer presiding again, and the two were again found guilty.

For six years, appeals, protests, and denunciations raged. Future Supreme Court Justice Felix Frankfurter wrote an eloquent demand for a new trial. Protest rallies against the execution took place in Boston and in London, and bombs were sent to American embassies. Judge Thayer's house was bombed, and he had to be guarded 24 hours a day until his death.

In 1926, Massachusetts Governor Alvin Fuller appointed a committee of two academics and a retired judge to study the case. Using more modern technology to study the weapons, they determined that the original verdict stood. Sacco and Vanzetti were executed in the electric chair on August 23, 1927.

Fifty years later, Massachusetts Governor Michael Dukakis issued a proclamation saying that the execution had been unjust. Modern historians believe that Sacco was indeed innocent, but that Vanzetti may have been guilty.

normally a sleepy fishing community, became jammed with warehouses full of liquor. Launches packed with Canadian whiskey raced across the Great Lakes and rivers near Detroit. In winter, when lakes and rivers froze, enterprising bootleggers drove cars across the ice. Canadian politicians and police were in on the game—payoffs went up to the House of Commons in Ottawa.

Once the imported liquor reached its American destination, it was often watered down to expand profits, so that one gallon of Scotch could fill three bottles. That, mixed with locally-produced beer, filled barrels at speakeasies and whiskey flasks of consumers, as well as the pockets of increasingly powerful gangsters, whose reign of bloodshed and terror defined the decade.

GANG VIOLENCE

In 1920, Johnny Torrio, a Brooklyn native, was running gangs in Chicago for Big Jim Colosimo, ensuring that Colosimo's $500,000 network of gambling joints and bordellos operated smoothly. Torrio was frustrated because Colosimo was more interested in his girlfriend, singer Dale Winters, than in criminal operations.

Torrio quickly realized that illegal liquor was the next massive source of income. He needed only to break his wide array of competition, including Dion O'Banion and Hymie Weiss, who despite his Jewish name was a Polish Catholic. To take command, Torrio shot Colosimo through the head on May 11, 1920, in his South Wabash Street nightclub. Torrio wept crocodile tears at a funeral that cost $50,000, then bribed Chicago's municipal government to leave him alone.

That did not take much work—two-time Chicago Mayor "Big Bill" Thompson and his cronies were utterly corrupt. Newspapers inside and outside Chicago decried Thompson as one of the stupidest politicians in America, but he was adept at winning votes. Thompson was reelected mayor in 1919. He fell to reformer "Big Bill" Dever in 1923, but returned to power in 1927. Each time he became mayor, he shut down his police department's Morals Squad, ending all prosecution of Torrio's gambling, prostitution, and alcohol rackets. With the politicos in his pocket, Torrio needed only to eliminate his competition. In order to accomplish this, Torrio brought to Chicago a pal from Brooklyn, 23-year-old Alphonse Capone. Torrio offered Capone a big income and half the profits. Scar-faced, huge in build, and quick with a quip, Capone needed little prompting. He set up an office, printing business cards that read, "Alphonse Capone, Second Hand Furniture Dealer." Capone soon assembled an army of thugs and goons. Using the two new technologies of the time, automobiles and automatic weapons, Capone butchered his enemies and gained massive power.

In 1924, O'Banion sold his interest in the Sieben Brewery, which made near-beer for cover and real beer for mobsters, to Torrio for $500,000. Some 500 police officers at the nearby Maxwell Street Station were paid as much as $125 a month to keep the brewery secure from raids and rivals. When Torrio and O'Banion went to inspect the place, however, other Chicago police, answering to Dever's order to clean up the city, raided the place, netting the two gang leaders. It was O'Banion's first federal bust so he had little to fear, but Torrio landed in jail and his brewery was padlocked. Torrio and Capone saw the incident as treachery by O'Banion, who had snickered about Torrio's plight. Torrio pleaded guilty to the federal charges and got a meager $5,000 fine and nine months in jail. While Torrio was in jail, Capone took charge.

On November 11, 1924, Capone sent three gunmen to O'Banion's flower shop. They gunned O'Banion down at point-blank range, launching the Chicago "beer wars." Soon rival gangs were waging battles with grenades, Tommy guns, and bombs, struggling for control of the city's liquor trade. Hymie Weiss took over the North Side gang after O'Banion's death. He proved ferocious, ambushing Torrio on January 24, 1925, and severely wounding the gangster. Traumatized and wounded, Torrio turned over the operation completely to Capone.

Gang violence continued, as mobsters discovered the high firepower of the Thompson submachine-gun. Frank McErlane and Joe Saltis tried to gun down Spike O'Donnell at 63rd St. and Western Ave. They missed, but the police were impressed by the huge barrage of bullets delivered from a speeding car. McErlane and Saltis did better two weeks later when they killed Charles Kelly. On April 27, 1926, Capone struck at a Cicero saloon, killing the Assistant State Attorney, William McSwiggin. Capone and his crew were probably intending to knock off a rival bootlegger named Doherty, but McSwiggin, who was having a drink with the boys, simply got in the way. As usual, there were no convictions in these cases.

Tension between Weiss's North Siders and Capone reached a peak on September 20, 1926, when the determined Pole brought 10 gunmen in nine cars to Capone's Cicero headquarters at the Hawthorne Inn. Weiss's men poured more than 1,000 rounds into Capone's building, but missed the Big Guy, who was sipping coffee in the hotel restaurant. The gunmen drove off unharmed. Incredibly, they had shot at

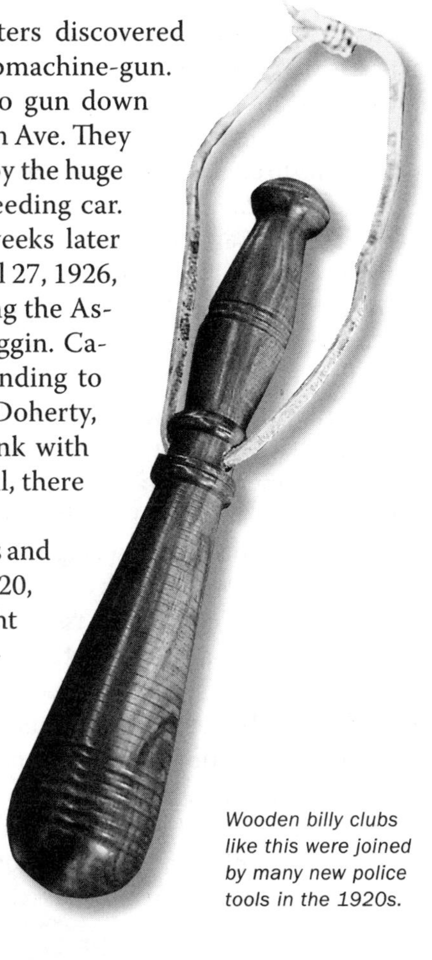

Wooden billy clubs like this were joined by many new police tools in the 1920s.

35 cars but had not killed anyone; they only wounded four people. Capone paid the hospital bills of the four victims, then plotted revenge.

Capone's revenge was spectacular. On October 11, 1926, as Weiss and four companions emerged from a car next to the Holy Name Cathedral, two Capone gunmen opened fire from separate apartments across the street. Their crossfire put 10 slugs into Weiss, killing him and his bodyguard, and wounding the rest. "I'm sorry Weiss was killed," Capone told reporters that afternoon at the Hawthorne, "But I didn't have anything to do with it. It's getting to be a joke, this pinning all the murder on me. Hymie Weiss is dead, because he was a bull-head." By then, Capone was famous for his power, flamboyant lifestyle, and colorful quotes.

AL CAPONE'S POWER AND WARS

With Weiss gone, Bugs Moran took over, and the beer wars continued. Moran hated Capone's organization because it supported bordellos, drug peddling, and jazz music. Capone feared Moran, calling him a homicidal maniac. The battles between the two gangsters reached their climax on the morning of February 14, 1929. The facts remain in dispute, but the generally accepted theory is that Capone and his lieutenants, Jake "Greasy Thumb" Guzik and Frank "The Enforcer" Nitti, agreed that Moran had to be eliminated no matter the consequences. Capone assigned "Machine Gun" Jack McGurn to the task, and he brought in "outside torpedoes" from New York and even Tennessee. McGurn and his crew rented an apartment opposite Moran's 2122 North Clark Street garage, the S.M.C. Cartage Company, to monitor the gang's activities. Then they paid freelance Sicilian bootleggers to offer to sell a load of stolen bootlegged Canadian whiskey to the Moran gang. Since such deals were common in Chicago gangland, Moran accepted.

On the morning of the 14th, six members of the Moran crew convened at the garage for the "sale," awaiting the bootleggers, minus Moran, who was apparently late. Joining them, however, was a local optometrist, Dr. Reinhart Schwimmer, who was a gangster "groupie" and part-time bootlegger. He showed up wearing a coat and hat that resembled Moran's.

McGurn and his killers, seeing Schwimmer enter the garage, followed him in a stolen Chicago police truck and wearing stolen Chicago police uniforms. The Moran crew and Schwimmer assumed they had been betrayed by the bootleggers, and a police raid was about to ensue. They stood by the wall, waiting to be searched and cuffed. Instead, McGurn's killers took out their Thompsons and gunned down the seven men. To make a statement, McGurn's men fired shotguns into their victims' faces. Missing was Moran, who saw the stolen police truck enter his garage, and wisely fled. Lying dead were his six top lieutenants. Moran roared, "Only Capone kills like that," and vowed revenge.

"They don't call him 'Bugs' for nothing!" was Capone's rejoinder when reporters asked him about the massacre, but Capone knew that having missed

Al Capone's jail cell at the Eastern State Penitentiary, where he purposely had himself locked away in 1929 to avoid Bugs Moran. His influence was such that he acquired the luxuries shown here.

his primary target, he was likely to be next. Indeed, Moran pulled together what was left of his organization and ordered assassination attempts on Capone and McGurn. "Machine Gun Jack" was killed on February 14, 1930, in a bowling alley, but Capone arranged to have himself jailed in Philadelphia on May 16, 1929, on a gun-carrying charge. This put the Eastern State Penitentiary's massive walls between him and Moran's killers until March 17, 1930, when he was released. He headed for his Palm Island estate in Florida.

By 1928, Prohibition was regarded as a failure and a joke across America. Yet it remained the law of the land and politicians made no effort to repeal the Volstead Act. It had been created to attack crime and vice, but instead had inflamed it on a massive scale.

As the decade ended, Capone's power seemed firm and his invulnerability to rivals and the law absolute. Chicago's Crime Commission proclaimed the Big Fellow the city's Public Enemy Number One, but Bill Thompson's corrupt administration, and Capone's combination of lavish bribery and ruthless violence cemented his position. Capone drove around Chicago in an armored Rolls-Royce, dined on lavish meals at the Lexington Hotel, sat in box seats at Cubs and White Sox games, and entertained reporters with colorful quotes like, "When I sell liquor, they call it bootlegging. When my patrons serve it on silver trays on Lake Shore Drive, they call it hospitality."

Reckoning for Capone and his machine would come in another decade, but the systems he built for organized crime would become the standard for America for decades to come. As he said, "My rackets are run on strictly American lines and they are going to stay that way."

The new tabloid newspapers, locked in fierce competition with each other and with radio, waged their battles for circulation by putting mayhem on the front page. This shocked, titillated, and entertained readers. In one such story, Americans became familiar with the trial of Ruth Snyder in 1928. Snyder had allegedly murdered her husband, art editor Albert Snyder, so that she and her lover, corset salesman Judd Gray, could live on the insurance money. Writers covering the trial included D.W. Griffith and Will Durant. Snyder became the first woman to face electrocution in New York State. A news reporter who had equipped himself with a camera strapped to his ankle successfully obtained a blurry, but shocking front-page shot of the historic execution.

Crime raged across America in many forms during the 1920s. While Capone was the premier figure, mobsters rose to the foreground in other states and cities. New York mobsters dominated the liquor trade and the docks, making vast payoffs to police officials, leading to investigations that brought down Mayor Jimmy Walker in 1929. Arnold Rothstein, the "Big Bankroll," dominated illegal gambling until he was shot to death in 1928. British-born Owney Madden controlled breweries, nightclubs, taxis, laundries, and with Rothstein, a piece of the legendary Cotton Club in Harlem. Lucky Luciano, Albert Anastasia, and other key figures of organized crime also began their rise in the 1920s. Luciano claimed to pay $10,000 to $20,000 a week to cops and politicians to protect his beer shipments from Europe on the New York waterfronts.

The electric chair known as Old Sparky, which was first used in 1923 in Florida.

Another crime that rose was the Ponzi Scheme, named for its chief proponent, Charles Ponzi. These were investment scams in which absurd profits were promised to investors. Instead, investors were called upon to provide increasingly large sums of money, until they were bankrupted, or until the con man was arrested or simply vanished. These cons continued to evolve over the following decades and are still around today.

THE POLICE AND THE FBI

Fighting crime required more tools than police raids and hysteria, and new ones were developed during the 1920s. The biggest was motorizing the police. In 1919, the New York police department owned 33 cars. Six years later, it had more than 600. Police cars meant that officers did not have to spend time "on reserve" in precincts, and could instead work on three-shift rotations. By 1930, New York eliminated reserve duty.

Communications were also improved in the 1920s, with the development of telephone call boxes. Two-way radio for patrol cars was introduced in 1929. Criminal investigation also improved, with science providing investigators with microscopes, blood tests, firearms testing technology, and X-rays for autopsies. Police departments began developing crime-scene investigation procedures and analyses of *modus operandi*, the means by which criminals committed their crimes. Carbon paper and typewriters enabled police agencies to prepare reports and evidence more professionally.

One of the biggest developments in the war on crime came in 1924, when President Calvin Coolidge, cleaning up the scandals of the Harding administration, appointed Harlan Fiske Stone as attorney general. A former Columbia Law School dean and future chief justice, Stone had a mandate to clean up the Justice Department and the Bureau of Investigation, which was so corrupt that it was known as the Bureau of Easy Virtue. The bureau was led by Gaston Means, who ended up in jail. Stone decided to imitate Scotland Yard, manned by agents with training and intelligence.

J. EDGAR HOOVER

To run the new and improved Bureau of Investigation, Stone hired one of its attorneys, J. Edgar Hoover. He had gained high marks for compiling detailed indexes and lists of radicals during World War I, providing the Palmer raiders with the information they needed. Despite the questionable events surrounding the Palmer raiders, Hoover was highly regarded for efficiency, honesty, and integrity. On May 10, 1924, Stone summoned Hoover to his office, and said, "Young man, I want you to be the acting director of the Bureau of Investigation."

Hoover said he would take the job under "certain conditions."

"What are they?" Stone asked.

"The bureau must be divorced from politics and not be a catch-all for political hacks. Second, promotions will be based on proven ability, and the bureau will be responsible only to the attorney general."

"I wouldn't give it to you under any other conditions," Stone said. "That's all. Good day." With 441 agents, 216 support employees, and a $2.3 million budget, the modern FBI was born.

CONCLUSION

Crime and the efforts to control it were changed by Prohibition in the 1920s. It led to a shift in self-image for Americans as hundreds of thousands of otherwise law-abiding citizens engaged in criminal behavior, a legacy that would never be completely forgotten. Respect for government regulation faltered, and reformers encountered real limits to their attempts to enforce changes in behavior. While Prohibition changed national attitudes on some levels, on others the country continued in entrenched patterns. Racial violence, heightened by anxiety over immigration, remained brutal and relentless.

David H. Lippman

Further Readings

Allen, Frederick Lewis. *Only Yesterday*. New York: Harper and Row, 1931.

Behr, Edward. *Prohibition: Thirteen Years That Changed America*. New York: Arcade Publishing, 1997.

Clark, Norman H. *Deliver Us from Evil: An Interpretation of American Prohibition*. New York: W.W. Norton, 1976.

Courtwright, David T. *Forces of Habit. Drugs and the Making of the Modern World.* Cambridge, MA: Harvard University Press, 2001.

Friedman, Lawrence M. *Crime and Punishment in American History*. New York: Basic Books, 1993.

Jeffreys-Jones, Rhodri. *The FBI: A History.* New Haven, CT: Yale University Press, 2008.

Kessler, Ronald. *The Bureau*. New York: St. Martin's Press, 2002.

Lardner, Thomas and James Reppetto. *NYPD*. New York: Henry Holt, 2000.

McDonald, Brian. *My Father's Gun*. New York: Penguin, 1999.

Murdock, Catherine Gilbert. *Domesticating Drink: Women, Men, and Alcohol in America, 1870–1940*. Baltimore, MD: Johns Hopkins University Press, 2001.

Reuter, Edward B. *The American Race Problem*. New York: Thomas Crowell, 1927.

Schoenberg, Robert J. *Mr. Capone*. New York: William Morrow and Company, 1992.

Wade, Wyn Craig. *The Fiery Cross: The Ku Klux Klan in America*. New York: Simon and Schuster, 1987.

Chapter 12

Labor and Employment

"There are two ways of making money — one at the expense of others, the other by service to others."
—Henry Ford

IN THE UNITED States, the 1920s were characterized by rapid change. The 1920s were a period of ostensible prosperity, a time in which technological and psychological advances led to the introduction of mass production and new definitions of the workplace and workers' rights. Following a tumultuous year of business-labor confrontations in 1919, the second decade of the 20th century was a relatively peaceful period in which the business community joined with three Republican presidents and the courts to promote the belief that business was the key instrument for realizing the American dream. Touted by conservatives as the New Era, Presidents Warren G. Harding (1921–23), Calvin Coolidge (1923–29), and Herbert Hoover (1929–33) collectively insisted that giving business free rein was essential to continued prosperity. Their claims appeared to hold legitimacy because the federal budget was balanced, and the national debt declined. The standard of living for many Americans was higher than it had been at any previous point in history.

Despite the image of the prosperous 1920s, from 1920 to 1922 the United States experienced a period of economic depression. In 1920 five million workers out of a workforce of 40 million were unemployed. The following year that number rose by nearly a million. At some point during the decade, one-half of all men and two-thirds of all women were unemployed for longer than a 10-week period. In addition to the workers who were let go, tens of thousands were forced to take wage cuts. The 1920s ended with the Great Depression, the most cataclysmic economic event in American history.

PROSPERITY AND PRODUCTION

After a period of post–World War I depression, the United States entered 1923 with a booming stock market and rapidly increasing productivity. On November 11, 1924, the New York Stock Exchange reported that a record 2.2 million shares had been bought and sold in a single day. Between 1910 and 1920, productivity had risen by only 12 percent. By comparison, in the 1920s productivity increased by 64 percent. At the same time, business profits increased by 62 percent, and real incomes of Americans earning over $3,000 a year rose by as much as 35 percent. Incomes of those drawing six-figure incomes doubled between 1920 and 1928. The number of millionaires increased five-fold between 1914 and 1928, climbing from 7,000 to 35,000. Among middle-class Americans, wages and salaries remained relatively stable, but so did prices. The Eighteenth Amendment went into effect in January 1920, and the legal system was inundated with crimes connected to violations of liquor laws. Prohibition also set the stage for the rise of organized crime in the United States. Throughout the 1920s mobsters bought or forced their way into positions of influence in American business, particularly in banks and unions.

A 1920s time clock made by the International Time Recording Company.

The success of the 1920s was in great part due to the automobile industry. Between 1919 and 1929 sales climbed from 1.5 to 4.8 million. By the mid-1920s one in eight American workers was involved in production, selling, servicing, or fueling automobiles. The steel, rubber, chemical, and construction industries also made significant gains during the 1920s. Electrification played a major role in transforming the American workplace. Between 1919 and 1929 the number of industries that were electrified rose from 30 to 70 percent. Much of the growth of the 1920s was a response

Women, most with bobbed hair, assembling radios in a factory in 1925. Most female workers in the 1920s were single, under 25, and earned only $13–$14 a week.

to advancing technology that allowed companies to produce more products with fewer workers.

Other factors involved in the transformation included utilization of the assembly line, which allowed even unskilled workers to perform intricate tasks through repetition, and so-called scientific management. First devised by Fredrick Winslow Taylor (1856–1915), what became known as Taylorism transformed the workplace through shifting control of production to engineers and away from supervisors. By precisely timing worker actions and fine tuning every tool utilized in production, Taylor established standards that were designed to increase productivity while maximizing efficiency with the added benefit of lower costs and enhanced benefits. Thousands of businesses hired their own efficiency experts and consultants to implement Taylorism. Although it was intended for use in industry, Taylor's system spread to offices, department stores, libraries, and government, and was adopted by countries around the world.

While the business community hailed scientific management, workers often felt alienated by the monotony and experienced stress brought on by the scientific management. This dissatisfaction was epitomized by an event that

Henry Ford (1863–1947)

No single individual more aptly symbolized the 1920s than Henry Ford, the founder of the Ford Motor Company, who revolutionized American industry and helped to launch consumerism in the United States. Although he was a man of extreme prejudice, Ford's resourcefulness made him one of the most popular Americans of the decade. He was also one of the richest. Ford plants used specialized machinery designed to cut labor cost and reduce industrial waste. Production was increased by instituting assembly lines on which products were transported to workers at waist height to avoid wasted time spent in stooping and walking. By repeatedly performing the same task, workers gained skill, speed, and dexterity. Ford bragged that his workers could turn out a Model T every 24 seconds.

Ford was called the "mad socialist of Highland Park" in 1914 when he increased wages to an unprecedented $5 a day. In December 1929, Ford increased its minimum wage from $6 to $7 a day. Over the next two decades, real wages in Ford's plants quadrupled. The practice of improved production coupled with savings for both workers and consumers became known as Fordism, a practice that was adopted around the world. Despite Ford's reputation as a generous employer, workers labored under strict rules. They were forbidden to sit, whistle, sing, lean against machinery, smoke, or talk while working. Employees learned to get around the prohibition of no talking by perfecting a method of communicating without moving their lips. This practice became known as the "Ford whisper," and the tendency to assume a frozen expression while under observation came to be known as "Fordization of the face." Customers also joked about Ford motor cars, claiming that Fords needed no speedometers because the windshield rattled at 15 mph, the fenders at 20 mph, and the teeth at 25 mph. Fillings allegedly dropped out at 30 mph.

While producing automobiles that were within the means of the average American, Ford improved the lot of his workers. On September 29, 1926, he announced that he was instituting an eight-hour, five-day work week. Ford also instituted what became known as the "family wage" that has consistently been used to justify paying men a higher wage than women. In the 21st century, this "family wage" has impoverished female-headed families around the world. When sales of the Model T began to decline in the late 1920s, Ford laid off 40,000 workers, closed his plants, and began renovations to produce the Model A. This layoff caused unemployment in Detroit to rise to more than 60,000. From Ford's point of view, the strategy was successful. Hundreds of thousands of orders for the Model A poured in even before the prototype was ready. On December 1, 1927, the new model was placed on display in Madison Square Garden in New York to accommodate the crowds flocking to see it.

occurred in Gastonia, North Carolina, in 1929. Workers constructed an effigy of an unpopular plant superintendent and placed it in a coffin that was paraded through town. At intervals, the figure sat up and inquired about the number of workers carrying the coffin. When he was told there were eight, he bellowed out that two should be laid off because six were sufficient for the task.

During the 1920s, over 1,000 mergers took place in the manufacturing and mining industries. Banking also profited by the prosperity. In 1927 one percent of American banks controlled 46 percent of all banking resources. By 1929 approximately 200 large corporations owned 20 percent of the national wealth. Banks also entered the business world. In the largest business transaction in U.S. history up to that time, Dillon Read, a banking firm, paid $146 million for Dodge Brothers on August 1, 1925.

As the rich got richer, real wages increased for middle-class Americans, and purchasing power rose accordingly. However, certain segments of the population, including blacks, recent immigrants, and workers in those industries identified as "sick" never participated in the prosperity of the Roaring Twenties. Workers in textile mills and shoe factories in northern states were hit hard by a mass move to the south where profits could be increased with little effort because wages and overhead were lower, and unions rarely had to be taken into account. Because of these factors, working-class southerners were also left out of the prosperity of the 1920s.

The southern migration led to the closing of many mills, and sent some states into early economic depression. In Lawrence, Massachusetts, the American Woolen Company was forced to close its mills for two months. Even when it reopened, production and wages were cut. In Akron, Ohio, some 50,000 unemployed workers left the city to seek work elsewhere. Unemployment in affected areas rose to more than 20 percent, and wages were cut by a fifth in some industries. Depression in the textile industry almost annihilated the Amalgamated Textile Workers of America (ATWAP) because workers were unable to pay their dues. By 1923 the economic tide began to turn for many

A carpenter's hand drill from the early 20th century. In the 1920s productivity increased by 64 percent, with some of the gains coming from construction.

Americans, and working conditions improved. In August U.S. Steel announced that it would institute an eight-hour workday. Standard Oil followed suit in July, 1925, paving the way for other industries to institute shorter workdays.

WORKERS AND WORK

At the turn of the century 24 million workers had been involved in industrializing the United States. Approximately 40 percent of those workers were foreign-born, and recent immigrants had been generally willing to take any job at any wage to feed themselves and their families. American workers, who tended to divide into skilled and unskilled, had often turned to labor unions to promote their interests in the frequently volatile relationship between business and labor. The first American labor union had been established in 1866, but the American Federation of Labor (AFL) could claim only moderate success at that time. During World War I, the number of American workers increased significantly as the United States attempted to fulfill the needs of European nations at war. Efforts further intensified when America entered the war in 1917. By 1920 the labor force had reached 48 million workers. Nevertheless, unemployment never fell below five percent throughout the 1920s.

The number of white-collar jobs continued to expand. By 1920 more than a fifth of the total workforce was made up of salaried, white-collar workers. Because white-collar workers were paid higher wages, worked fewer hours,

In the 1920s, trends toward larger and more efficient organizations affected industries besides manufacturing, driving out smaller farms and food producers like bakeries.

The Hawthorne Works Experiment and Industrial Psychology

In 1924 the Hawthorne Works, a Chicago branch of the Bell Telephone Company, which mass produced telephone equipment, became the scene of a major study examining the workplace of the 1920s. Some 30,000 male and female workers, unskilled and semiskilled, made up the workforce at the Hawthorne Works. Employees were considered successful if they could meet the joint demands of speed and dexterity. Compared to most American workers of the 1920s, those at the Hawthorne Works were well treated. They worked 48 hours a week for good pay and had a pension plan and recreational facilities. Despite this, supervisors had observed that employees were experiencing a tendency toward on-the-job fatigue. Psychologist Elton Mayo (1880–1949) was hired to identify the ideal working environment for optimizing production.

Mayo separated volunteers into two groups to observe worker responses to changes in pay increases, hours worked, number and frequency of breaks, benefits offered, and lighting conditions. Mayo first compared a group working under conditions of improved lighting to those who worked with no lighting changes. Surprisingly, he found improvement in both groups. Subsequent experiments revealed that production consistently rose whether lighting was increased or decreased.

Production increased even when no changes were made after workers were told that they would be instituted. Mayo then examined changes in humidity and temperature, discovering that both those who worked under changed conditions and those who did not increased production levels. He subsequently instituted longer rest periods, free lunches, and shortened workdays for one group and compared them with a second group who continued to work under usual conditions. Again, production rose in both groups. Mayo also allowed one group to work at their own pace rather than meeting management-established standards. He found that absenteeism declined by 80 percent among this group, and levels of fatigue accordingly dropped.

Mayo's overall conclusions led to what became known as the Hawthorne Effect, the notion that the chief factor in determining production levels was the attention employers paid to workers, because this attention gave workers hope for improved conditions in the future. The Hawthorne study paved the way for the emerging field of industrial psychology. Frederick Herzberg (1926–2000), a noted industrial psychologist, subsequently identified five elements that affected job satisfaction among American workers: achievement, recognition, the work itself, responsibility, and advancement.

Religion and Labor

Because labor unions were often unable to combat the marriage of government and business in the 1920s, other groups frequently attempted to negotiate when employee/worker confrontations reached a crisis stage. Such was the case on September 23, 1929, when James Myers, the industrial secretary of the Federal Council of Churches, arrived in Marion, North Carolina, to investigate the facts behind the labor unrest that had been building steam since the previous spring, when mill workers had unsuccessfully tried to force mill owners to improve harsh working conditions, raise wages, and allow mill workers to organize. After Myers's arrival, workers picketing the local textile mill were met with armed sheriff's deputies intent on protecting the interests of mill owners. During the course of the confrontation, six workers were killed and another 25 wounded. To head off further hostilities, Myers met with government representatives who investigated the strike and worked with local churches to organize relief efforts to meet the immediate needs of workers and their families.

Myers, a Presbyterian, represented a group of Protestant churches. However, it was the Catholic Church that had historically been the most visible religious force engaged in supporting the rights of American workers. Generally, churches engaged in labor struggles advocated social reforms that recognized the rights of workers as essential in American industrialization and supported workers' rights to a living wage, shorter work days, and collective bargaining. Churches were also opposed to the exploitation of children in the workforce. However, because socialists were highly visible in the labor movement, religious support for labor unions was often tempered by the commitment to opposing radicalism.

labored under better working conditions, and had highly desirable leisure time, their relationships with employers tended to be far less volatile than those of the working class. Some of that tension was a result of financial stress. Between 1919 and 1927 the average industrial wage rose slowly, from $1,158 to $1,304 annually. It was estimated that $2,000 was needed for a family to meet basic living expenses. Many families solved the wage gap by putting wives and children to work.

Women made up a larger percentage of the labor force in the 1920s than ever before, but they made only one-half to two-thirds of what male workers earned. Many women earned only $13 to $14 a week, working nine and a half hours a day, six days a week. This trend was partly due to the tendency of women to cluster in low-paying, female-dominated occupations such as teaching, nursing, and social work. After World War I, there was a backlash against women workers who were believed to be taking jobs that rightfully be-

A wood-shaving plane from the 1920s that could have been used by a child laborer. In 1922, the Supreme Court overturned a child labor law in a case of a furniture maker in North Carolina.

longed to returning veterans. To deal with the particular interests of women workers, the Women's Bureau was established in 1920 under the auspices of the Department of Labor with Mary Anderson as its first director. Most female workers of the 1920s were single women under age 25 who voluntarily left the labor force to marry and have children. Contrarily, women of lower economic status often continued to labor at low-paying jobs after marriage and childbirth. For African-American women, domestic work was often the only option. In the agricultural sector, even women who did not engage in the physical side of farm work often participated in the labor force by selling eggs, cream, chickens, butter, and handcrafts, and sometimes supplemented family income by boarding schoolteachers.

The introduction of the assembly line drastically increased American production. On May 10, 1921, the Ford Motor Company manufactured a record 4,072 automobiles in a single day. However, the monotonous work often led to major stress on employees who performed the same task hour after hour, day after day, year in and year out. Instead of allowing workers to set their own pace, scientific management systems required workers to perform particular functions in a designated time period, following proscribed motions. Workers were closely watched by supervisors with stop watches. Nowhere was the assembly line more essential to increased production than in the automobile industry. Production increased from 300,000 automobiles in 1914 to almost two million in 1923 and 1924. By using the assembly line, Ford was able to produce the Model T Touring car for $290, a price that was in the reach of average Americans for the first time. As a result, more than half of all cars on American roads were Model Ts.

Because they understood that satisfied and loyal workers were more productive, employers of the 1920s instituted a number of measures to convince their workers that they were valued. Two of the most common practices of promoting contentment among employees and fulfilling social responsibilities were known as paternalism and welfarism. In both instances

Private Detectives

The 1920s were considered the Golden Age of the private detective in the United States. Some detectives were associated with companies such as Pinkerton, but many operated on their own. These detectives had become essential to many employers during the heavy labor activity of the previous decade, allowing them to be exempted from the draft during World War I on the grounds that they were engaged in an essential occupation. Large companies frequently hired hundreds of private detectives to keep workers in line and deal with strikes. On the latter occasion, detectives were used to protect strikebreakers and company property when crises occurred. Consequently, violence often accompanied their activities. Unions were forced to develop their own tactics for preventing private detectives from sabotaging efforts to protect American workers. In 1924, for instance, workers were unnecessarily injured and exposed to gas while building a dam and tunnel in Seattle, Washington. After employers refused to rectify problems, the local union sent representatives undercover to work as strikebreakers to prevent detectives and employers from violating worker rights.

Detectives were permanently on the payroll of mine owners in West Virginia, Kentucky, and Colorado. The most powerful cadre of detectives was found in Pennsylvania's coal industry where they managed to circumvent union activity for a number of years. Even the Ford Motor Company, which was considered an enlightened employer, hired hundreds of private detectives by putting them on the payroll as employees of their service department. Private detectives also frequently engaged in industrial spying and regularly issued reports on workers that could lead to employees being fired for smoking or talking on the job, being even a few minutes late for work, or for gossiping and complaining. A major part of the private detective's job was to present union organizers as Communist sympathizers who wanted to ease the way for Russian entry into the American system.

workers were "rewarded" with benefits such as unpaid vacations, pensions, unemployment benefits, stock options, company housing and stores, medical and dental care, health insurance, increased wages, and improved working conditions. Company newspapers, recreational facilities, lunchtime entertainment, and uniforms with company logos were viewed as ways to promote goodwill and *esprit de corps*. Certain company initiatives targeted the "Americanization" of immigrants. From the employer's view, all such actions had the added benefit of undercutting the lure of unions.

The practice of blocking labor activities by continued opposition to closed shops, which required all workers to belong to unions, and to collective bargaining, which forced employers to negotiate with union officials, became known as the American Plan. Business justified the implementation of this widespread plan by arguing that unions interfered with property rights of employers and with the right of workers to negotiate individual contracts. Company unions also proved to be a highly successful method of limiting the influence of organized labor. These unions gave employees the sense of worker protection, even though workers were not allowed to take part in decision-making.

THE COURTS

The road toward business ascendancy during the 1920s was paved in large part by President Harding's appointment of four conservative Supreme Court justices and Republican appointments of a number of lower-court judges who were chosen for their pro-business positions. Supreme Court decisions overturned a number of Progressive reforms, including those that had guaranteed minimum wages to women and restricted child labor. The shift toward a pro-business mentality in the courts also resulted in decisions that interfered with the ability of unions to protect the interests of members, publicly protest, and engage in collective bargaining. In 1921 the Supreme Court struck a major blow to labor unions by declaring that unions could be prosecuted for interfering with interstate trade, and that unions could be sued under antitrust laws. Lower courts freely used injunctions to prevent labor unions and workers from engaging in strikes and picketing. Organized labor did not make up the ground it lost in the 1920s until after the stock market crash of

A wooden typesetter's chest from the 1920s.

October 1929 and the subsequent election of Democratic President Franklin D. Roosevelt (1882–1945) in 1932.

Reformers were particularly appalled at court decisions that overturned barriers to child labor. In 1920 official reports indicated that 11 million children between the ages of 10 and 15 were gainfully employed. Tens of thousands of other younger children were working without being reported to authorities. The National Child Labor Committee estimated that children under the age of five were laboring in a large number of American industries. In the sugar beet industry, for instance, two of every three workers were believed to be small children. Child laborers worked long hours for as little as $.20 an hour, rarely seeing the sunshine. During the previous decade Progressive reformers had been adamant in ending, or at least limiting, the exploitation of children in mines, factories, and mills where children as young as seven or eight were used to perform dangerous tasks.

The result of Progressive efforts had been the passage of child labor laws in a number of states. The age at which children could begin regular employment was raised to 15, and young workers were limited to eight-hour workdays and 48-hour workweeks. Children were also banned from hazardous employment and night work, and proof of age was required. On May 15, 1922, the court overturned the child labor clause of the War Revenue Act of 1919 in

A 1920s courtroom. The Supreme Court overturned a number of Progressive reforms in the 1920s, and was assisted by Republican appointments of pro-business judges in the lower courts.

Bailey v. Drexel Furniture. As a result, reformers began advocating a child labor amendment to the U.S. Constitution. When Congress passed the amendment in 1924, it was sent to the states for ratification, giving opponents ample time to rally their arguments. Opponents of the amendment used the threat that Socialists, Communists, and Bolsheviks were behind it to help defeat the amendment. Some states, including Massachusetts, rescinded support for the amendment and lobbied against it.

In *United Mine Workers v. Coronado Coal Company,* the Supreme Court decided that labor unions could be held liable for damages incurred by their members during union protests and strikes. One of the most devastating blows to labor in the 1920s resulted from the court's decision in 1923 in *Adkins v. Children's Hospital,* in which justices determined that a minimum wage law for women in Washington, D.C., was unconstitutional. The case had widespread effects because 17 states had already enacted similar laws. By mid-decade the court had also overturned minimum wage laws in Arizona, Kansas, Minnesota, Wisconsin, and Puerto Rico. Only in eight states were minimum-wage laws left intact. Some states tried to circumvent the court's decision by rewording their laws. Massachusetts, for instance, encouraged voluntary compliance with a minimum wage, and Wisconsin based its new law on an employer's ability to pay a minimum wage.

On January 20, 1920, the Department of Justice launched a nationwide effort to target known radicals, anarchists, Socialists, and Bolsheviks. In New York, Chicago, and Detroit, some 5,000 warrants were issued. Overall, officials targeted individuals in 30 eastern and midwestern states. Political and business leaders managed to weaken labor unions considerably by linking them in the minds of the public to anti-American radicalism. Since the Supreme Court had upheld the use of such contracts in 1908 in *Adair v. United States,* scores of workers were forced to sign "yellow dog" agreements, swearing that they would not join unions.

LABOR UNREST

Between 1920 and 1929 union membership in the United States fell from 5.1 million to 3.4 million members. Most remaining union members were concentrated in the fields of printing, public service, transportation, building, and entertainment. In the latter half of the previous decade, there had been approximately 100 strikes per year. In the first half of the 1920s the number of strikes per year dropped to 34; only half that number took place in the latter half of the decade. At the same time that labor influence was declining, large numbers of American workers continued to labor in unsafe environments, on farms and in mines, mills, factories, and sweatshops.

Although incidences of labor unrest declined significantly during this period of increased prosperity, American workers continued to press for what they considered the basic rights of humane working conditions, a living wage, and the right to collective bargaining. The relationship between employers and railroad workers, longshoremen, miners, and textile workers was particularly volatile. In the mining industry where workers were exposed daily to a host of dangers that resulted in the deaths of 2,000 to 2,500 miners each year, the United Mine Workers union was considered powerful. However, union officials were unable to protect their members from wage cuts and abbreviated work days. Conditions were particularly bad in non-union mines where workers faced life-threatening conditions while earning approximately $2 a day.

In the spring of 1920, worker unrest resulted in a major strike. On April 17, 50,000 Chicago railroad employees walked off their jobs. Attorney General A. Mitchell Palmer accused the Industrial Workers of the World (IWW), also known as the "Wobblies," of using strikes to further the cause of Socialism in the United States. Consequently, strikers lost a good deal of public support. This pattern of government support for business over workers continued throughout the 1920s. A week after the Chicago strike, police fired into a crowd of IWW strikers in Butte, Montana, injuring 14 strikers. In May, Pinkerton representatives killed 12 people in a confrontation with West Virginia miners. Three months later, a fight broke out between police and streetcar workers in Denver, Colorado, leaving three strikers dead.

In February, 1922, amid local support, 60,000 textile workers walked off their jobs for a nine-month period in New Hampshire, Massachusetts, and Rhode Island to protest a wage cut of 22.5 percent. Workers in New Hampshire and Rhode Island were also protesting a proposed workweek increase from 48 to 54 hours. After mill owners received an injunction to prevent further worker protests, the wage cut was rescinded. However, New Hampshire workers were forced to agree to extended hours.

In April, 500,000 coal miners struck in response to an announced wage cut. Two months later a riot broke out in Herrin, Illinois, during a coal miners' strike. Mine owners responded by hiring nonunion workers and private detectives. After three strikers were killed during confrontations, miners responded by kidnapping several strikebreakers and shooting them as onlookers cheered. Despite 214 indictments, no one was ever convicted of any of the murders. In July, during the Great Railway Strike, some 400,000 railroad shop workers walked out on their jobs to protest a series of wage cuts that had been approved by the Railway Labor Board. President Harding received an injunction to force strikers back to work. On August 31, 1925, 150,000 Pennsylvania coal miners also went on strike.

Workers in the south were generally not unionized, in part because employers had a ready cadre of "spare hands" who were ready to step in when workers were fired for complaining too much or for engaging in protest. Nevertheless, strikes and protests sometimes spontaneously occurred. What became known as the Piedmont Revolt began in Elizabethtown, North Carolina, in late 1929. After the United Textile Workers union, which had joined the fray, was unable to win concessions for striking workers, labor unrest spread to Marion, North Carolina, and Danville, Virginia. Despite the labor failures of the 1920s, significant groundwork was laid that led to increased union activity and militancy during the 1930s.

NATIONWIDE DEPRESSION

By 1929 American wealth was concentrated in the hands of the richest 24,000 families, who held 34 percent of all savings. Some 21 million American families had no savings at all. The much touted prosperity of the 1920s came with a high price that was exacted in the United States and throughout much of the world in the 1930s. One of the first signs of the coming depression occurred in December 1928 when the New York Stock Exchange suffered a decline of 22 points. The Department of Labor acknowledged that 1.9 million Americans were unemployed, but one senator insisted that the number was closer to eight million. When Ford Motor Company announced in December 1928 that 30,000 workers would be hired to produce the Model A, many more workers arrived to apply for the openings. Many hopefuls who had stood in line overnight in 14-degree weather were hospitalized for exposure. When workers stormed Ford offices, employers turned fire hoses on them, despite the cold. Only 600 out of thousands were hired. Early in 1929 in an effort to curtail stock market speculation, the Federal Reserve Bank banned member banks from lending money to individuals interested in buying stocks on margin. By August, automobile factories had laid off thousands of workers. For the next five months, factory employment continued to decline. Some three million Americans were officially out of work by fall. Between October 24 and October 29, 16 million stock market shares were traded at a reported loss of eight billion dollars.

Despite growing desperation among American workers during the early days of the Great Depression, President Herbert Hoover continued to insist that the downturn was temporary. He believed the problem could be solved with tax cuts, business cooperation, reduced wages, an increase in public works, and efforts by the private sector. The president announced in December that public confidence had been restored and predicted that the unemployment problem would be solved by the first quarter of 1930. Early indications suggested that Hoover may have been justified in his predictions. In the long term, however, he was proved to have drastically misjudged the seriousness of the situation. That error in judgment ultimately led to his defeat in 1932, and it was left to Franklin Roosevelt to turn the country around with his New Deal and the subsequent transformation of the United States into a social welfare state. The official end of the depression did not come until World War II with the rise of America to the world's leading industrial power.

Elizabeth R. Purdy

Further Readings

Allen, Frederick Lewis. *Only Yesterday: An Informal History of the 1920s*. New York: Wiley, 1997.

Arnesen, Eric, et al. *Labor Histories: Class, Politics, and the Working Class Experience*. Urbana, IL: University of Illinois Press, 1998.

Blake, Angela M. *How New York Became American, 1890–1924*. Baltimore, MD: Johns Hopkins University Press, 2006.

Burgan, Michael. *The Great Depression*. Mankato, MN: Compass Point Books, 2001.

Dumenil, Lynn. *The Modern Temper: American Culture and Society in the 1920s*. New York: Hill and Wang, 1995.

Eyvig, David E. *Daily Life in the United States, 1920–1940: How Americans Lived through the "Roaring Twenties" and the Great Depression*. Chicago, IL: Ivan R. Dee, 2004.

Fischer, Claude S. and Michael Hout. *Century of Difference: How America Changed in the Last One Hundred Years*. New York: Russell Sage, 2006.

Goldberg, David J. *Discontented America: The United States in the 1920s*. Baltimore, MD: Johns Hopkins University Press, 1999.

Goldberg, Ronald Allen. *America in the Twenties*. Syracuse, NY: Syracuse University Press, 2003.

Green, Harvey. *The Uncertainty of Everyday Life, 1915–1945*. New York: Harper Collins, 1992.

Jacoby, Daniel. *Laboring for Freedom: A New Look at the History of Labor in America*. Armonk, NY: M.E. Sharpe, 1998.

Kronzberg, Melvin and Joseph Gies. *By the Sweat of Thy Brow: Work in the Western World*. New York: Putnam's, 1975.

Perrett, Geoffrey. *America in the Twenties: A History*. New York: Simon and Schuster, 1982.

Smith, Robert Michael. *From Blackjacks to Briefcases: A History of Commercialized Strikebreaking and Unionbusting in the United States*. Akron, OH: Ohio University Press, 2003.

Stearns, Peter N. *Encyclopedia of Social History*. New York: Garland, 1994.

Streissguth, Tom. *The Roaring Twenties: An Eyewitness to History*. New York: Facts On File, 2001.

Taylor, Benjamin and Fred Whitney. *US Labor Relations Law: Historical Development*. Englewood Cliffs, NJ: Prentice-Hall, 1992.

United States Department of Labor. *Growth of Labor Law in the United States*. Washington, D.C.: Government Printing Office, 1967.

Chapter 13

Military and Wars

"In war, the heroes always outnumber the soldiers ten to one."
—H.L. Mencken

AMERICAN MILITARY AFFAIRS in the 1920s represent only one portion of a longer period of transition in the era between the two world wars. Throughout the decade the United States confronted a number of issues involving the size and modernization of the armed forces, and the role that the nation would play in a postwar world as a wave of isolationism swept the country. The 1920s were in many ways a period of retrenchment, as the wartime army demobilized and America turned its back on large-scale military action, confining itself to the goals of trying to keep the peace in various places in which it had a particularly strong interest in political or economic stability.

President Woodrow Wilson had led the United States into World War I with lofty goals. Not only would Germany and its partners be defeated, but the war would lead to a better world through a system of fair treaties, an end to colonialism, and the adjustment of national boundaries to reflect the aspirations of previously subject populations. The League of Nations, an international association, was designed to prevent future conflicts through mediation of member states and collective security. The results were less than hoped for. The Treaty of Versailles, signed in 1919, reflected a series of compromises and the outright rejection of most of Wilson's Fourteen Points. Wilson was no more successful at home. Both the treaty and American membership in the League were rejected by Congress.

Following the rejection of the treaty and the end of a reluctant American participation in an Allied intervention in Russia, the United States resolved to stay out of future European conflicts while returning to the pursuit of its own goals and interests. This included its ongoing occupations of Haiti and the Dominican Republic, a new intervention in Nicaragua, and continuing protection of an Open Door policy in China. Efforts at maintaining international peace were pursued by various conferences on peace and arms limitations. In the meantime, as the armed services demobilized following the end of the war, plans were made to prepare for the dreaded possibility of another major conflict through modernization of both organization and technology.

EFFORTS AT PRESERVING THE PEACE

Although the United States refused to join the League, it participated in major conferences designed to limit naval expansion and maintain a balance of power among the victors of World War I. Although initially the United States desired to continue its pre-war program of naval expansion, the realities of paying off the nation's huge war debt dovetailed with the desire to prevent another naval arms race of the sort that had contributed to the outbreak of war. This led to a goal of establishing a naval balance through negotiation. In 1921 and 1922 the Washington Conference was held, resulting in the Five Power Treaty between the United States, Britain, Japan, France, and Italy. It established a ratio of naval strength based upon ship tonnage for capital ships (battleships and battle cruisers). Britain and the United States were allowed total limits of 500,000 tons of water displacement each, Japan 300,000 tons, and France and Italy 175,000 tons. Battleship size was limited to 35,000 tons per vessel. The size of naval guns was also limited. The treaty nations were required to scrap existing vessels to get within their assigned limitations and could not build new capital vessels for 10 years. Afterwards, they could only build new ones to replace outdated ships. The individual tonnage of new vessels had to fall within the total tonnage allotted for each nation.

Often used in World War I, the 4.5 in.-howitzer was upgraded in the 1920s.

While the Washington Conference limited the ability of the United States to expand its capital fleet to the sort of organization dreamed of by naval enthusiasts of previous decades, it left plenty of room for the development of naval strength in other ways. Destroyers, submarines, and naval air forces could

The Russian Intervention

The end of hostilities between the Allies and Germany did not lead to a cessation of military activity on the part of the United States. At the time of the signing of the Treaty of Versailles, American forces were already involved in an Allied intervention in a Russian civil war that was itself the by-product of the global conflict. The autocratic regime of Czar Nicholas II, slow to adopt modernizing reforms, had enjoyed little support among the Russian populace, and the high costs of participation in World War I, especially in human lives, had proved to be the breaking point. A series of revolutions had erupted in February 1917 that had overthrown the Czar, and by November had brought the Bolsheviks to power. The new Soviet government withdrew Russia's participation in the war, which among other things freed up thousands of German troops for use on the western front. It also meant the potential loss to the Allies of a substantial number of war supplies stockpiled for use in the war at such ports as Archangel on the Baltic Sea and Vladivostok on the Pacific. To protect these interests, Allied governments began to send troops and warships to Russia in 1918. By this time, a civil war had erupted between the government and various anti-Bolshevik "White Russian" factions. Hopes that the Bolsheviks might be overthrown, leading to a Russian reentry into the world war, led to a change in Allied policy toward active support of the rebels. The Allies shifted their support from one White Russian leader to another as each proved unsatisfactory or was defeated.

The United States reluctantly became involved in Russia in the second half of 1918. The primary American concern was the protection of the masses of supplies that were threatened by the chaos, including much material originally provided by the United States. In August 1918, 9,000 American troops landed at Vladivostok, where British and Japanese forces were already operating. An additional 5,000 American soldiers landed in northern Russia in September, where they joined British and French forces. The U.S. forces in Russia saw limited action. In Siberia, part of the task facing the Americans was the protection of the long Trans-Siberian Railroad, the major supply line for the White Russian forces operating in the region. This assignment led to some clashes with Soviet partisan forces.

The Allied intervention was operating on borrowed time, however. The various White Russian factions never became a viable alternative to the Soviet regime, and although different commanders enjoyed some success in battle, they were eventually worn down and defeated by their better-organized and better-led opponents. In contrast, policy differences grew among the war-weary Allies about the intervention's goals, and the number of troops was never large enough to make a permanent impact. As the Soviet military and political situation stabilized and the White Russian cause declined, America soon tired of its involvement. The American troops in northern Russia left in July and August 1919, while those in Siberia departed early in 1920.

be built, and the treaty allowed the United States to convert two large cruisers into aircraft carriers. Although heavy cruisers (the next ship size below battle cruiser) were limited to 10,000 tons, there were no limits on the numbers that could be constructed.

A second naval conference was called for by President Calvin Coolidge in February 1927. It was intended to address the issue of limitations on vessels not covered in the first conference. The meeting was held in Geneva during the summer. France and Italy refused to participate, although they sent observers. The United States proposed a plan dividing non-capital vessels into three categories: cruisers, destroyers, and submarines. Total tonnage in each type of ship would be restricted along the lines of the ratio between the nations in the Washington Conference.

The British had a different idea, suggesting that all three remaining categories of ships should be divided into two classes each. Within each class, there would be limitations on tonnage and gun size for each ship, as well as on the number of ships in each category. The reasons for the conflict between the American and British positions lay in the different needs and financial limitations of the respective navies, with the Royal Navy desiring to have more light cruisers at the expense of the heavy cruisers favored by the Americans. The Japanese wanted a halt on further naval construction altogether. Efforts at compromise failed, and the conference ended without result; in the aftermath, the U.S. Navy requested and received from Congress authorization for building more cruisers.

A more ambitious and idealistic effort at securing peace was signed in Paris on August 27, 1928, and eventually ratified by 57 countries. The Kellogg-Briand Pact, known more formally as the International Treaty for the Renunciation of War, was primarily the work of U.S. Secretary of State Frank B. Kellogg and French Foreign Minister Aristide Briand. Those nations who committed to the treaty agreed to renounce war as an instrument of national policy, with certain exceptions such as self-defense, violation by a participating nation, or to protect certain national spheres of influence. As the 1930s would show, getting aggressive or unscrupulous leaders to live up to both the terms and the spirit of the treaty would prove a major problem.

ORGANIZATION AND MODERNIZATION

Efforts were made to modernize the various armed services, incorporating the experiences gained during World War I and integrating the new technology that had been introduced in that conflict. Congress passed the National Defense Act of 1920. The standing army would remain small, consisting of 280,000 officers and men. The National Guard would provide the chief reserve force of the nation, with an allowable upper limit of 435,000 officers and men. As compulsory service of any sort was not included in the plan, the Army would build itself quickly in time of war through mobilization of the Organized Reserves. During peacetime, the latter would be a small token force of veterans, organized around the headquarters of otherwise non-existing military units organized as far up as the divisional level. Once a conflict broke out and mobilization was activated, these units would become fully functional, with the headquarters providing training for the newly-arrived conscripts who would flesh out the ranks. Reserve officers would be trained and commissioned on a regular basis during peacetime, utilizing a series of seasonal training camps and the newly-organized Reserve Officer Training Corps (ROTC) on college campuses.

The National Defense Act of 1920 represented a number of compromises between those who favored a system of compulsory military training based on one or another European model, traditional American celebration of the citizen-soldier and hostility towards the idea of large standing armies, and the realities of postwar budgeting. It nevertheless marked a major step in developing a modernized standing army with a supplementary reserve system that could quickly be mobilized and filled up in the event of another major conflict. Efforts were also made to plan for industrial mobilization in the event of war, although these plans did not begin to come to fruition until 1930.

The adaptation of technological change was also a feature of the era. Modernization of ship design, armor, and armament was conducted within the confines of the agreed-upon guidelines of the Washington Conference. Two new technologies that faced some resistance to acceptance within the peacetime armed services were aircraft and tanks. Both technologies had shown their worth during World War I, but neither had reached their full potential, and questions lingered among more conservative officers over their proper function. Despite the melodramatics that surrounded the efforts of Brigadier General William "Billy" Mitchell to promote air power, which ended his own career, air power won gradual acceptance. The tank faced a tougher road to acceptance and, regulated to an adjunct of the infantry, it languished until the events of World War II demonstrated more fully its potential as a weapon.

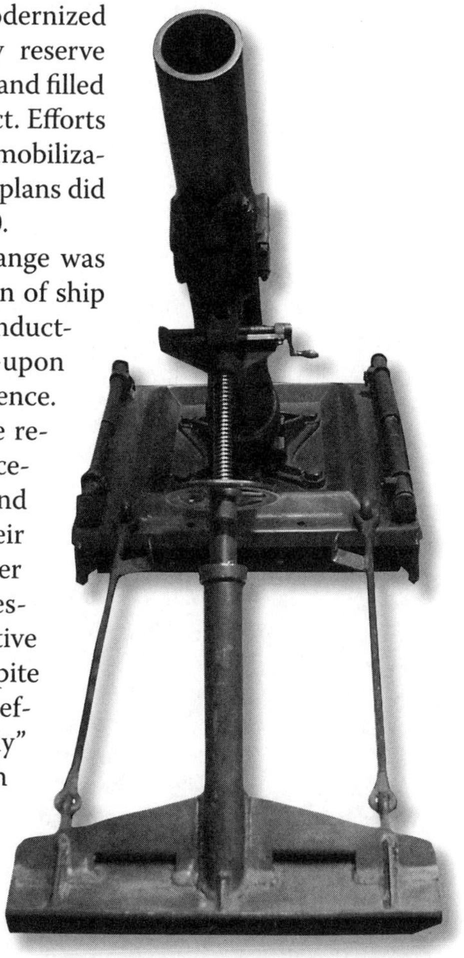

The 4.2-in. chemical mortar had its origins in World War I, and was used in World War II to fire high-explosive or chemical mortars.

Billy Mitchell and the Future of Air Power

Air power was one of many recently-introduced technologies that saw widespread military use for the first time during World War I. Its use was originally limited to reconnaissance, but as the war progressed, planes and gas-filled dirigibles were used to bomb ground targets. Other planes were used as fighters to attack enemy bombers. Although air power became more integrated into overall strategy as the war progressed, the use of aircraft for military purposes was still relatively limited by the time the conflict ended. This did not stop many aerial specialists from theorizing about the prominent and perhaps decisive role that air power would have on future warfare. Much as Alfred Thayer Mahan and other naval theorists of earlier decades had promulgated the use of sea power as the ultimate means of insuring military superiority, now supporters of air power made similar claims for their new and evolving branch of service.

In the postwar United States the most prominent proponent of air power was William "Billy" Mitchell. After serving in a number of different military posts, he became an assistant instructor at the new Signal School in Fort Leavenworth. While there, he first became intrigued about the potential use of air power in warfare, speculating on the possible battlefield roles that dirigibles might play. After a tour of duty in the Philippines, during which he conducted reconnaissance and observation missions in the Pacific, he was appointed to the Army General Staff. His growing interest in the use of air power as an adjunct to the operations of land forces coincided with the outbreak of World War I, and he helped develop the nation's fledgling aerial force. In 1917 Mitchell was sent to Europe as an observer. There he gained first-hand knowledge of the state of aerial warfare through observation and through contact with such figures as Major General Hugh Trenchard, who commanded the British air forces in France. Mitchell was later placed in charge of the American air forces in France, although many of his ideas on aerial strategy were slow to be adopted due to conservative attitudes and limited equipment.

After the war, Mitchell continued to advocate the expanded use of air power. He was not alone, as the Joint Board of Aeronautics believed that both the Army and the Navy should develop their own aerial forces to secure battlefield supremacy and bombard enemy armies and land targets. Mitchell dismissed their ideas as too conservative. By 1919 he was openly challenging the prevailing military policies toward air power. A bit of a showman, Mitchell pressured the Navy into allowing him to test his theories regarding the threat that planes posed to ships during exercises conducted off of Chesapeake Bay in 1921. Mitchell's planes sunk an old German battleship, but he won few friends due to his ridicule of the Navy's commanders. His public criticism of Army policy led to tensions with his own superiors, resulting in his effective demotion from brigadier general to colonel. This was followed by a court-martial for insubordination. Mitchell left the Army in 1926 to avoid dismissal.

LATIN AMERICA AND THE CARIBBEAN

During the period following the end of World War I, the United States continued its occupation of Haiti and the Dominican Republic, while embarking on another intervention in Nicaragua. In the Dominican Republic an American military governor ran the country and introduced a series of reforms and public works. Not all of its efforts were successful, as the provost court system introduced by the Americans was often ineptly managed and unfair to the Dominicans who came before its bench. The occupiers replaced the corrupt Republican Guard by a police force that was known successively as the *Guardia Nacional Dominicana* and the *Policia Nacional Dominicana*. Its rank and file was made up of Dominicans, but the officers were U.S. Marines. It never evolved into an efficient organization, and was viewed by the populace with suspicion. Its most dubious legacy was that future dictator Rafael Trujillo emerged from its ranks. The U.S. Marine contingent, the real backbone of American power in the country, was also inadequate, consisting increasingly of short-term enlistees as its more veteran officers and soldiers were siphoned off for duty in World War I and other assignments. Military action was limited to operations against rural bandits. The occupation ended in 1924 when the last of the Marines withdrew.

A rebellion against the American presence in Haiti erupted in October 1918, led by a former Haitian general named Charlemagne Massena Peralte. Initially, responsibility for handling the violence was in the hands of the *Gendarmerie d'Haiti*, a constabulary that had replaced the Haitian army under the terms of a 1916 treaty with the United States. The *gendarmerie* was a larger counterpart of the *Guardia Nacional Dominicana*, and was made up of Haitians under American command. The *gendarmerie* was unable to put down the revolution, so a brigade of U.S. Marines stationed in Haiti went into action. Like its fellow unit in the Dominican Republic, however, the Marines did not have many veteran troops or officers, and consisted mostly of short-term enlistees who had signed up for the duration of World War I. Reforms were made to make

Billy Mitchell in 1925 during his struggle to promote American air power.

the *gendarmerie* into a more effective force, while veteran Marines gradually replaced the enlistees.

In October 1919, Peralte launched a major attack against Port-au-Prince, the Haitian capitol. The Marines and *gendarmes* knew of the attack ahead of time, which was repulsed. Peralte was dead by the end of the month, killed by a mixed force of Marines and *gendarmes* who infiltrated his camp. The rebellion continued, however, under the leadership of Benoit Batraville. The Americans went on the offensive at the beginning of 1920. Batraville attacked Port-au-Prince in the middle of January, but was driven off with heavy losses. Small clashes continued in the countryside through May, when Batraville was killed. The rebellion fell apart afterward. This did not bring an end to unrest in Haiti, however. Abuses and killings of Haitian civilians and rebel prisoners by members of the *gendarmerie* were covered up by American officers, but eventually came to light. Criticism of the occupation grew in the United States. The Marine presence was gradually reduced as the *gendarmerie* took on more of a role in keeping the peace. The policies of Haitian President Louis Borno led to a new round of unrest in 1929, with violence breaking out in the following year. Tiring of the situation, U.S. President Herbert Hoover initiated the withdrawal of U.S. forces from Haiti, which was completed in 1934.

In 1927 the United States once again occupied Nicaragua due to a crisis that had been developing for two years. The country had remained relatively quiet in the years following the end of the previous intervention in 1912, although tensions between the American-backed government and its opponents remained high. The Marine legation guard was a focal point of anger

Troops training with an ambulance. At the start of World War I, horse-drawn ambulances were used on the battlefield, but the Red Cross helped replace many with motor ambulances.

A GM K-16 military ambulance. The U.S. military used both Ford Model T and General Motors ambulances in World War I.

among many Nicaraguan nationalists. After a clash between a small party of Marines and policemen in Managua resulted in six deaths in 1921, the decision was made to withdraw the legation guard, depending upon maintenance of peace by the government. The Nicaraguan army was in bad shape, however, and declined steadily in size. In 1925 a constabulary was established under American prompting and guidelines, similar to the ones in Haiti and the Dominican Republic. Like those bodies, the Nicaraguan *Guardia Nacional* was made up of citizens of that nation, trained and led by American officers. Although intended to eventually replace the Nicaraguan armed services, nationalist protest led to their retention and subordination of the *Guardia Nacional*'s American officers to the Nicaraguan government.

In August 1925, the United States finally withdrew the Marine legation guard. Within weeks, anti-government violence broke out. Emiliano Chamorro, a former army commander and president, quickly emerged as leader of the opposition, seizing control of the La Loma fortress in Managua. The coalition government of President Carlos Solorzano refused to act, despite pleas from the American commander of the *Guardia Nacional*. Solorzano resigned

The National Defense Act of 1920 disbanded the Tank Corps and integrated tanks within the infantry as support units. These 28th Infantry troops were training with tanks in 1921.

in January 1926, and was succeeded by Chamorro. A government-in-exile was established in Washington, D.C., by Solorzano's vice president, Dr. Juan Sacasa of the Liberal Party, but the U.S. government refused to recognize either it or Chamorro's regime. A revolution broke out against Chamorro in 1926, leading to his resignation from office in November. American-backed Adolfo Diaz eventually emerged as the new president. The civil war continued, however, with Sacasa receiving recognition and arms from Mexico. Diaz skillfully played upon American fears of Bolshevism regarding Mexico's leftward-leaning ideology to drum up concern about the latter country's involvement in the revolt.

Early in 1927 the United States became more directly involved in the civil war, lifting an arms embargo to support the Diaz government and sending in additional contingents of Marines. The government forces suffered some major defeats, however, and the British government began to hint at a possible intervention to protect its interests. The United States stepped up its own military commitment to forestall the possibility of European intervention. Henry Stimson, Wilson's former secretary of war, was sent to negotiate a peace settlement between the government and Sacasa's military commander, General Jose Moncada (but not Sacasa himself). In May Moncada and Stimson came to terms, agreeing to keep Diaz in power while providing for mutual disarmament and the inclusion of Liberal politicians in the government. American forces had the responsibility of insuring the disarmament and securing the countryside.

One of Moncada's officers, Augusto Cesar Sandino, refused to abide by the terms and launched a counterrevolution of his own. Initially Sandino attempted to gain American support, asking that a U.S. military governor be

The Uncertain Future of the Tank

Another major military development during World War I was the introduction of the tank. In 1914 Lieutenant Colonel Ernest D. Swinton advocated the armoring and arming of tractors as war weapons. The idea found an interested backer at the cabinet level, First Lord of the Admiralty Winston Churchill, who sponsored tests on an armored vehicle by the Royal Navy. The early connection with the British Admiralty resulted in the permanent use of naval terminology for some portions of the vehicle. Likewise, the name "tank" derived from the fact that early armored vehicles sent to the continent for field testing were disguised in cargo manifests as water tanks bound for Russia. Tanks were introduced into combat by the British during the bloody battle of the Somme in 1916. The French and the Germans soon introduced their own vehicles, developed independently of the British model. The first heavy use of tanks occurred at the battle of Cambrai in November 1917, when the British launched a surprise mass attack of the vehicles in an effort to punch a hole in the German trench system. As in the case of so many attacks in World War I, the initial assault succeeded, but the momentum was soon lost. Nevertheless, armored vehicles had shown their worth.

When the American Expeditionary Force arrived on the western front in 1917, it was decided that the Americans would use tanks as well. General John J. Pershing, commander of the AEF, took a leading role in the development of an American tank force, authorizing the creation of 10 heavy tank battalions and 20 light tank battalions. A Tank Service was created under the command of Colonel Samuel D. Rockenbach. Among his officers was George S. Patton, a cavalry officer. Patton saw tanks as an extension of the role of the cavalry. After training at the French tank school at Chaumont, he was put in charge of organizing a tank school at Langres for training Americans in the use of light tanks. Under Patton's command, American tanks went into action for the first time during the St. Mihiel offensive in September 1918, and were successful in the face of light resistance. After the war, the Tank Corps was downsized. It would take World War II to fully prove the value of tanks.

An American 1917 model six-ton tank, closely copied from a 1917 French Renault model, and used through the 1920s in training.

The Colt "Alaskan" revolver, which was used by American forces in the Philippines.

appointed to run the country until free elections could be held, but the Americans refused, and he became determined to resist the occupation. In the meantime, unrest died down and American troop withdrawals began, their place filled by a reorganized and expanding *Guardia Nacional.* Sandino's activities began to expand, gaining support among disaffected liberals and much of the native peasantry. Sandino was badly defeated by American forces on several occasions, and many of his followers deserted him, but he managed to keep just enough of his forces intact to continue, gradually shifting from open confrontation to guerrilla warfare. Americans became divided on the issue of the intervention, with some favoring withdrawal and others urging a new troop buildup. Some additional Marines began to arrive in January 1928, and efforts to catch Sandino intensified. In November, U.S.-supervised elections were held, with Moncada and the Liberal Party achieving victory. Sandino left the country for Mexico in May 1929, and his movement temporarily declined. His return in 1930 sparked the beginning of a new anti-government campaign. By this time, the Great Depression and other troubles both at home and abroad precluded the possibility of a new American troop buildup, and plans began for a full-scale American withdrawal. With Sacasa's election to the Nicaraguan presidency in 1932, the way was paved for the end of the American occupation at the beginning of 1933. Negotiations between Sacasa and Sandino ended tragically, when the latter was kidnapped and murdered on the orders of Anastasio Somoza, commander of the *Guardia Nacional.*

ASIA AND THE PACIFIC

Following the end of World War I, American foreign and economic policy in the Pacific Ocean and Asia continued to be primarily concerned with maintaining an "open door" in China and other Asian markets while curtailing the growing strength of Japan.

The latter nation emerged from the war as the strongest naval power in the western Pacific, taking over Germany's former Pacific colonies and building a series of island bases that made the continuing defense of the Philippines problematic in the event of a war. The Washington Conference and the resulting Five Power Treaty established limitations to Japan's growing military power. A Japanese-backed clause inserted into the treaty, however, represented a setback for American strategic goals. It prohibited the construction or expansion of further bases in the western Pacific, leaving the Japanese with a distinct advantage as it prevented the Americans from responding to Japan's own recently established chain of bases. Two other treaties that emerged from the conference dealt more directly with power relations in the Pacific. In the Nine Power treaty, all of the countries with economic interests in China pledged to uphold its national integrity. The Four Power Treaty involved Great Britain, France, the United States, and Japan in a promise to respect the signatories' possessions in the Pacific.

In the years following the end of the Boxer Rebellion, American troops continued to be stationed in various parts of the Chinese countryside to protect U.S. interests. These included a strong force in Peking (Beijing), while a small flotilla of gunboats patrolled the Yangtze River. Coordination of activities was difficult, however, as the local Army, Navy, and Marine commanders answered to their own superiors, and efforts in the early part of the decade to create a unified force under the leadership of the local Army commander met with failure.

CHINESE WAR

China was marked by political upheaval during the 1910s and 1920s. The Manchu (Qing) Dynasty, which had ruled China since the 17th century, was overthrown in 1911. By 1912 a new government had been formed under of Sun Yat-Sen. Following Sun's death in 1925, a civil war erupted between the government of the Nationalist Party and the Communists.

By 1927 Nationalist forces were marching toward the port city of Shanghai, which included a large foreign enclave called the International Settlement. Although the United States held no direct concessions from China in Shanghai, pressure built upon the administration of Calvin Coolidge to send in forces to protect the city. A Marine regiment was sent to the city to help protect the settlement. In the event, there was no conflict between the Americans and forces of the Chinese government. There were moments of tension, however, between American forces and the various Chinese armies jockeying for local or national control. Sailors and Marines were sometimes put ashore by gunboats to protect various economic interests or foreigners in trouble, and these sometimes (if rarely) resulted in clashes. U.S. infantrymen assigned to guard the railroad network in northern China were caught amidst the conflict between three local warlords. Although there were occasional confrontations between the American soldiers and the warlords' troops, no major violence resulted.

The role of the U.S. military in China and the rest of the world during the 1920s was limited by the goals of American policymakers in the wake of a major conflict that had left much of the nation cynical about international involvement. The emphasis was on a purely defensive strategy and an avoidance of future conflict. Military involvement was limited to goals that had been established long before World War I: enforcement of the Monroe Doctrine and the promotion of economic and political stability in the Caribbean and Latin America; and enforcement of the Open Door policy in China. For most active duty members, it was a relatively quiet time. The continued downsizing of the armed services reflected these goals. As the armed forces demobilized, outdated ships were decommissioned, and postwar budget cuts went into effect, most members of the armed services were confined to life on bases in the United States. Such periods always had their share of tedium for full-time professional soldiers and sailors. Particularly frustrated were ambitious officers such as George S. Patton and Douglas MacArthur, whose dreams of higher rank were thwarted. For them, the Roaring Twenties did not live up to its name. In the 1930s, however, a new set of international tensions would arise, leading to an even more devastating international conflict than the one that had recently ended.

Michael W. Coffey

Further Readings

Blumenson, Martin, ed. *The Patton Papers 1885–1940*. New York: Houghton Mifflin, 1972.

Coffman, Edward M. *The Regulars: The American Army, 1898–1941*. Cambridge, MA: The Belknap Press of Harvard University Press, 2004.

Hurley, Alfred F. *Billy Mitchell: Crusader for Air Power*. New York: Franklin Watts, Inc., 1964.

Lincoln, W. Bruce. *Red Victory: A History of the Russian Civil War*. New York: Simon and Schuster, 1989.

Millett, Allan R. and Peter Maslowski. *For the Common Defense: A Military History of the United States of America*. New York: The Free Press, 1984.

Musicant, Ivan. *The Banana Wars: A History of United States Military Intervention in Latin America*. New York: Macmillan Publishing Co., 1990.

Noble, Dennis L. *The Eagle and the Dragon: The United States Military in China, 1901–1937*. New York: Greenwood Press, 1990.

Roskill, Stephen. *The Period of Anglo-American Antagonism 1919–1929*, vol. 1 of *Naval Policy Between the Wars*. New York: Waller and Company, 1968.

Chapter 14

Population Trends and Migration

"The 'need of expansion' is only another name for overpopulation."
—Margaret Sanger

"HOW YA GONNA Keep 'Em Down on the Farm After They've Seen Paree?" asked a Tin Pan Alley hit in 1919, at the close of World War I. After America's youth had seen so much of the world, how would they ever be happy returning to their humble farms? The question had an implicit value judgment, of course. It implied that the only people who would want to stay "down on the farm" were the ones who did not know any better. This was an increasingly common sentiment among urbanized Americans. Americans had been steadily moving from the country to the city, or making cities out of their small towns, since the Civil War. Even some of the migrations to the frontier had been peculiarly urban in character: when the Oklahoma land runs gave 160-acre lots to whoever got there first, new cities were created literally in an afternoon. Small cities, yes, even by 19th-century standards—but cities nonetheless, with multiple newspapers and a dozen banks, not the "post office and general store surrounded by farms" town that had characterized much of the frontier in years past.

In the 1920s America was a generation or two removed from those land runs, and even more urban in attitude. However the attrition from rural

This group of drug store employees in Washington, D.C., is representative of the trend toward white-collar and service jobs in urban areas in the 1920s.

America was not nearly so extreme as the Tin Pan Alleyist might have supposed, as many of those who left the farm moved up the road a little bit to the small town nearby. Nevertheless, this was the first period in which more Americans lived in cities than in the country. Much of the attrition that did occur owed a good deal to the development and popularization of automobiles, the state and federal construction of the roads to drive them on, and the prosperity that made such things affordable for so many Americans. The service sector began a pattern of steady growth, with banking and insurance in particular expanding and providing entry-level jobs that neither relied on the manual labor of manufacturing or farming, nor required the expensive training and education of the "professions."

Both the automobile and urbanization in general boosted the restaurant industry, as Americans now traveled farther and more often, and were more likely to do so for pleasure. Moreover, fewer of them lived with extended families that might include a grandmother spending the day cooking. Women entered the workforce in record numbers in this decade, leaving fewer of them in the home to cook and clean, which boosted the housekeeping industry nearly as much as the restaurant industry. Considered unsuited for factory or

"Cotton-pickin'"

The adjective "cotton-pickin'" is actually first attested in a Bugs Bunny cartoon, though it seems certain that it must have been in use before then and just failed to make it into print or film. Easier to track is the noun "cotton-picker," which first attained prominence in the 1920s. Though both terms sound like harmless euphemisms now, faux-curses to revert to in lieu of bluer language, they are tied up in the classist and racist feelings of the day.

"Cottonpicker" was probably not a race-specific word at first. It referred to any low, contemptible individual—cotton picking was difficult, painful, back-breaking labor that would be done only by people who could get no other work. Economically healthy societies have always had disdain for people who do unpleasant work, no matter how necessary that work is to the society's prosperity. To call someone a cottonpicker is to call them poor—and to call them poor is to call them ignorant.

That classist terminology soon took a racist turn. Southern whites did not migrate north in the same numbers blacks did. When they migrated, their passage was mostly westward, to seek out new opportunities in the frontier and former frontier, rather than to take up residence in the centers of industry. During the Great Migration, "cottonpicker" began to be used as a slur against blacks, and it is not hard to see how that evolution would occur. If most southerners migrating to an area were black, to denigrate southernness was to denigrate blackness—and vice versa.

Southernness and blackness have long been conflated in northerners' denigration of blacks. Just as foreign immigrants had an aura of "otherness" because of their accents, food, names, and the cultural practices they kept alive in their new homes, blacks relocating in the north differed from their white neighbors in ways that went deeper than skin color. They talked funny. They ate strange parts of the pig, or unfamiliar pickled vegetables. When they could plant, they planted things like okra and collard greens. They had strange words for things, and gave their children strange names or, by contrast, overtly white names (such as those of presidents) that seemed odd. Like the stereotypes of blacks that portray them eating fried chicken from a bucket and giant slices of watermelon, "cotton-pickin'" is an accusation not simply of race but of southernness.

laborer jobs, women mostly took clerical positions or worked in one form or another of customer relations.

Our modern-day white-collar society, in which a significant American middle-class earns a salary at a desk job, began in the prosperous 1920s, and helped enable the creation of the suburbs. Like many things characteristic of modern America, office culture essentially dates to this period. At the beginning of the

century, fewer than a fifth of Americans worked white-collar jobs, many of them in banks and restaurants. Of course, the expansion of government in the 1930s and the desk jobs that it entailed would provide the bigger push here, but the 1920s were the germination period.

Much of the urban growth in 1920s America took place in the cities of what used to be the westernmost bound of civilization—Chicago, St. Louis, Kansas City, all the gateways to the long-gone frontier. This was the fruition of the great push westward in the last third of the 19th century.

THE GREAT MIGRATION

The major trend of internal migration was the first Great Migration, in which from 1910 to 1940, 1.6 million blacks left the south for the rest of the country—sometimes for urban areas, sometimes not. In the late 19th century, when Reconstruction clumsily tried to elevate blacks while at the same time punish southern whites and restore the Union, the backlash against southern blacks was immense. As soon as southern self-governance was restored, that backlash became institutionalized, beginning the period of time historians call "the nadir [lowest point] of American race relations," or sometimes just "the nadir." Blacks had the legal right to vote, but were discouraged by any means possible, both by individuals and by state and local governments. Jim Crow laws were passed to further marginalize them, limit their participation in white society, and just plain punish them, as Reconstruction had punished the whites. White on black violence was accepted as a matter of course, even defended as a legal right of whites, and lynchings in American history reached their peak during the period from the 1890s to the 1920s.

Lynching is key to understanding race relations at the time, because above all, a lynching is a public murder. Rarely were the crimes of which the lynching victims were accused—never mind the question of whether or not they were even guilty—punishable by death in a court of law. Rather, the crimes ranged

Discrimination and Immigration

It appeared to observers that many African Americans had migrated to the north in search of a promised land and in hopes of escaping the oppression of lynching and segregation in the south. Disappointed to find their physical well-being little improved, with unemployment, discrimination, poverty, and bitter winter climates, and cut off from their traditional religious roots, they seemed ready to turn to the promises held out by charismatic leaders such as Marcus Garvey and others.

Other immigrants also faced discrimination and hostility, although as whites, their integration into mainstream American was somewhat easier to accomplish. Nevertheless, for first-generation migrants from southern Europe and the Middle East during this period, hostility and prejudice were commonplace. Like African Americans, the new immigrants tended to seek out enclaves where others from their homelands had taken up residence.

The Immigration Restriction Act of 1924 reflected an effort by Congress to establish immigration quotas that would favor those from the British Isles and northern Europe. Limiting immigration to two percent of the ethnic groups represented in the 1890 census, before the waves of southern Europeans and others had flooded into the United States in the first decade of the 20th century, the law also placed a total immigration cap of 154,000. The quotas allowed for Italians fell from 42,000 to just over 3,800. The law did not apply to countries in the Western Hemisphere, and it did not go into effect until 1929. Nevertheless, the meaning of the law was clear, both to immigrants and native-born citizens—the country had adopted a policy intended to reshape American ethnicity along the lines of 1890, not that of 1910 or 1920.

While much of the Great Migration was to northern cities, some African Americans went west, such as the group that founded the all-black town of Nicodemus, Kansas, shown above in about 1885.

from livestock theft, to vagrancy, to consensual sex with a white woman. Certainly many of those lynched had committed a crime—but instead of being punished as a white criminal would, or compelled to make amends, they were dealt with outside the official system. Sometimes their crimes were exaggerated, but often wronging a white man or sleeping with a white woman was considered perfectly sufficient grounds for death. Very often, the lynching was expected to teach a lesson to other blacks—to show what would and would not be tolerated. The issue was not just one black man sleeping with one white woman—but of tolerating interracial relations.

This family of African-American homesteaders farmed in Nicodemus, Kansas, in an early phase of the Great Migration after Reconstruction.

Black leader Booker T. Washington had said that the best way for black Americans to better their condition was to work hard and make do with what they had until the work paid off. The nadir seemed to prove the opposite—as blacks succeeded, they were driven out of town so that they could not compete with whites. Whether the situation was worst in the south or not, the south was where most blacks were, and therefore where the racism of the day was most likely to be institutionalized. During the rapid westward migrations of the late 19th century, many blacks left the south for the midwest. When segregation was upheld by the Supreme Court at the end of the century and the boll weevil infestation ruined the cotton crop in the teens, the north began looking better and better, and soon enough the Great Migration began, as blacks in record numbers abandoned the south. Most moved to northern cities because they were the easiest to get to—they simply bought their train ticket and traveled to where they could afford to go: Chicago, Philadelphia, New York, Boston, Detroit, Minneapolis, Milwaukee, and Cleveland all saw major increases in their black populations, and the overall black population in the north—even accounting for the rural areas and New England farms that saw little black settlement—rose by 20 percent in the 1920s.

The Nicodemus African Methodist Episcopal Church, photographed in 1983. The town is now a National Historic Site and is still inhabited.

Some companies actively recruited black labor. World War I had caused a boom in northern industry that persisted throughout the 1920s, increasing the demand for labor at a time when the anti-immigration acts of the era cut off the supply of cheap labor in the form of immigrants. As blacks settled and found jobs, they sent word to friends and family back south to join them. In the north, they were not prevented from voting, and the schools available to black children were significantly better than the marginalized schools created by southern segregation.

Northern whites reacted badly to the sudden influx of blacks. While they had long condemned the racism of the south, they had not coexisted with blacks themselves. Northerners bristled at what they perceived as a group of newcomers taking available jobs. But, whether because northerners lacked the resentments of Reconstruction, or because the prosperous decade meant there was less to fight over, overall blacks still found their lot considerably improved by the migration. There was still racial violence, much of it horrific, but the numbers never matched the lynching figures of the nadir, nor was it received so blithely by the public. For the most part, blacks were better able to integrate in the north than they had been in the south.

This family of 27 people were refugees from the Russian civil war and had just arrived in New York City by ship on September 16, 1921.

EUROPEAN IMMIGRATION AND QUOTAS

In the late 19th century, the term "new immigration" came into use to refer to the large numbers of immigrants who were noticeably different than the immigrants of previous decades. "Old immigration" consisted mostly of western and northern Europeans—British, Irish, Germans, French, Scandinavians, immigrants more or less from the countries that had settled this part of the New World to begin with—people with whom Americans had things in common, family ties, language, and cultural background. The new immigrants came from southern and eastern Europe, from Russia, and from Asia. A large number of Chinese immigrated to the United States in the second half of the 19th century, but their numbers were greatly exceeded by the millions of Italians and eastern Europeans. While old immigrants had mostly been Protestant, new European immigrants were mostly Catholic, with a substantial number of Jews from eastern Europe and Russia.

Many of these immigrants settled in the northeast and midwest, the urban centers of the country. A growing number of Americans talked about immigration with alarm, and anti-Catholic sentiments had informed politics since the previous century. Indeed, when the Ku Klux Klan was reformed, it was principally an anti-Catholic organization, more than a racist one. Americans perceived that the large number of immigrants from ethnically, religiously, and culturally different places would disrupt the balance of the country, and feared that they would change its character unfavorably.

After years of lobbying, action was taken. In May 1921, the Johnson Quota Act was passed by Congress, sponsored by Representative Albert Johnson of Washington State. "The United States of America," Johnson said, "a nation great in all things, is ours today. To whom will it belong tomorrow? The United States is our land. If it was not the land of our fathers, at least it may be, and should be, the land of our children. We intend to maintain it so. The day of unalloyed welcome to all people, the day of indiscriminate acceptance of all races, has definitely ended." The United States was explicitly no longer open territory to which all were welcome if they abided by the rules.

The frontier had closed in 1890, precipitating Frederick Jackson Turner's treatise on its formative role in American history and an ongoing discussion among American historians, philosophers, and politicians about the different direction a frontierless America would take. That, in addition to the Great Migration of blacks to the northern cities and the gradual change in the character and "otherness" of immigrants, contributed to the feeling that there was only so much America to go around and that it was time to start rationing. Occurring so soon after the end of World War I, perhaps a rationing mentality was exactly what was at work. Perhaps, too, the devastation of that war and the poor state of affairs that Europe found itself in at its close contributed to the general feelings of suspicion that surrounded these new Europeans. Certainly the socialist revolutions and movements around the world colored Americans' view of people from those parts of the world, even

The Mexican Revolution

Record numbers of Mexicans immigrated to the United States in the 1920s. One of the first large revolutions of the 20th century, the Mexican Revolution (which ended in 1920, with revolts and uprisings continuing throughout the decade) drove at least one million refugees over the border. Many of them sought only temporary shelter, while others remained permanently. Nearly half a million Mexican immigrants were recorded in the 1920s. Because of poor record-keeping—compared to the main processing center at Ellis Island—and the ease of unrecorded immigration, the real numbers were probably much higher, perhaps as high as two million.

Most of these Mexicans settled near the border of their native country, or elsewhere in Texas and the southwest, where there were already substantial Mexican-American populations, Spanish speakers, and in some cases, existing family ties. After the Great Depression, 100,000 or more Mexicans returned to Mexico, where the political situation had calmed down and the economic prospects were no worse than in America.

Anti-Catholicism

Though it would be wrong to call the United States a Protestant country or even a country of Protestant origins, it was certainly a country of Protestant founders. For many Americans in the 19th and 20th centuries, the insistence of those founders on a separation of church and state and the guaranteed freedom of religion made the country culturally Protestant. Because Catholic church leaders had been so instrumental in European politics for so long—because the Pope had for so long been seen as a figure more powerful than any monarch or other worldly leader—the American exclusion of religious institutions from political power was seen as directly at odds with Catholicism. Clearly this is not true. For one thing, there was as strong a relationship between church and state in Lutheran Prussia and Anglican England. For another, Catholics in American government are as capable of ignoring clerical attempts to influence them as Protestants are; if Catholicism was more involved in European politics than Protestant denominations were, it was only because it had had the time to be so involved. Regardless, it was easy to sow seeds of anti-Catholic sentiment in the United States. In the colonial era, there were a number of anti-Catholic laws in order to preserve the essentially Protestant nature of American faith at the time. The nativist movement was responsible for mob attacks, house burnings, and the founding of the mid-19th century Know-Nothing Party, but despite the active resistance to the Catholic influx, by 1900 the nation was about one-sixth Catholic. Immigration was responsible for much of this, but so too were the acquisitions of territory once controlled by Catholic Spain and France.

Presidents who met with the Pope faced criticism for doing so. As late as the 1960s, it was speculated that John F. Kennedy's campaign was doomed to failure because of his Catholicism—and indeed he remains the only Catholic president. Because anti-Catholic sentiments can be couched in terms of criticizing the worldly institution of the Catholic Church, anti-Catholic bigotry—that is, discrimination of Catholic individuals because of their Catholicism, as opposed to simply and directly criticizing specific actions of the Catholic Church—has often managed to thrive among people and communities who are otherwise tolerant of race, ethnicity, and freedom of religion. In the 19th and 20th centuries, Protestants widely mocked Catholics for the practices that differ so deeply from Protestants': the veneration of saints and the Virgin Mary, the sacrament of confession, the celibacy of priests, and the existence of the Pope. Catholicism was portrayed as primitive, uncivilized, superstitious, ritualistic rather than literate, hot-blooded rather than rational. Urban legends spread widely, claiming sexual abuse of parishioners and kidnapped children—long before the current spate of sex abuse scandals—and of dark rituals. Indeed, many conflated Catholicism with Satan worship. Over time, anti-Catholicism dampened, thanks in part to Kennedy's popularity, as well as the inclusion of Irish- and Italian-Americans in politics.

when the immigrants were fleeing those socialists, as in the case of many of the Mexican immigrants, and later the Cubans.

It is important to note that this was also called the Emergency Quota Act, and that is exactly how it was treated, as an emergency that had to be dealt with immediately, a flood that had to be stopped before it was too late. While there have been many discussions about illegal immigration in recent years, what was dealt with here was legal immigration—immigration of a sort that had traditionally been welcomed and depended on.

The act limited the number of immigrants who would be allowed into the United States each year, according to their country of origin. Professionals—doctors, lawyers, teachers, and the like—were exempt from the quotas, but otherwise the number of immigrants admitted from any given country would be limited to three percent of the number of Americans from that country as recorded in the 1910 census. In determining who would be allowed the spaces allocated by those quotas, preference was given to relatives of existing Americans so that cousins, grandparents, spouses, and so on, could join those who had already made a new life in America. The goal, in other words, was to more or less preserve the ethnic balance of the United States, to freeze it in place (although truly freezing it would depend on making sure immigrants continued to arrive from desirable countries like Great Britain and France, or undesirable Czechs and Poles would still tip the scales). The vote in the House of Representatives was not recorded, but was probably not substantially different from the vote in the Senate, which passed the bill with only one vote against.

This proved too wide a sieve for Americans. The Johnson-Reed Act, also known as the National Origins Act, was enacted in 1924 in order to refine the exclusionary system. That three percent in the 1921 act was reduced to two percent. Instead of the 1910 census, the 1890 census was used to establish the figures upon which that two percent would be based, which meant not only deriving a quota based on a smaller portion of a smaller population, but deriving it based on a population that much more closely resembled the "old immigration" Americans. Exempt from the quotas were spouses and children of U.S. citizens if they were under 18; if they were over 18, they were merely given preference. Skilled farmers were given preference, along with their families if they immigrated together.

The Johnson-Reed Act included a number of wrinkles that the Johnson Act had not. Any immigrant who was ineligible to become a naturalized citizen—which meant that Asians were excluded entirely, and indeed the Japanese—was the primary target of those provisions. Unlike previous exclusionary acts, the Johnson-Reed Act did not have to be renewed; it was intended as a permanent law, and remained unchanged for 41 years. The numbers of immigrants from Italy dwindled from 200,000 a year to 4,000. Eastern European immigration trickled virtually to a halt, compared to the large waves of eastern European Jews fleeing pogroms, who had come to America after 1890.

In 1927, the Johnson-Reed Act was slightly modified. In response to pressure from business owners who needed cheap labor sources, and eastern European–American groups, Congress changed the census used to determine quotas from 1890 to 1920. Regardless, the major wave of immigration had ended.

CONCLUSION

While one population trend after World War I had originated in native-born Americans' search for jobs and opportunities in urban, rather than rural, areas, the other two great trends in migration in the United States in the era had darker origins. Both the Great Migration of African Americans to the north and the end of the massive waves of immigration had been caused or shaped by blatant racism and hostility toward foreigners. It would take time for southern and eastern Europeans to become accepted, and the discrimination against them would only be replaced by fears of other groups. Meanwhile, both African Americans and new immigrants went about building their mostly urban communities and continuing their own pursuit of jobs and opportunities in America.

Bill Kte'pi

Further Readings

Alexander, Michael. *Jazz Age Jews*. New York: Princeton University Press, 2003.

Arnesen, Eric. *Black Protest and the Great Migration: A Brief History with Documents*. New York: St. Martin's, 2002.

Grossman, James. *Land of Hope: Chicago, Black Southerners, and the Great Migration*. Chicago, IL: University of Chicago Press, 1991.

Jackson, Kenneth T. *The Ku Klux Klan in the City, 1915–1930*. New York: Oxford University Press, 1967.

Kyvig, David. *Daily Life in the United States, 1920–1940: How Americans Lived Through The Roaring Twenties and the Great Depression*. New York: Ivan R. Dee, 2004.

Lemann, Nicholas. *The Promised Land: The Great Black Migration and How It Changed America*. New York: Vintage, 1992.

Lemay, Michael, and Elliott Robert Barkan, eds. *U.S. Immigration and Naturalization Laws and Issues: A Documentary History*. Westport, CT: Greenwood Press, 1999.

Lescott-Leszczynski, John. *The History of U.S. Ethnic Policy and Its Impact on European Ethnics*. New York: Westview Press, 1984.

McCaffrey, Lawrence. *The Irish Catholic Diaspora in America*. Washington, D.C.: Catholic University of America Press, 1998.

McWhiney, Grady. *Cracker Culture: Celtic Ways in The Old South*. Tuscaloosa, AL: University of Alabama Press, 1989.

Meager, Timothy. *Inventing Irish America: Generation, Class, and Ethnic Identity in a New England City, 1880–1928*. South Bend, IN: University of Notre Dame Press, 2000.

Merwin, Ted. *In Their Own Image: New York Jews in Jazz Age Popular Culture*. New Brunswick, NJ: Rutgers University Press, 2006.

Scott, Emmett J. *Negro Migration During The War*. New York: Arno Press, 1969.

Sernett, Milton. *Bound For The Promised Land: African American Religion And The Great Migration*. Durham, NC: Duke University Press, 1997.

Zeitz, Joshua. *Flapper: A Madcap Story of Sex, Style, Celebrity, and the Women Who Made America Modern*. New York: Three Rivers Press, 2007.

Zolberg, Aristide. *A Nation by Design*. New York: Russell Sage Foundation, 2006.

Chapter 15

Transportation

"When once you have tasted flight,
you will forever walk the earth
with your eyes turned skyward."
—Anonymous

THE DECADE OF the 1920s was the period when America became a mass society. The decade did "roar" when it came to artifacts (material objects), mentifacts (thoughts and words) and sociofacts (institutions and processes that form society). The culmination of the mass production/assembly line approach was carried over to all industries as interchangeable parts became part of industrial production, while industrial production replaced agricultural production as the mainstay of the economy. The scientific management approach to business supported the investment of millions of dollars into research to streamline production and increase efficiency and productivity. In part this was a response to World War I, which had increased spending on industry. Modern appliances such as vacuum cleaners, washing machines, toasters, refrigerators, irons, and even the party line for telephones became part of life for all segments of society. Cars were central to consumer buying, as car production rose from 2 to 5.5 million from 1920 to 1929. The consumer revolution hit the country as people began to pay on installment and on layaway, especially for cars. About 75 percent of all automobile purchases were on the installment plan.

Sociofacts altered as political participation increased with votes for women. Economic participation also increased as consumers could use credit through layaway. Marketing and advertising became facets of American life.

A 1928 Star automobile. The Star Car was a short-lived brand built in the 1920s in an attempt to compete with the Ford Model T.

Women, at least in some cities, were seen smoking and drinking (if illegally), wore lipstick, and raised their hems. People paid lip service to Victorian morality, which they characterized as pre-Freudian. Yet fundamentally the country remained conservative as evangelicals made a comeback. Nativism revived with the limitations on immigration in 1921 and 1924 through a quota system that favored the composition of the people resident in 1890 and gave the edge to people from northern and western Europe. America was exhausted by World War I and the flu pandemic. A desire for normalcy took precedence over idealism, particularly as a number of the reforms that had been on the progressive agenda had already been enacted. The last gasp of progressivism as a political movement came in a failed presidential party attempt in 1924. African Americans felt alarmed by the revival of the Ku Klux Klan and supported the ultimately abortive "back to Africa" movement of Marcus Garvey.

Mentifacts changed as radio, film, records, and mass circulation magazines made their appearance as part of American culture and the purveyors of contemporary trends. Franchise sports such as baseball, football, and later basketball and jazz came to be viewed as characteristic of American life. Sports and popular music became integral to popular American culture.

As the country went from rural to urban and suburban according to the 1920 Census, transportation became ever more important as it became tied to the urban way of life. Access to the variety of services as well as economic, social, and leisure activities in a metropolitan area via transportation was all-important. In this aspect, the automotive revolution, which produced vehicles

The Great Ocean Liners

The competition among ocean liners for the "blue riband" as a symbol of the fastest crossing was a device for publicity and for maintaining interest in shipping. Speed records for the ocean crossing had been meticulously maintained since 1838. The record set by British Cunard liner *Mauretania* in 1909, at 26.06 knots for an Atlantic crossing, was not surpassed until 1929 by the German liner *Bremen* at 27.83 knots, so through the 1920s, travelers could expect to cross the Atlantic at better than 20 knots, resulting in a five-day trip from Queenstown in Ireland to New York. Ocean liners continued to reflect the class structure, with first, second, and third class accommodations. Third class was quite economical and provided the means for the great waves of immigration through the first decades of the 20th century.

Until the outbreak of World War I, most shipping lines had relied on emigration for revenue, and they all suffered setbacks, first with the war, and then when Congress passed the Immigration Restriction Acts of 1921 and 1924. As a consequence, some of the transatlantic lines reduced their schedules, rerouted ships to less expensive runs, or experimented with "cruises," carrying passengers on vacation trips to a variety of destination ports. Less expensive cabins on some liners were refitted to "tourist class." Furthermore, the prohibition of alcohol aboard U.S. ships put American-registered ocean liners at a competitive disadvantage, and British and French lines tended to dominate the transatlantic routes in the 1920s. Ships of those lines would close the bars and wine cellars as they approached the 12-mi. limit off the American coast. W.A. Harriman, who owned several ships, transferred the registry of two of them to Panama in this period to avoid the effect of the Prohibition laws.

Even with these issues, and with the loss of the *Titanic* on April 14, 1912, after a collision with an iceberg, and the torpedoing of the *Lusitania* on May 7, 1915, enthusiasm for ocean liner travel remained high. In the 1920s regularly scheduled lines left the United States for Europe, Latin America, Hawaii, and the Far East. The newer liners of the era reflected the current fad for art deco design, led by the French. Some of the greatest art deco artifacts and designs were found aboard such liners as *Ile de France*, launched in 1926. Other ships followed the pattern, as art deco, echoing the modernism of the machine age, seemed well suited to the mechanical marvel of the great ocean liners. This trend reached its culmination in the 1930s with the launching of the *Normandie* in 1932, and the *Queen Mary* in 1936.

Through the 1920s, the only means of transatlantic crossing remained ship travel, as regular passenger air crossings by dirigible and large sea plane did not begin until the 1930s.

Seven women known as Sennett Bathing Beauties posed on a car for a film by Mack Sennett, whose slapstick comedies featured wild car chases.

Cars and Youth Culture

Although cars permeated culture, they had a special attraction for youth. Cars often gave the impression of youth and speed, mixed with sex appeal. It was a part of an emerging national culture that emphasized youthful music (jazz/swing), youth-oriented films (*Six Cylinder Love*), and architecture (art deco). Contemporary surveys of college life found that car terminology affected slang. Students referred to unpopular girls as "fat tires" or "tin cans." During the 1920s, films on college life were quite common with automobiles and motorcycles often playing a key role. The "keystone cop" series with comic policemen and equally comic car chases also appealed to a youthful sensibility.

Since young people could drive at age 16, the fascination with automobiles was understandable. What was unexpected was the influence of cars on children. By the 1920s, over 20 books had been written for children about the Motor Boys, who traveled the world in various automotive vehicles—motorcycles, powerboats, cars, even the then novel flying machines. Their rivals, called the Noddy Noxious, also traveled in various motor conveyances. Soon there were other serials, such as the Auto Boys. Not to be outdone, girls had a series of books called the Automobile Girls, the Motor Girls, and the Motor Maids. In line with the increasing democratization of automobile ownership, the protagonists progressed from originally upper-class families to characters from all backgrounds. The Roaring Twenties were based on the "roar" of the car or motorcycle, and youth responded to the siren song.

that ran on cheap energy, and the development of paved roads and highways to serve this newly-dominant form of transportation, became the critical factors determining where people chose to live.

ROAD TRANSPORTATION

Various aspects of American life in the 1920s were affected by the emergence of automotive culture. By the end of the decade, the number of Americans who owned cars, buses, and trucks had reached 26.5 million. Taking into consideration the under-16 population and extrapolating for those few who owned buses and trucks only, this is a better than one in five figure. By this period, America produced 85 percent of all automotive vehicles. Directly or indirectly, car-related production was an increasingly important part of the economy. Over 500,000 people were directly employed by the automotive industry. The largest car manufacturing company, General Motors, kept adding to its models with new cars such as the Dodge, DeSoto, and Plymouth. It also added new brands such as Oldsmobile to its family of cars so that by the mid-1920s, it competed with U.S. Steel and Standard Oil of New Jersey (later ESSO and now EXXON), for the role of largest industrial corporation in the world.

Indirectly, the automobile companies had a multiplier effect on the overall economy, because they provided a market for other suppliers. The automotive sector purchased 20 percent of all steel, 25 percent of machine tools, 75 percent of glass, 80 percent of rubber, and 90 percent of petroleum (oil and gas) products. In all more than 1.2 million people were employed in these areas. The ripple effect went beyond basic supplies. Related industries such as gas stations, repair shops, dealerships, auto parts stores, used car lots, roadside restaurants and food outlets gave employment to hundreds of thousands of people. In all, close to three million people depended on the automotive industry for their livelihood.

Human ecology continued to be influenced by the automotive boom. More people moved to the fast-growing suburbs, which residents found to be more convenient places to live. With more cars available and extremely cheap gas and oil, people found it even more feasible to go back and forth between city and suburb.

There were other consequences of the revolution in car-making. There was a new impetus to road construction as cars became universal, and as laws such as the Highway Act of 1921 were implemented. Paved roads more than doubled while the population increased only 16 percent. With traffic fatalities and accidents rising at an alarming rate, safety measures were instituted. Traffic signs and traffic lights soon littered the rural and urban landscape. Speed limits were introduced, followed by one-way streets in the cities to cut down on the ever increasing congestion. Commercially, both parking lots and driving schools made their appearance. Insurance now became a requirement for licenses and vehicle registration. On a positive note, innovations occurred to make driving safer: hydraulic brakes (1920), safety glass and windshield wipers (1926), antifreeze for all automotive vehicles (also 1926), and four-wheel drive (1929). The American Automobile Association (AAA) became even more influential because it supported the first Rand McNally national atlas in 1924, which detailed the emerging state and federal highway system.

Car consciousness swept throughout the nation. Almost every aspect of popular culture appeared affected. Automobile scenes routinely showed up in pictures published by mass magazines and newspapers, particularly in newly fashionable periodicals such as the *Saturday Evening Post*. Auto motifs found their way into comic strips such as *Gasoline Alley*. Cars even appeared in popular novels such as *The Great Gatsby*, where they functioned as plot devices. Cars were identified with loose behavior in films where characters were described as "fast." Automobile jargon even found its way into everyday language. "Drive" went far beyond car usage. "Let's take a spin" became a common phrase, and a luxury car, the Duesenberg, gave birth to the expression "it's a doozy."

The new fields of advertising and marketing were used for mass mobilization as automotive companies advertised on radio, in movie theaters, and in print media. No outlet was neglected; advertisements for products appeared on the sides of buses and in subways. When highways such as the famous Route 66 (which opened in 1926 and stretched from Chicago to Santa Monica—a distance of nearly 2,500 miles) opened, a new, very American form of advertising appeared on the road: the billboard. Travelers at regular intervals would see advertisements on these signs for accommodations, gas, food, and other information. It was estimated that the information on a billboard could be viewed within 18 seconds at 35 mph.

The wooden spokes on this wheel from a "tin can camper" evoke earlier wagon wheels.

There were other economic developments as well. As roadside restaurants proliferated, lodges for sleepovers also opened. Ultimately, they amalgamated and the motor hotel or motel was born. For those road travelers who could not afford motels, there were auto courts—the predecessor to the trailer court—where people could sleep in their vehicles or nearby cabins at night. Within a few years, these auto courts and trailer courts would furnish running water and laundry services. City and town businesses also established

"Tin can campers" like this were early incarnations of travel campers. They were developed as families became able to vacation at such attractions as Yellowstone National Park.

drive-in restaurants and laundries with drive-in facilities. The first drive-in movie did not appear until 1933.

During this decade, the road now became accessible to motor vehicles. As a result new practices appeared. One of the more dubious was hitchhiking. Another one was parking. Young men and women would now "park" without chaperones and the backseat or rumble seat became a prized object as men and women began to "double-date." Soon lover's lanes with parked cars became quite common, much to the chagrin of law enforcement officers.

Buses served as conduits of both sports and recreation. Emerging sports franchises in baseball and football would now travel by bus to have games on the "road" against other teams. Big time bands with band leaders and crooners made famous by records and radio would tour by both rail and road, as did theatrical companies. Summer stock productions often called "bus" tours would present summer offerings of Broadway productions. Movie stars and opera stars would also tour and take the train or bus depending on the budget.

Truck-like vehicles called trailers were used by families during summers and holidays in national parks. Yellowstone National Park went from 52,000 visitors to 228,000 visitors between 1917 and 1929. Recognizing the inevitable, railroads teamed up with Fred Harvey of "Harvey Girls" fame, who had hotels and restaurants throughout the line of rail in the Southwest to entice travelers to take the train to Native-American reservations. Once there, they could take a three-day trip to Taos, New Mexico, by motor, and then hire a car with chauffeur to tour the *pueblo*. Not everyone could afford these arrangements, however, so less affluent people would take the bus. By this period car races had become a national pastime as a spectator sport. Then as now, the Indianapolis Speedway with its 500-mi. race on Memorial Day was a national institution made even more famous by radio and film shorts.

Nonetheless, the car market was becoming segmented. From the beginning, luxury cars had been available for the wealthy. Pierce Arrows, Rolls-Royces, Bentleys, and Mercedes-Benzes became quite common. Not to be outdone on this potentially lucrative market and recognizing the status symbol possibilities, domestic producers began producing luxury cars. In addition to the Cadillac, limousines made their appearance. By the late 1920s, the Lincoln Continental had made its debut and had joined the Duesenberg as a long-lasting American-made prestige car.

THE ADVENT OF THE TRUCK

In contrast to other automotive vehicles (the luxury cars and elaborate touring buses), trucks basically remained work vehicles. With pneumatic tires and smoother roads, trucks encroached upon rail and water freight traffic. Businesses might be located far away from rail depots or rivers, but a truck could go anywhere, especially on the rapidly growing roads and highways. Unlike rail and water, trucks could offer door-to-door delivery. Small businesses such as florists and bakeries soon made truck deliveries a major part of their operations. Large businesses saw their mail-order units boom. It was because truckers were becoming reliable customers that truck stops along highways that offered food, gas, and rest stops for the long-distance hauler came into existence on highways, as did truckline cafes along roads. Independent "gypsy" truckers began making a living by delivering goods.

Public services became almost entirely dependent on automotive vehicles. In addition to the use of such vehicles in municipal sanitation, fire, police, street cleaning, snow removal, and medical services, buses, cars, and trucks reduced the isolation of people in small towns and rural areas. The country doctor was not quite as essential, as a local consolidated clinic could be within driving distance. Obviously, the availability of automobile transportation made it less of a hindrance for medical personnel to set up practices and see patients in their homes. Much the same could be said for teachers. With paved roads and automotive vehicles, better teachers would be more eager to go to a rural area. The institution of the consolidated school and the school bus meant that there would be no shortchanging school children. The same held true for consolidated libraries and bookmobiles. In general, professionals of all occupations no longer felt as reluctant to locate outside of a big city. Agricultural agents could reach the most remote farmstead to give advice on farming. Even traveling salespeople found their careers easier with road and

The Ben Franklin Bridge carries traffic across the Delaware River. When it was finished in 1926, it was the world's longest suspension bridge.

auto access, as did potential customers who could get a demonstration of new products. Mailmen in mail trucks in conjunction with rural free delivery also felt the benefits of the change.

Sadly, there was a downside to the triumph of the car and other automotive vehicles. By 1930, approximately 32,500 people had died in auto-related accidents. Prohibition's failure led to drunk driving, which increased the incidence of accidents. Gangsters also made use of cars to rob banks and make fast getaways. On balance, though, most people took a positive view of the car, apart from a few clergymen who deplored its influence on young people. In *Middletown,* a famous sociological study undertaken in Muncie, Indiana, during the 1920s, people were interviewed about the possession of a car. No matter what their class, the car received the highest priority. One woman put it above clothes, while another put it above food. It was now as essential to many people as air and water.

RAIL AND WATER TRANSPORTATION

Rail transportation during this decade saw its dominance decline. It had peaked during the war because it was an essential supplier for the war effort under the War Mobilization Board. Thereafter a slow decline began. Whereas there were 254,000 rail miles just before 1920, by 1930 rail miles had decreased to

249,000. During the same period, railroad employment shrank from over two million to a little over 1.5 million in 1930. The slow decline was reflected in freight carrying numbers, which fell from 413 billion tons to 385 billion tons per year. Passenger traffic also decreased by approximately four percent during the decade. The railroads fought against this fall-off by giving the federal government a 50 percent discount for its business. However, even much of this was threatened in the mid-1920s when newly functional airplanes began to receive more federal contracts.

To combat the reductions in quantity, trains sought to attract upscale customers through upgrading the locomotives and initiating the replacement of some of the steam engines with diesels at the very end of the decade (this became common from the late 1930s onward). These engines were less expensive and speedier. The forerunner of this in the 1920s was the sleek locomotive. It had a trim look and was fashioned in the newly-popular art deco style, combining machinery with artistic motifs. These streamlined and speedy locomotives came to be called "streamliners" by the end of the decade, and they had names like Twentieth Century Limited and Zephyr. Over time, these trains reached speeds of 80 mph. Subways, which now sped to and from the continually growing suburbs, had their equivalent in express trains as well.

The decline in water transportation varied. Canals were the hardest hit because much of their barge traffic now went to trucks, which could function in all seasons. To a lesser extent, river traffic and Great Lakes traffic also suffered, although some of the slack was taken up by petroleum tankers that supplied fossil fuel. Fossil fuel was rapidly replacing

As train traffic declined in the 1920s, train companies sought to appeal to more customers by upgrading locomotives and railroad cars like this one.

This early 20th-century railroad station, complete with waiting room, ticket office, and freight room, is preserved at the Railroad Museum of Pennsylvania.

coal as both a fuel and energy source. Gulf ports soon compensated through the oil and gas business so that by 1930, Lake Charles, Baton Rouge, and especially New Orleans, Louisiana, were among the largest ports in the country. Other large ports included Houston, Corpus Christi, and Port Arthur, Texas; Tampa, Florida; Mobile, Alabama; and Biloxi-Gulfport, Mississippi. Riverboats still plied the Mississippi, but to progressively less business, as touring and summer stock entertainment, along with the radio, records, and film, cut into their customer base. Only cruises along the river remained popular.

Recreation led to one area of increase especially in the west. The Colorado, Columbia, and Snake rivers were soon the scene of holiday travel, including adventure sports as people "shot" the rapids. The inland waterway from Seattle to peninsular Alaska also proved popular.

Schooners continued to be popular for coastal traffic and ocean liners continued to be the fastest non-military form of transport (being able to cross the Atlantic in five days, for instance). The military transportation importance of oceangoing ships in wars, which had led to the development of American-owned liners after World War I, continued to ensure the survival of Navy yards such as that in Philadelphia, Pennsylvania; Coast Guard training at Groton, Connecticut; and marine training facilities at Quantico, Virginia. The oil tanker business also was a plus for coastal and ocean traffic.

AIR TRANSPORTATION

The other major transportation development (in addition to the triumph of the automotive vehicle) affecting life in America during the 1920s was the arrival of air travel as a mainstream option for travel. Between 1903 and 1925, air travel went through three stages: mail, cargo, and passenger. Until the 1920s the basic function of airplanes was carrying mail. Although its role in military operations had shown potential in World War I, air travel continued to be looked on as merely a curiosity until the mid-1920s, when a combination of technological breakthroughs, enabling legislation, and financial backing allowed it to break through as a realistic option for travel and transportation.

In 1927, only 46,000 lbs. had been shipped by air by cargo and freight planes. By 1929 this had ballooned to 2.3 million lbs. per year. Even more impressive was American Railway Express, backed by Henry Ford, which carried both mail and freight loads of up to three million lbs. by 1929. National Air Transport, which later became one of the units of United Airlines, was the first airline in 1926 to contractually fly freight as well as mail from Dallas

Airmail Routes in the United States, 1927

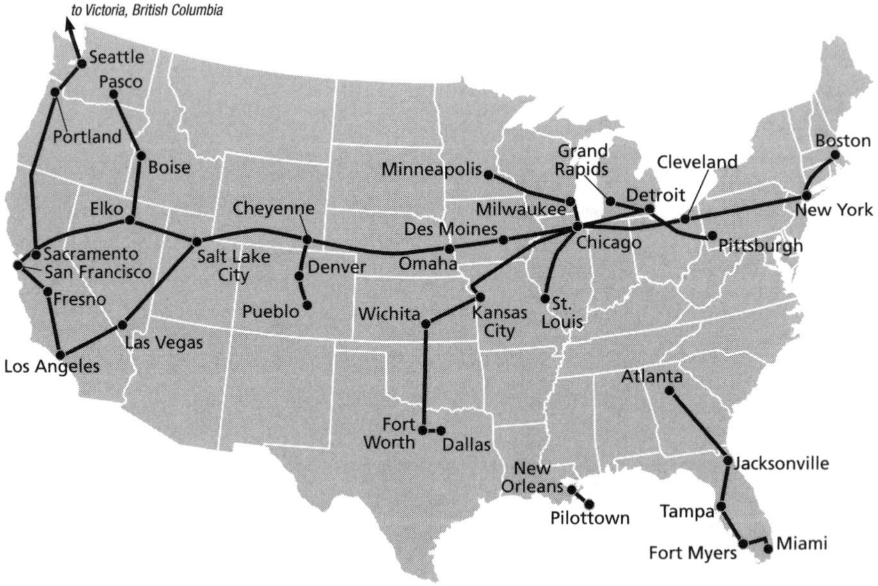

Note: The first U.S. airmail flight took off in 1918. By 1927 mail was flown on 24 major routes. To beat the trains, mail planes had to fly at night and in all weather, which led to the development of instruments that made flights more reliable. Airmail service also accelerated the development of air routes, airports, and navigation systems.

Source: Historical Atlas of the United States, Centennial Edition. Washington, D.C.: The National Geographic Society, 1988

to New York on a nationwide basis. It joined with American Railway Express and was renamed Railway Express (so as to encompass international aspirations). However, it could never be a real competitor with trains or even water transport for bulk mail. Nevertheless the development of the DC-3 (Douglas) engine combined with an enclosed and pressurized air cabin cut the cost of flying, increased speed, and made travel more bearable for passengers. By the end of the 1920s, planes such as the Ford Trimotor as well as a variant, the 5AT, and Boeing's Model 80, both of which were introduced in 1928, could carry a limited number of passengers through the use of these engines.

Two pieces of legislation proved crucial in the establishment of the air industry. The 1925 Air Mail Act gave exclusive mail contracts to airlines and permitted the hiring of private air carriers to deliver the mail. The guarantee of these contracts gave a basis for the survival and consolidation of airlines such as American, United, and TWA. With the money from the mail contract, the airlines could develop better equipment, train personnel, travel by night, and cultivate popular patronage. With both cargo and mail patronage, 33 companies were operating, with 23 carrying mail and cargo, while 10 others were also carrying passengers by 1929. Altogether 10 million mi. were racked up in 1928 and 1929. By 1929, cargo planes flew 125 mph, passenger planes 150 mph, and mail planes 175 mph for regular and express mail.

The crucial piece of legislation for the development of air passenger transportation and travel was the Air Commerce Act (Kelly Act) of 1926, which created regulations for licensing pilots, as well as for all airline flying. It established supervision of airlines under the Department of Commerce (later under the Department of Transportation) under an aeronautics branch (later the Civil Aeronautic Board). The CAB, as it came to be called, created and awarded air routes, set up lighting beams for air strips and airports, equipped airways and airlines for night flying, and reinforced the new radar communications.

In response, airlines embarked upon a campaign to enlist new passengers and keep old ones in a mode of transportation previously geared toward mail and freight. By 1928, American, United, Pan-American, and TWA had initiated passenger flights. Pan-American had begun international flights to Latin America, especially the Caribbean via Miami. By that year, airlines flew nearly 53,000 passengers, nearly four and a half times the number from the previous year. The price worked out at about 10 cents a mile.

Nevertheless, the emergence of the airlines as a successful competitor to railroads in long distance travel still faced obstacles as the decade ended. The airplane models considered the most advanced of the time still had drawbacks. Usually, they could not accommodate more than 20 passengers at a time. The Ford Trimotor and the 5AT had no air conditioning and no air circulation. It was cold in winter and hot in summer; windows had to be opened to get fresh air. This constituted a danger of its own. The Boeing 80 did have forced air ventilation along with hot and cold running water. Nonetheless, planes were limited in their scope. Since planes were not yet able to fly at an altitude high enough to avoid turbulence, passengers experienced airsickness.

To reassure passengers, in 1926 airlines began to hire male stewards who also tended luggage and helped people get around the air cabins. In some cases, the co-pilot was made to tend to passengers, serve food or beverages, and reissue tickets for cancelled or delayed flights. His main job was also to reassure the passengers during turbulence. By 1928, stewards were required to have extensive first aid as well as seamanship training in order to cope with emergency landings on water.

The evolution of the airline industry in the 1920s is representative of American industry's move toward streamlining tasks and increasing efficiency through scientific management. New technology and processes changed not just the means of transportation, but the running of national transport businesses. The growth of highways, long-distance trucking, and airlines, as well as the survival of older rail and water transport, eventually brought improved access to manufactured goods, fresh foods, and rapid communication. These changes occurred behind the scenes, however, compared to the dramatic transformation the automobile wrought on American culture and daily life in the 20th century.

NORMAN C. ROTHMAN

Further Readings

Bourne, Russell. *Americans on the Move.* Golden, CO: Fulcrum, 1995.

Coffey, Frank et. al. *America on Wheels: The First Hundred Years.* New York: General Publishing Group, 1996.

Finch, Christopher. *Highways to Heaven: The Auto Biography of America.* New York: HarperCollins, 1992.

Flink, James J. *The Car Culture.* Cambridge, MA: MIT Press, 1975.

Goddard, Stephen B. *Getting There: The Epic Struggle between Road and Rail in the American Century.* New York: Basic Books, 1994.

McNally, Bruce. *Model T Ford: The Car that Changed the World.* Osceola, WI: Motorbooks Publishing, 1994.

Mowry, George. *The Twenties: Fords, Flappers and Fanatics.* Englewood Cliffs, NJ: Prentice-Hall, 1963.

Rae, John B. *The Road and Car in American Life.* Cambridge, MA: MIT Press, 1971.

Sandler, Martin W. *This Was America.* Boston, MA: Little, Brown, 1980.

———. *Flying Over America: Airplanes in American Life.* New York: Oxford University Press, 2004.

Taaffe, Edward and Howard L. Gauthier. *Geography of Transportation.* New York: Prentice Hall, 1973.

Chapter 16

Public Health, Medicine, and Nutrition

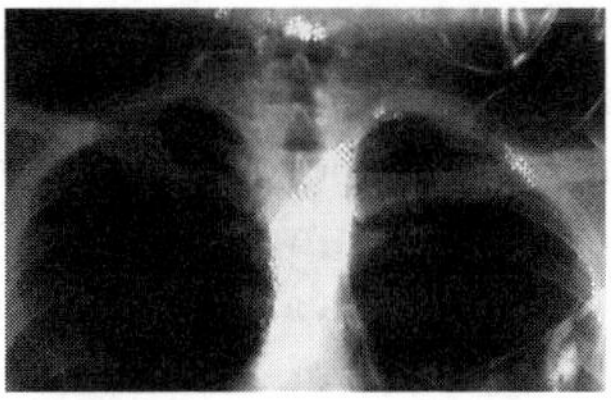

"My own experience has been that the tools I need . . . are paper, tobacco, food, and a little whiskey."
—William Faulkner

THE DECADE OF the 1920s was a boom time in the United States, and lifestyles improved accordingly. Important advances were made in public health, medicine, and nutrition, and fears over most communicable diseases faded in response to widespread vaccination programs. Better health coupled with increasing knowledge of sanitation and nutrition made day-to-day living safer and more pleasant for most Americans. In the 1920s physicians were receiving better training than in the past. Armed with the knowledge needed to deal with a wide variety of conditions and diseases, preventive medicine was emphasized. By 1920 the number of hospitals in the United States had grown to more than 6,000. Children were viewed as unique individuals with needs different from those of adults, and social programs were instituted to protect children and ensure their well being. In 1923 Congress approved an amendment outlawing child labor in the United States. Although the amendment was never ratified, legislation at the federal and state level subsequently placed restrictions on the employment of children.

Between 1900 and 1920 the death rate in the United States dropped from 19 deaths per 1,000 to 14 per 1,000. Life expectancy, which had stood at 47 years at the turn of the century, rose to 53.6 years for males and 54.6

for females. Childbirth was safer in the 1920s because of improved prenatal care, and most middle-class women gave birth in hospitals. Improved antiseptics and a greater understanding of how germs were spread decreased the number of infections contracted in hospitals. Physicians washed their hands between treating patients, and surgical instruments were sterilized. The use of X-rays, diagnostic laboratories, and anesthesia made surgery safer and less frightening. Almshouses were established to meet the needs of the poor in response to reform movements that also lobbied for improved public health, conservation, improved housing, and worker safety and rights. Some reformers began insisting that smoking was a major health hazard.

In 1926 Henry Ford set the stage for what would become common practice by establishing an eight-hour a day, five-day workweek. Between 1926 and 1929 the number of Americans with mechanical refrigerators in homes wired for electricity rose from two to nine percent. As a result illnesses from spoiled and tainted food declined. Maintaining clean clothes also became easier as the number of Americans boasting washing machines rose from 21 percent in 1925 to 33 percent in 1929. Governments became more heavily involved in financing schools, libraries, museums, zoos, parks, playgrounds, and summer concerts. Other public services included police and fire protection, sanitary inspections, garbage collection, paved streets and sidewalks, hospitals, asylums for the mentally ill, and relief for the poor.

SOCIAL DIVISIONS

Despite improvements in the overall American standard of living, great disparities in incomes continued to create social divides. In 1924 cultural anthropologists Helen (1894–1982) and Robert (1892–1970) Lynd, the authors of the *Middletown* books that detailed life in middle America, studied families in Muncie, Indiana, to determine the standard of living for a typical American family. The Lynds estimated that a family of five needed $1,920.87 to cover basic living expenses such as rent, food, fuel, clothing, insurance, and union dues. They concluded that 70 to 88 percent of all families in Muncie were unable to provide for these basic necessities. In 1929 a more comprehensive study by the Brookings Institution revealed that 59 percent of all American families were unable to afford the basic necessities that allowed them to live "decently."

Three weeks after the 1920s began, the Eighteenth Amendment took effect. As a result, the prohibition of beverages that contained at least .5 percent alcohol was in full swing throughout the decade. With the outlawing of the beer that was the staple of working-class saloons, and the wines, liquors, and champagnes favored by the upper classes, speakeasies of various sizes flourished throughout the country. In New York City, for example, police reported the existence of at least 32,000 speakeasies. One third of the inmates in federal prisons in 1929 were charged with violating Prohibition laws. The

A collection of soaps and cleansers from the early 20th century. The number of Americans who owned washing machines rose from 21 percent in 1925 to 33 percent in 1929.

restrictions of Prohibition could be bypassed by homegrown cider and wine, and enterprising individuals also discovered that California grape juice transformed into wine after fermenting for 60 days. Consequently, the California wine industry grew 400 percent over the course of the decade. While most small-town Americans viewed Prohibition with equanimity, this was far from true in large cities.

The economic boom of the 1920s ended abruptly on October 29, 1929, on what became known as Black Tuesday, a day on which 10 million shares were sold on the stock market. The Great Depression that followed this stock market crash paved the way for the election of President Franklin Roosevelt (1882–1945) in 1932 and the transformation of the United States into a social welfare state. However, the depression did not officially end until the 1940s when World War II revitalized the American economy and propelled the United States into the position of the leading world power.

DISEASE AND EPIDEMICS

Although vaccinations had virtually eradicated many diseases by the 1920s, epidemics continued to threaten the health of Americans. The peak period for smallpox outbreaks occurred in the United States between 1920 and 1921 when some 200,000 people contracted the disease. Because of a greater understanding of the disease and its ramifications, the death rate in the 1920s was proportionately lower than that in earlier epidemics that had proved so devastating (0.43 percent in 1920 and 0.55 in 1921).

By this time, the federal government had accepted the responsibility for all quarantining activities on the American mainland, the Hawaiian Islands, the Philippines, Puerto Rico, and the Virgin Islands. Ships were now routinely quarantined whenever cholera, typhus, the plague, smallpox, leprosy, or

Poliomyelitis

Poliomyelitis, also known as "infantile paralysis," continued to be a major problem in the United States during the 1920s. Polio is an acute viral infectious disease that is spread through direct contact. It was first identified by German orthopedist Jacob Heine (1800–79) in 1840. Cases of polio had occasionally surfaced over the years, but it was not until the 1880s that polio became epidemic in the United States. At the time, it became evident that the disease was more likely to strike white, affluent individuals, causing researchers to believe that improved sanitation and new standards of cleanliness had prevented many 20th-century Americans from building up natural immunities. The most well known case of polio during the 1920s involved Franklin Roosevelt (1882–1945), who developed symptoms of the disease in 1925 after a swimming outing with his children. Roosevelt was left paralyzed for the rest of his life, and the disease continued to take a heavy toll on his health throughout his years as president of the United States (1932–45). Roosevelt died without finishing his fourth term in office as World War II was drawing to a close.

In approximately 95 percent of all cases, polio appears in its asymptomatic form. Researchers believe that it is this type of polio that was so common in crowded tenements during the early days of the Industrial Revolution that many infants developed immunity to the disease. Three types of symptomatic polio have also been identified. Type 1, also known as abortive polio, is the most common form and is highly contagious. It is characterized by low fever, headache, sore throat, and a general malaise. Many people with this type never know they have contracted polio. If antibiotics are administered, recovery generally occurs within three days. Affected individuals are thereafter immune to the disease. Around one percent of infected individuals develop Type II polio, which may be either paralytic or nonparalytic. Type III, in which the disease reaches the spinal cord and brain, is much more devastating. The deterioration of motor nerve cells may lead to paralysis. In the most severe cases, the deterioration of breathing muscles proves fatal.

In 1952 around 60,000 cases of polio were documented in America, resulting in 3,000 deaths. The disease was not checked until the introduction of a vaccine developed by Jonas Salk (1914–95) in 1955. Today, American children receive four doses of polio vaccine between the ages of two months and six years. Polio was eliminated from the United States in 1979 and from the Western Hemisphere in 1991. In 2006 2,001 cases of polio were reported in developing countries, but international sponsorship of National Immunization Days provides hope for worldwide eradication in the 21st century.

anthrax were suspected. In 1921, for instance, the federal government inspected approximately two million ship passengers and crew on 20,000 separate vessels. At least 5,000 of those ships were fumigated and disinfected. Of 3,986 vessels arriving in the United States from foreign ports, 47 harbored infected individuals. Consequently, 50,000 passengers and crew members were detained and disinfected, and 4,800 were required to be vaccinated or to undergo bacteriological examinations.

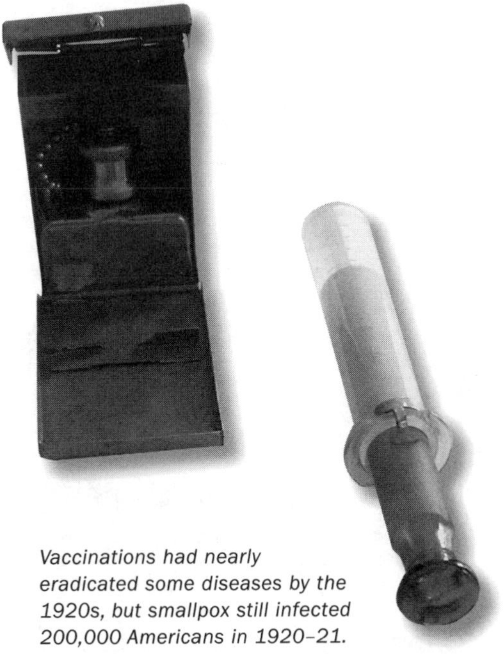

Vaccinations had nearly eradicated some diseases by the 1920s, but smallpox still infected 200,000 Americans in 1920–21.

Between 1870 and 1920, deaths from most communicable diseases dropped rapidly. However, diphtheria continued to plague Americans during the 1920s. Although it was becoming less common, children under the age of five were particularly vulnerable to the disease. In 1920 Massachusetts reported a diphtheria death rate of five per 10,000 persons, a decline of 61 percent over the last four decades. In 1825 in Alaska, a dog team performed a historic rescue to provide children with the serum needed to stave off an epidemic in Nome. Typhoid also continued to be a problem in the United States in the early 1920s; however, incidences declined drastically. In Massachusetts, for instance, the death rate from typhoid was 5 per 100,000 persons. Rates of other diseases also declined. For example, in Philadelphia, the death rate from tuberculosis was more than halved, dropping from 320 per 100,000 persons to 151. In response to the availability of a reliable vaccine, the death rate from typhoid fever fell to 64 per 100,000 persons. Deaths from dysentery and malaria were virtually halted, dropping to 15 per 100,000 persons, and seven per 100,000 persons, respectively.

MEDICINE AND HEALTH

By the 1920s the United States was a medically advanced nation. Views on public health now included a focus on extending life spans by promoting overall good health and disease prevention. During the 1920s specialists were available in virtually every area of medicine, and most Americans had easy access to medical care by trained physicians, druggists, dentists, nurses, and veterinarians. Even though medical care was widely available, it was not always

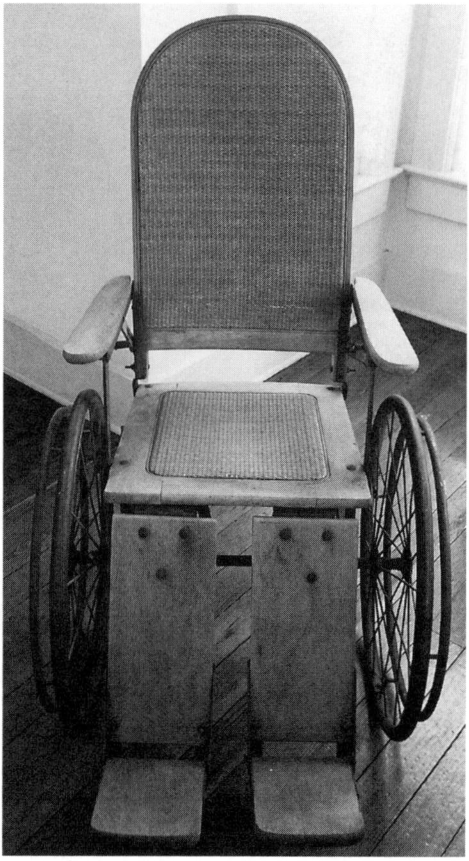

This wood and wicker wheelchair is typical of designs from around 1920.

affordable. As late as 1920, the medical profession continued to lead the campaign against health insurance, arguing that it would precipitate economic disaster by raising both wages and prices.

Hospitals and clinics had been established around the country. Due to increased government and private support for research, medical technology was constantly advancing. In the summer of 1927, for instance, the so-called iron lung, an artificial respirator, was used for the first time in New York's Bellevue Hospital. The federal government was heavily involved in assessing present realities and future needs of American health through extensive research and surveys. The sanitation movement had been highly successful in precipitating a healthier environment. In response to the new emphasis on cleanliness, American families changed sheets more often, and many men gave up detachable collars and cuffs in favor of shirts laundered after each wearing. Bathrooms and kitchens were kept scrupulously clean to avoid the breeding and spreading of germs.

As a result of all these changes, Americans of the period were generally a good deal healthier than their ancestors. The population rose from 106 million in 1920 to 122 million by the end of the decade. Unfortunately, as the death rate from communicable diseases continued to decline, deaths from cardiovascular and renal diseases continued to rise. These conditions had accounted for around one-fifth of all deaths at the turn of the century. By 1925, however, the number of deaths resulting from cardiovascular and renal diseases accounted for around one-third of all deaths in the United States. On the positive side, the number of heart-related deaths in children had been greatly reduced in response to medical advances concerning rheumatic fever and its complications. Cancer, which had been the eighth leading cause of death in 1900, rose to second place.

Infant mortality had been a major problem in the United States since colonial times, but an improved understanding of medicine, sanitation, and nutrition resulted in declining rates of infant mortality. However, socioeconomic status remained a key factor in determining life expectancy of infants. During the early 20th century, one in 16 infants of wealthy families died, but one in six poor infants died in the first year. In 1924, an extensive study of infant mortality conducted by Robert Morse Woodbury in seven cities established correlations between infant mortality and low paternal income, the level of neonatal care, housing and sanitary conditions, the status of maternal employment, and feeding methods. Laboratory studies in the 1920s led to the discovery that many American infants were dying unnecessarily because diarrhea was accompanied by fluid loss, electrolyte imbalance, and circulatory failure. By preventing dehydration, most infants could be saved. Infant mortality dropped drastically around the country in response to this discovery. In Connecticut, for example, the death rate for infants under one year of age dropped from 23.1 per 1,000 live births in 1916 to 8.6 per 1,000 live births in 1923.

In 1921 Grace Abbott (1878–1939) succeeded Julia Lathrop (1858–1932) as the head of the Children's Bureau. Under Abbott's guidance, over the next few years the bureau was responsible for the opening of around 3,000 child health and prenatal clinics in the United States. Despite continued progress in children's health, in 1929 Congress eliminated the controversial grants for maternal and children's programs that had been authorized by the Sheppard-Towner Maternity and Infancy Protection Act of 1921.

In the 1920s, rickets, a disease caused by a deficiency of Vitamin D, calcium, or phosphates, continued to be a major problem among poor children. In 1921 E.V. McCollum (1879–1967), professor of biochemistry and molecular biology at Johns Hopkins University, insisted that at least one half of all urban children had contracted rickets at some point in their lives. While rickets was not normally fatal, many children died from complications such as pneumonia or convulsions. The disease could also render females infertile. McCollum worked with British physician and pharmacologist Edward Mellanby (1884–1995) to solve the problem of rickets through proper nutrition.

Researchers of the Roaring Twenties continued to advance the study of vitamins and minerals in a variety of ways by studying their effect on health and disease. For instance, American Glen King (1896–1988) and Hungarian Albert Szent-Györgyi (1893–1986) were successful in isolating and chemically identifying Vitamin C. As a result, scurvy virtually disappeared in the developed world, although it continues to pose a major health risk to the poor of the developing world.

PUBLIC HEALTH

In 1921 the American Public Health Association (APHA) identified a number of major areas that should be of concern to local health officials: housing,

Dogs Save Lives of Alaskan Children

During a winter blizzard in 1924, Dr. Curtis Welch was called to a home in Nome, Alaska, where two Eskimo children had become ill with fever, sore throat, and labored shallow breathing. Welch considered and discarded diphtheria as a diagnosis. In the absence of lab facilities, he was unable to test the children. They died the next day. On January 21, Welch was called to the home of a white Alaskan child who had also become ill. The diagnosis of diphtheria was unmistakable in this case.

The physician was well aware that an epidemic could devastate the population of Nome where residents had no immunity to the disease. Welch concluded that the only way to treat the ailing children and prevent a possible epidemic was to obtain 300,000 units of serum that had been located at the Railroad Hospital in Anchorage. Unfortunately, blizzard conditions made delivery of the serum difficult.

It was ultimately decided that the serum would be shipped from Anchorage to Nenana, located on the Tanana River, by train. Twenty dog sled teams were assigned to relay the serum the 675 mi. from Nenana to Nome. Ultimately, it took the teams less than five days to bring the serum to the home of Dr. Welch. The first leg of the journey was conducted by musher "Wild Bill" Shannon. The final team, led by musher Gunnar Kaasen and lead sled dog Balto, traveled 53 mi. in 7.5 hours to arrive in Nome at 5:30 A.M. on February 2. Five days after the arrival of Kaasen's team, a second batch of serum arrived in Nome from Seward, Alaska.

A statute of Balto is located near the zoo in New York's Central Park, and the husky was immortalized in *Balto*, an animated fictionalized version of the story, in 1995. Two sequels followed: *Balto II: Wolf Quest* (2002) and *Balto III: Wings of Change* (2004). Today, the annual Iditarod Sled Dog Race begins on the first Saturday in March, following the same route taken by the original dog sled teams. The first team generally arrives in Nome from nine to 11 days after the race begins. The historical celebration includes sporting events, and arts and crafts booths.

plumbing nuisances (including animal control, cesspools, privy vaults, and manure piles), vital statistics, contagious diseases, vaccination, infant hygiene (including pasteurization of milk), school inspections, industrial hygiene, health centers, public health nursing, food and drug regulation, garbage collection, health education, and publicity (including disease prevention and control). Because of the new emphasis on children's health, most local health departments hired nurses to work in schools and instructed them to monitor outbreaks of diseases and to educate children about health issues, proper sanitation, and good nutrition.

Those who lived in small communities had the least access to indoor plumbing in the 1920s and often used outhouses like the one shown above.

During the Roaring Twenties, sanitary reforms were widespread, and Americans demanded basic health and sanitation protection and services from all levels of government. Outdoor privies of past generations were almost entirely replaced with sanitary indoor plumbing. At the turn of the century, only around a million Americans had had access to filtered water. During the 1920s, however, water treatment plants were erected around the country to cleanse water of various minerals and pollutants. Chlorine was added to municipal water supplies. These measures were so effective that typhoid fever was nearly eradicated. Milk was regularly pasteurized and inspected, and meat and poultry required government certification. Sewage systems were built, and garbage was collected on a regular basis. Required inoculations were designed to prevent the spread of diseases such as diphtheria. Other local government measures included general pollution control and the promotion of groups concerned with health issues and child welfare and protection. Most schools regularly weighed children to monitor possible malnutrition and began serving hot lunches. Children's organizations such as Girl Scouts, Boy Scouts, Camp Fire Girls, and the Little Mother's League regularly taught health and hygiene.

By 1926 95.3 percent of all American communities over 100,000 residents offered public garbage collection. Among communities with 10,000 to 25,000 residents, 56.3 percent provided this service. Throughout the country, communities of 10,000 or more residents provided water piped directly into homes. More than three-fourths of Americans living in areas that boasted 100,000 or more residents had sanitary bathtubs, as did 66.9 percent living in communities of 10,000 or more. More than 90 percent of all residents in communities of 100,000 or more had flush toilets, and 78.1 percent of Americans living in communities of 10,000 to 25,000 had this service. Flush toilets were also available to more than a fourth of Americans

Shifting Images of the Ideal Female

In the 1880s, entertainer Lillian Russell (1860–1922) was considered the feminine ideal. Russell maintained her "hourglass figure" by dining at New York's Delmonico's restaurant several times a week. Russell was still considered attractive when her weight reached 200 pounds. However, the lessons learned during the food shortages of World War I led to a revamping of ideas on proper nutrition in the 1920s.

By 1929 the average American was consuming five percent less calories than before the war. Dieting became popular among the upper class in the 1920s, and weight loss books were readily available. Gimmick diets were common; one involved eating three meals a day consisting of one-half a grapefruit, Melba toast, and coffee. Other diet plans consisted wholly of baked potatoes and buttermilk, or raw tomatoes and hard-boiled eggs. Tobacco companies began advertising smoking as a way to lose weight while improving digestion and nerves. In response, the rate of female cigarette smokers rose dramatically. The image of the ideal female changed from rosy and plump to thin and trim. The impact of this change became strongly evident in novels written for middle-class adolescent girls. Every protagonist was portrayed as slim and smart. Either a best friend or an adversary was portrayed as fat and comical. These depictions influenced young girls' perceptions of the "right" kind of female body shape.

This image of the ideal female body persisted for decades. Studies have revealed that the inability to measure up to this ideal lowered self esteem among young girls, who often began dieting as young as seven or eight years old. In 2007, a study of 1,000 seventh and eighth graders conducted by Dr. Eliana Miller Perrin revealed that among white girls, self esteem was seven times higher in girls who were highly satisfied with their bodies than in those who expressed less satisfaction. Among black girls, self esteem was three times higher in those who were highly satisfied with their bodies.

By the time Lillian Russell died in 1922, the ideal female figure had changed, as had attitudes toward food.

Cans of coffee and other staples from the 1920s. Innovations in transportation and packaging revolutionized America's food supply in the 1920s.

who lived in small communities of 1,000 or more. Water heaters and central heating were also widely available.

The lives of many American women changed considerably during the Roaring Twenties. The fight for suffrage had galvanized the women's movement, culminating in 1920 with the ratification of the Nineteenth Amendment, which gave women the right to vote for the first time. Feminist reformer Margaret Sanger (1879–1966) opened the nation's first birth control clinic in Brooklyn, New York, on October 16, 1916. Sanger was later arrested and charged with keeping a "public nuisance." Undaunted, she formed the Birth Control League on November 2, 1921. Birth control continued to be a controversial issue in the United States until the 1960s when the Supreme Court determined in *Griswold v. Connecticut* that access to birth control was protected by an inherent right to privacy. Over the previous decades, changing dress styles had provided women with an unprecedented freedom of movement and eradicated the deformities caused by corsets and other tight clothing.

Midwives continued to be an integral part of the birthing process in rural areas and immigrant communities. In 1923 a survey of 31 states conducted for the Children's Bureau by Anna E. Rude revealed that 26,627 midwives were registered in the United States. Rude estimated that more than 17,000 unregistered midwives provided services in the remaining states. The 1920s ushered in a period of great involvement by the Children's Bureau in improving the lives of children through a greater emphasis on maternal health. For the first time, prenatal care became widely available in the United States, partly through the efforts of Arthur B. Emmons, II, of the Boston Lying-In Hospital who joined with the Women's Municipal League to establish outpatient prenatal clinics. Puerperal septicemia (commonly referred to as toxemia), the leading cause of maternal health problems (34 percent), was considered entirely preventable by the 1920s. As the secretary of the American Public Health Association, in 1926 Emmons extended his attention to discovering the link between employee absences and conditions such as the common cold. As a result, ventilation in the workplace improved, and sanitary drinking fountains and closed containers for discarded paper towels were instituted.

NUTRITION OF AMERICANS

The years between 1914 and 1945 were a time of great change for Americans. During World War I, food shortages had forced Americans to cut back on the amount of food consumed; the government had promoted "wheatless" and "meatless" days. A number of studies of the period had revealed that as long as the right food, containing the proper balance of proteins, carbohydrates, minerals, and vitamins was consumed during the shortage, there would be no lasting effect from cutting back on overall calories. Although the suggested daily calorie consumption of from 3,000 to 3,500 may seem high by today's standards, it was a major deduction for many Americans of that time. Extensive studies of American diets revealed that eating lower quantities of more nutritious foods had made many Americans healthier than in the past.

Breakfast cereals continued to be popular in the 1920s, and companies such as Post promoted their products like Grape Nuts as ideal sources of iron, calcium, phosphorus, and other essential minerals. Many product advertisements added the words "health" to increase sales. For instance, Morton promoted "health salt," and Welch's grape juice was touted as having enormous "health values." Even chocolate was advertised as a source of vitamins. Sealtest and Borden, the leading diary companies, assured Americans that milk was essential to their good health. As a result, by 1925 800 pounds of milk per capita were being consumed in the United States. Despite this trend

Large-scale bakeries, such as this one from 1923, became a staple of communities in the 1920s, but many mass-produced breads lost nutritional value through excessive processing.

toward healthy eating, bread, meat, and sugar products made up the bulk of the American diet in the 1920s. Most working-class families had entirely given up on making homemade bread. Instead they purchased breads that had lost most nutritional value through excessive processing.

Americans were advised to eat three meals a day. Breakfasts generally consisted of fruit and cereal or eggs and toast. Most students and workers carried light lunches with them, but those who could afford to do so ate at the lunch counters and restaurants that appeared around the country. In most American homes of the 1920s, the main meal of the day was consumed in the late afternoon or early evening. Farmers, however, continued to eat the main meal at midday, followed by a light evening meal. Typical dinners of the period included roast or broiled meat or poultry, potatoes, a vegetable, and a dessert such as cake, pie, cookies, or pudding. Salt continued to be the chief American seasoning. One-dish meals were also popular, consisting of meat, potatoes, pasta, beans, rice, and vegetables thickened with condensed tomato soup, cheese, or milk. Salads made of a variety of produce such as crisp lettuce, tomatoes, celery, and carrots appeared in the early 20th century. Other popular salads were made with canned fruit, vegetables, Jell-O, and/or mayonnaise. By the late 1920s, baby food and formulas were considered safe, and infants over six months were generally fed a combination of prepared baby foods and home-cooked mashed and pureed fruits and vegetables. Many immigrant families adopted the traditional American diet, except for holidays and special occasions.

ACCESS TO FOOD SUPPLIES

Few families had cadres of servants after World War I, and food preparation was focused on convenience. A plethora of electrical kitchen appliances were sold. The ways that food arrived in American households was also transformed. Large-scale bakeries and dairies became a staple of most communities, and many smaller businesses were driven out of business. Likewise, large agricultural establishments became the order of the day, and new technologies allowed farmers to increase production while employing fewer workers. Advances and innovations in transportation revolutionized America's food supply and made even exotic foods available throughout the country.

Although general stores still existed in some areas until the middle of the century, specialty stores began replacing them in many areas. A typical shopping trip might include a trip to the butcher, the greengrocer, the confectionary, the delicatessen, and a grocery store. Items were often purchased on credit, and many stores offered home delivery. In 1922 the opening of the Crystal Palace in San Francisco paved the way for the advent of the modern supermarket. Covering 68,000 sq. ft., the Crystal Palace boasted 110 sepa-

The modern supermarket emerged in the 1920s. This photo shows the Memphis, Tennessee, Piggly Wiggly self-service grocery store during that period.

rate departments to serve its clientele of 150,000 shoppers per week. The first self-serve grocery store had opened in Memphis in 1916. By 1920 the company now known as Piggly Wiggly had expanded to 400 stores. By 1928 when Safeway and Kroger purchased the Piggly Wiggly chain, the franchise had expanded to 2,700 stores. As supermarkets with large parking lots became the norm in the 1920s, home delivery declined.

Frozen foods became widely available during the 1920s in response to a discovery by Clarence Birdseye (1886–1956) that food could be frozen in cellophane wrappers and thawed without loss of quality. In 1925 Birdseye formed the General Sea Foods Company, which became General Foods three years later. By 1928 restaurants had begun buying large quantities of frozen foods. After the Post Company took over General Foods in 1929, Birdseye continued to oversee what became the Birdseye Frozen Food Division. Within the first year of operation, Birdseye developed 16 different varieties of frozen poultry, meats, fruits, and vegetables. During the next decade, Birdseye began repurchasing the patents that he had sold under General Foods and improved the quality of frozen food products. Commercial freezers were leased to grocers to encourage them to sell frozen foods.

World War I had led to inflationary food prices, reaching the highest point in 1920. Over the next three years, prices dropped sharply before leveling out. The price of some foods dropped in response to new methods of production. For example, a loaf of bread that had cost 11.5 cents in 1920 cost Americans 8.6 cents in 1929. The price of eggs dropped from 68.1 cents a dozen to 52.7 cents during that same period. Likewise the price of milk decreased from 16.7 cents in 1920 to 14.4 cents in 1929. The price for a pound of potatoes dropped from 63 cents to 32 cents over the course of the decade, and the price of sugar fell from 97 cents a pound to 32 cents a pound. Despite price reductions, the overall cost of living continued to rise during the 1920s. Between 1921 and 1929, the percentage of household expenditures spent on food rose from 16.8 to 23.4 percent. At the same time, the cost of housing and utilities rose from 12.3 to 14.5 percent, and the cost of medical care rose from 1.5 to 3.0 percent.

The elaborate restaurants of previous decades virtually disappeared in the 1920s because of Prohibition. They were replaced with smaller establishments that offered affordable menus. Of the restaurants operating during the 1920s, 48 percent were lunch rooms, 26 percent were coffee and sandwich shops, and eight percent were cafeterias. Only 11 percent of American eating places of the period were considered full-scale restaurants.

Despite the embarrassing failure of Prohibition, other government actions in the 1920s had more success, such as increased government support for medical research. Important advances in health and nutrition had been made in the era, and a number of diseases were even headed toward eradication.

Elizabeth R. Purdy

Further Readings

Bennett, James T. and Thomas J. DiLorenzo. *From Pathology to Politics: Public Health in America.* New Brunswick NJ: Transaction Publishers, 2000.

Bullough, Bonnie and George Rosen. *Preventive Medicine in the United States 1900–1990: Trends and Interpretations.* Canton MA: Science History Publications, 1992.

Cassedy, James H. *Medicine in America: A Short History.* Baltimore, MD: Johns Hopkins University Press, 1991.

Foy, Jessica H. and Thomas J. Schlereth, eds. *American Home Life, 1880–1930: A Social History of Spaces and Services.* Knoxville, TN: University of Tennessee Press, 1992.

Grob, Gerald N. *The Deadly Truth: A History of Disease in America.* Cambridge, MA: Harvard University Press, 2002.

Husband, Julie and Jim O'Laughlin. *Daily Life in the Industrial United States, 1870–1900.* Westport CT: Greenwood, 2004.

Kiple, Kenneth F. *Plague, Pox, and Pestilence.* London: Weidenfeld and Nicolson, 1997.

Kyvig, David E. *Daily Life in the United States, 1920–1939: Decades of Promise and Pain.* Westport, CT: Greenwood, 2002.

Leavitt, Judith Walzer and Ronald L. Numbers, eds. *Sickness and Health in America: Readings in the History of Medicine and Public Health.* Madison, WI: University of Wisconsin Press, 1999.

Lerner, Monroe and Odin W. Anderson. *Health Progress in the United States 1900–1960: A Report of Health Information Foundation.* Chicago, IL: University of Chicago Press, 1963.

Levenstein, Harvey A. *Revolution at the Table: The Transformation of the American Diet.* New York: Oxford, 1988.

Oshinsky, David M. *Polio: An American Story.* New York: Oxford, 2005.

Pillsbury, Richard. *No Foreign Food: The American Diet in Time and Place.* Boulder, CO: Westview, 1998.

Rosen, George. *Preventive Medicine in the United States 1900–1975: Trends and Interpretations.* New York: Science History Publications, 1975.

Ross, Gregory. *Modern America 1914 to 1945.* New York: Facts on File, 1995.

Sealander, Judith. *Private Wealth and Public Life: Foundation Philanthropy and the Social Reshaping of American Social Policy from the Progressive Era to the New Deal.* Baltimore, MD: Johns Hopkins, 1997.

Taylor, Lloyd C., Jr. *The Medical Profession and Social Reform, 1885–1945.* New York: St. Martin's, 1974.

Waverly, Root and Richard de Rochemont. *Eating in America: A History.* New York: William Morrow, 1976.

Wolf, Naomi. *The Beauty Myth: How Images of Beauty Are Used Against Women.* New York: W. Morrow, 1991.

index

Index note: page references in *italics* indicate a figure or illustration; page references in **bold** indicate main discussion.

D

PHOTO CREDITS. Library of Congress: vii, 1, 2, 6, 8, 10, 13, 14, 16, 18, 20, 24, 32, 36, 41, 45, 47, 48, 51, 54, 56, 58, 59, 60, 64, 66, 69, 74, 77, 78, 79, 84, 87, 88, 91, 92, 102, 105, 113, 115, 121, 123, 128, 132, 138, 139, 141, 143, 146, 148, 149, 153, 155, 158, 163, 173, 187, 188, 191, 193, 194, 196, 201, 202, 206, 207, 208, 218, 238, 242. Loretta Carlisle Photography: 5, 19, 22, 27, 29, 30, 31, 33, 34, 35, 39, 51 inset, 68, 70, 80, 81, 95, 97, 99, 106, 109, 110, 112, 120, 125, 140, 145, 156, 159, 160, 165, 168, 171, 172, 175, 176, 179, 181, 182, 195, 197, 198, 215, 216, 220, 221, 223, 224, 225, 229, 231, 233, 234, 237, 239, 241. Wikipedia: 119, 127, 131, 167. Photos.com: 53, 63, 58, 124, 135.

Produced by Golson Media

President and Editor	J. Geoffrey Golson
Layout Editors	Oona Patrick, Mary Jo Scibetta
Managing Editor	Susan Moskowitz
Copyeditor	Ben Johnson
Proofreader	Mary Le Rouge
Indexer	J S Editorial